THE MENTAL HEALTH OF CARE-EXPERIENCED CHILDREN AND YOUNG PEOPLE

A Guide for Social Workers

Christine Cocker

First published in Great Britain in 2026 by

Policy Press, an imprint of
Bristol University Press
University of Bristol
1–9 Old Park Hill
Bristol
BS2 8BB
UK
t: +44 (0)117 374 6645
e: bup-info@bristol.ac.uk

Details of international sales and distribution partners are available at policy.bristoluniversitypress.co.uk

DOI: 10.51952/9781447365617

British Library Cataloguing in Publication Data
A catalogue record for this book is available from the British Library

ISBN 978-1-4473-6559-4 paperback
ISBN 978-1-4473-6560-0 ePub
ISBN 978-1-4473-6561-7 ePdf

Cover design: Liam Roberts
Front cover image: iStock/ivetavaicule
Bristol University Press and Policy Press use environmentally responsible print partners.
Printed and bound in Great Britain by CPI Group (UK) Ltd, Croydon, CR0 4YY

Bristol University Press' authorised representative in the European Union is: Easy Access System Europe, Mustamäe tee 50, 10621 Tallinn, Estonia,
Email: gpsr.requests@easproject.com

FSC
www.fsc.org
MIX
Paper | Supporting responsible forestry
FSC® C013604

To Nesha Nicol (1987–2022), my brother and sister-in-law's foster daughter, whose life ended too soon. With love always.

Contents

List of figures and tables

Figures

Tables

Acknowledgements

Thank you to all the people who have supported me in the writing of this book. Firstly, thanks to the young people who met with me and talked all things 'mental health' over dinner that they prepared. I'd also like to say a huge thank you to staff in Suffolk's leaving care services for their support. Similarly, colleagues at the University of East Anglia in the School of Social Work, Sociology and Education have been generous with their time and support, particularly Anna Wright, Dr Carlene Cornish and Dr Cynthia Okpokiri. Thanks to Professor Helen Minnis and Dr Helen Sweeting from the University of Glasgow for being the best PhD supervisory team I could have wished for. Finally, I would like to thank my partner Dr Adi Cooper OBE for her unwavering support always, and to our wonderful family for constantly inspiring me to do my best.

Introduction

This book examines the main debates about the mental health of care-experienced (previously termed 'looked after') children and young people. It provides an overview of research, examining issues arising in multidisciplinary working, and hears from young people themselves about what matters to them in relation to mental health support.

Mental health affects everyone. It is integral to our own self-worth, it affects every aspect of our lives, including our relationships, our behaviours and how we interact with our environment. Mental health is not a constant – it continuously changes. It is somewhat perplexing then that there is often significant stigma around mental health difficulties. At some point in our lives, we will all experience emotional distress, and for some, this may lead to a period of feeling we are struggling to cope. It may also lead to mental illness. How we are supported during this period can make all the difference to recovery or to living with a significant mental illness for a longer term.

Many different factors affect our psychological and social wellbeing. These include:

- the number of demands and stressors we have;
- our physical health;
- significant life events;
- how much sleep we get;
- relationships with other people, including in online spaces;
- our diet/nutritional intake;
- environmental, societal and cultural factors;
- how much we engage in leisure activities, hobbies and interests.

(Hampshire CAMHS NHS website, 2025)[1]

Since 2015, there has been an increase in public awareness of mental health issues affecting children and young people and this has become a social policy priority area for several recent governments. In 2015 the Conservative government committed an extra £1.4 billion to Child and Adolescent Mental Health Services (CAMHS) over a period of five years (Department of Health & Department for Education, 2017). This was partly in recognition of the impact of social media on young people's mental health, rising rates of problems from exam stress which led to young people reporting high levels of anxiety and mental health struggles, and experiencing long waiting times for services (Young Minds, 2018). Additionally, in response to the impact of the COVID-19 epidemic on mental health, further funds were allocated to CAMHS provision under the Conservative government. However, successive governments have been criticised for not being ambitious enough, and targets that have been set in terms of funding and of expanding the mental health workforce have been missed (Rainer & Abdinasir, 2023). Demographic data evidences that one in ten children and young people in the general population have a mental disorder (Meltzer et al, 2000). A growing body of research shows that care-experienced children and young people have much higher rates of mental ill health than their peers, with rates of mental disorder for this group of children at just below 50 per cent (Meltzer et al, 2003, 2004a, 2004b; Ford et al, 2007). The mental health of care-experienced children and young people is therefore something that all social workers and foster carers working with these children and young adults should understand and be confident and competent in addressing.

The book is written for social workers, so there is an emphasis on this professional lens throughout, although other practitioners working with care-experienced children and young people will find the content helpful for their practice. During their qualifying training and education, all social work students should learn about the issues affecting care-experienced children and young people. Understanding and supporting their mental health is key and critical to this learning. This book provides social workers, student social workers and other allied health and social care professionals with the information they need to understand mental health issues relevant for supporting care-experienced children and young people, including:

- the kinds of mental health problems that care-experienced children and young people are likely to have;
- the contribution that social workers and other professionals can make to the lives of care-experienced children and young people of all ages;
- how to work effectively with CAMHS professionals;
- the views of care-experienced children and young people about how social workers can best support them with their mental health issues;
- how racism affects the experiences of Black and minority ethnic children and young people, including its effect on their mental health.

The contribution of social workers to improving the mental health of care-experienced children and young people, both in the context of children's physical environment as well as of their relational world, should be core elements of social work practice. It is important that social workers have knowledge and understanding about the mental health of children and young people: the Mental Health Act 1983/2007 applies to all ages, including children, and the Mental Capacity Act 2005 applies to everyone 16 years of age and older. However, the knowledge of social workers working with care-experienced children and young people about mental health is not always sufficient.

Different terms and meanings

Language and terminology matter when discussing mental health. Often different terms are used interchangeably when each concept has a specific meaning. For example, we often talk about mental health when we mean mental ill health. Emotional distress is different from a mental illness, as are emotional and behavioural difficulties. It is best to understand mental health as a continuum, and our position on this continuum changes.

Mental health

The World Health Organization (WHO) defines mental health as 'a state of wellbeing in which the individual realises his or her abilities, can cope with the normal stresses of life, work productively and fruitfully, and is able to make a contribution to his or her community' (World Health Organization, 2001).

Emotional and behavioural difficulty or mental health problems

'Emotional and behavioural difficulties' and 'mental health problems' are terms that are used interchangeably and frequently to describe many different situations. Even though these terms are rooted in different social and medical approaches to mental ill health, it is assumed that these are both broad categories that refer to the same things. However, it is important to note that different definitions and thresholds for what constitute 'problems' have produced very different estimates of the number of children with emotional or behavioural difficulties (Scott, 2004).

Mental disorder

A mental disorder is a diagnosable mental illness which is internationally recognised in one of two classificatory systems. The *Diagnostic and Statistical Manual of Mental Disorders*, 5th edition (DSM-V) is published by the American Psychiatric Association (American Psychiatric Association, 2013). This is the main diagnostic reference for mental health professionals in the US. The International Classification of Diseases – Mental Health Disorders (11th edition) (ICD-11) (World Health Organization, 2024) came into use in World Health Organization Member States from 2018. The classification of 'mental disorders' has become increasingly sophisticated. The original DSM published in 1952 listed 60 types and subtypes of mental disorder, while the current edition contains well over 200. Difficulties experienced by children and young people represent one of the areas of classificatory expansion that has both reflected and inspired research interest in the field (Cocker and Scott, 2006).

Specific mental disorders

Both the DSM-V and ICD-11 classification systems use a number of broad categories to classify mental disorders. I have used the list of specific disorders that Meltzer et al (2003) identify in their prevalence study of the mental health of children looked after by local authorities in England:

- *Anxiety disorders.* Examples include separation anxiety; specific phobias; panic; agoraphobia; post-traumatic stress disorder (PTSD); and obsessive-compulsive disorder (OCD).
- *Depression.*
- *Conduct disorders.* Examples include oppositional defiant disorder; conduct disorder (family context); unsocialised conduct disorder; and socialised conduct disorder.
- *Hyperkinetic disorder.* Examples include attention deficit hyperactivity disorder (ADHD).
- *Less common disorders.* Examples include pervasive development disorder (for example, autism); psychotic disorders; tic disorders; eating disorders; and other psychiatric disorders.

This list is not exhaustive – they are examples only of some of the most common.

What do social workers need to know about the mental health of care-experienced children?

All care-experienced children and young people have an allocated social worker while they are in the care system. My own view, based on extensive experience, is that mental health issues for all care-experienced children and young people are critical, yet often underplayed or inadequately understood by social workers. While there is a substantial literature for social workers about working with care-experienced children, there is very little literature that focusses on the role of the social worker in terms of the assessments they make regarding a child or young person's mental health and the influence that they may have over decisions made about the child or young person in terms of treatment or support offered. Social workers are significant people in the lives of care-experienced children and young people. They act as a 'corporate parent' for the council (Department for Education, 2018), which means they have responsibilities for a care-experienced child or young person's wellbeing while in care, and this includes the child or young person's emotional, social, physical and educational wellbeing.

For social workers, carers and other allied professionals working with care-experienced children and young people, having an understanding about the issues which affect their mental health is crucial in ensuring that if children or young people have more serious needs in this area, they can access the services they require as soon as possible. There are behaviours that care-experienced children and young people may exhibit which will immediately be of concern to carers and social workers (for example: uncontrollable anger and outbursts; self-harming behaviours; physically hurting other children; smearing faeces; fire starting). Care-experienced children and young people may also be upset or angry because of their experiences but present these feelings in different ways (for example: not being able to make and/or sustain friendships at school; lack of concentration at school affecting their ability to learn; being quiet and withdrawn; not engaging with foster carers, teachers and/or friends; having sleeping and eating problems). Not all care-experienced children and young people will require specialist CAMHS intervention to process their experiences and improve their mental health. All will require good experiences of supportive parenting, but some children may require additional support and services. Social workers need to develop the skills and confidence to be able to identify when specialist support is required, and to refer appropriately. We know that some care-experienced children and young people may self-harm or have suicidal thoughts. Research on this topic is rare and social workers do not routinely have access to suicide prevention guidance tailored to young people in care and care leavers (Göbbels-Koch and Gupta, 2025).

Every child and young person has essential needs that should be met in order to reach their potential for physical and emotional growth and development. Examples of these needs are: basic physical care, affection, security, stimulation of innate potential, guidance and control, responsibility and independence (Talbot,

2002, pp 84–5). However, there are many factors which can influence how children and young people will respond to difficult life circumstances.

A child/young person's mental health is not 'fixed' – if children or young people develop emotional and behavioural problems, then it is quite probable that, with support and treatment, much can be done to alleviate the symptoms children and young people exhibit. However, being able to understand the cause of these problems, including the implications of abuse and neglect on the mental health of care-experienced children and young people, is vital to a social worker's role with children and young people in care. The experiences of loss and separation are common across all care-experienced children (Fahlberg, 2012) and yet the impact of these life experiences can affect individual children very differently.

Howe (2005, p 278) believes that *if relationships are where things developmental can go wrong, then relationships are where they are most likely to be put right.* In the majority of instances, the people with the most contact with care-experienced children are their carers (either foster carers, residential carers or extended family members), their social worker and their teacher. In recognising the role of teachers, mentors and other significant professionals, Werner (2000) describes a follow-up study of 24 child survivors of the Nazi Holocaust. As children these survivors were sent from concentration camps to a therapeutic nursery in England at the end of the war.

> Excerpts from follow-up interviews after 30–40 years reveal an extraordinary affirmation of life. Furthermore, all of the resilient survivors considered one woman to be among the most potent influences on their lives – the nursery school teacher who provided warmth and caring and who taught them to behave compassionately. (Moskovitz, 1983, cited in Werner, 2000, p 126)

Howe's views are that 'those who can stay with and touch these children, emotionally and psychologically, have the capacity to heal young minds' (2005, p 278).

What kinds of mental health problems do care-experienced children and young people have?

From the turn of this century, a number of seminal research studies about the mental health needs of care-experienced children showed that the number of children in care with a diagnosable mental disorder was much higher than the national average for all children (McCann et al, 1996; Dimigen et al, 1999; Meltzer et al, 2003, 2004a, 2004b). McCann et al (1996) showed that there were a considerable number of children in residential care with undiagnosed psychiatric disorders. This is an issue picked up more recently by Hiller et al (2025). What has remained a constant issue is the number of care-experienced children and young people who face lengthy delays in accessing much needed mental health services (Hiller et al, 2025).

The first prevalence study about the mental health needs of looked after children in England (a research study with a large enough sample size to give an indication of the total number of cases of diagnosable disorders in a given population at a specific time) was published in 2003 (Meltzer et al, 2003). Similar studies were published soon afterwards with care-experienced children in Scotland and Wales (Meltzer et al, 2004a, 2004b). These studies compared the mental health (as identifiable 'disorders') of children looked after by the state and children in the overall population. Meltzer and colleagues had completed a study about the mental health of children and adolescents in Great Britain a number of years earlier (Meltzer et al, 2000). In this general study, information was collected on 10,000 children, and it found:

- among 5- to 10-year-olds, 10 per cent of boys and 6 per cent of girls had an identified disorder;
- among 11- to 15-year-olds, 13 per cent of boys and 10 per cent of girls had an identified disorder;
- conduct disorder accounted for half of all cases – boys were twice as likely as girls to be identified as having a conduct or hyperkinetic disorder.

In the comparable study about care-experienced children and young people in England (Meltzer et al, 2003), the sample size was much smaller – information was collected on 1,039 children. This was enough to enable comparison with the general study, as the same methodology was used. It found:

- among 5- to 10-year-olds, 50 per cent of boys and 33 per cent of girls had an identified disorder;
- among 11- to 15-year-olds, this figure was 55 per cent of boys and 43 per cent of girls;
- conduct disorder was identified in 42 per cent of boys and 31 per cent of girls.

At that time, research showed that one in ten of all children had a diagnosable disorder. In 2023, about one in five children and young people aged between eight and 25 years had a probable mental disorder (Newlove-Delgado et al, 2023). This rises to almost half of all care-experienced children and nearly three quarters of those in residential care having a probable disorder. The answer to address this is often articulated as more CAMHS staff – such as child psychiatrists, psychologists and primary mental health care workers to work with care-experienced children and young people and more in-patient beds. However, even if it were forthcoming, this provision is unlikely to provide a complete solution. The reasons for this lie in the origins and causes of most emotional and behavioural difficulties in care-experienced children, as well as issues of the appropriateness and accessibility of traditional mental health services (Cocker & Scott, 2006).

The work of Meltzer et al (2003, 2004a, 2004b) is particularly helpful because it includes information about looked after young people's physical health, use of services, placement type, educational achievement, social networks and lifestyle issues alongside the prevalence of mental disorders. Two thirds of all looked after children were reported to have at least one physical complaint, the most common being eyesight, speech and language problems, coordination difficulties and asthma. Only 44 per cent of those identified as having a mental disorder were in touch with child mental health services (Meltzer et al, 2003).

About 60 per cent of all looked after children had difficulties with reading, spelling or maths. Children identified as having a 'mental disorder' were more than twice as likely as other looked after children to have marked difficulties, and a third were considered to be three or more years behind in their intellectual development. These children were also four times more likely than their looked after peers to report not spending any time with their friends. Such correlations remind us that emotional and behavioural difficulties are inseparable from numerous other aspects of life (Meltzer et al, 2003).

Trauma-informed care and adverse childhood experiences (ACES) are now common parlance in a strengths-based social care landscape of interventions supported by organisations working with care-experienced children and young people. It is important to ensure that these terms are not used in a tokenistic manner, but in such a way that recognises the individuality of every child and young person. This includes paying attention to cultural needs.

In 2014 the National Society for the Prevention of Cruelty to Children (NSPCC) published an international literature review of what is known about the research evidence informing mental health interventions for care-experienced children and young people (Luke et al, 2014). The review looked at 106 individual studies of interventions aimed at preventing or treating mental health issues in looked after children. It also looked at 'ordinary care' provided via a foster placement, and what makes a foster placement 'a good one', as this was noted to be a powerful influence on wellbeing (Luke et al, 2014, p 3 of the executive summary).

The main findings are identified below (Luke et al, 2014, p 2):

- Many 'problem' behaviours develop in response to living in a dysfunctional and unpredictable family environment. Responses that can help children to survive very harsh conditions, such as withdrawing, can be less adaptive in the wider world.
- The earlier children are placed in any kind of permanent placement, where that is the appropriate decision, the more likely that placement is to succeed.
- Wellbeing tends to be better among children who remain in care compared with apparently similar children who return home. The 'success rate' of children who do return home is not high: around half return to care.
- We lack proven models for selecting, training, supervising and quality-assuring carers and staff in such a way that the quality of care is enhanced.

- Structured programmes focusing directly on the child appear to be more effective when they have core components with some flexibility to meet individual needs.
- One size does not fit all. Multidimensional Treatment Foster Care (MTFC) for example benefits highly antisocial young people but might be the wrong fit for others.
- There is promising evidence on approaches which are underpinned by a combination of attachment theory and social learning theory e.g. Fostering Changes, the foster care training programme.
- Interventions for behavioural and emotional issues are more likely to be effective when they include some focus on developing relationships and understanding. They should target both the caregiver's understanding of the causes of children's behaviour and the young person's understanding of their own emotions and identity.

My journey

Having worked as a local authority child and family social worker and manager in various different children's teams for over a decade after qualifying, in 1999 I applied for a job as the manager of a team being set up in the London Borough of Southwark to oversee the mental health of looked after (now care-experienced) children. This team (Care Link) was jointly funded by the local authority and Department of Health (DH) Mental Illness Specific Grant. This DH funding provided an opportunity for the development of 24 pilot projects for local authorities and health services in England to deliver joint specialist CAMHS provision for care-experienced children (Richardson & Joughin, 2000; Kurtz & James, 2003). These projects paved the way for the development of specific jointly commissioned and funded mental health services for care-experienced children and young people across England in the early 2000s (Cocker, 2003; Kurtz & James, 2003; Cocker & Scott, 2006).

The experience of setting up and managing this project for two years influenced my career in several ways. I became curious about how it might be possible to improve care-experienced children and young people's mental health generally. Although there were pockets of excellence within the system itself, including very good social workers and other child and adolescent mental health professionals dedicated to working with this group of children and young people, as a group, care-experienced children and young people are overrepresented in the mental health statistics about children and young people who have diagnosable disorders (Meltzer et al, 2003). I began to understand that if the mental health of a child/young person was not prioritised from the moment they came into care, then the consequences were significant for the child/young person during their time in care, the rest of their childhood and their adult life.

This book is based on my PhD research, which examined the views of English social workers and CAMHS clinicians about how social workers use the Strengths and Difficulties Questionnaire (SDQ) with care-experienced children. I have published one article about my research (Cocker et al, 2018), but the content of this article reported quantitative aspects of my research, whereas this book details the qualitative findings of my PhD research. The book also includes information not covered in my PhD. I asked a group of care-experienced young people about their experiences of mental health services (see Chapter 1) and have used their insights to support my thinking about how social workers can address their mental health needs. I have also included a chapter that explores how racism affects children and young people's experience of mental health services (see Chapter 7). In addition to this, other equality and diversity issues are embedded throughout each of the chapters.

What does the book cover?

Chapter 1 has been written with two care-experienced young people and their personal adviser. It presents their views and experiences of the mental health support they received while in care. The aim of this chapter is to ensure that the voices of young people are central tenets that run throughout the book. It is important that social workers hear what young people who are care-experienced have to say about how social workers acknowledge, assess and support children and young people who have mental health issues. This chapter provides these young people with an opportunity to present their perspectives about the support they have received or would have liked to receive. The chapter is presented in a strengths-based way, with an approach that encourages social workers and sets out young people's suggestions concerning how to improve services for them.

Chapter 2 presents the research evidence from several systematic and narrative reviews about what is known about the mental health of care-experienced children and what interventions are informed by this evidence base. A systematic review is a summary of existing research that provides an overview about what is known on a given topic (Critical Appraisal Skills Programme, 2025). They are reasonably common in health circles as there is a strong link to evidence-based practice. Systematic reviews have become more frequent in social care as social care embraces the use of evidence in its interventions, but the emphasis in social care is more on evidence-informed practice, as many social care studies utilise qualitative methods, alongside 'practice wisdom' and the experiences of people who use services (Research in Practice, 2025). A narrative review is a review of previously published studies in a given area. The views of children and young people are largely missing from studies about mental health provision for care-experienced children and young people, which is why a narrative review is necessary here. The chapter presents information from these reviews about what factors are important in determining how well a child may do in placements and what factors intrinsic to the child and to the carer are important in supporting a good attachment pattern between the child/young person and carer.

Chapter 3 discusses the importance of the SDQ for social work practice in routinely assessing the mental health of care-experienced children and young people. The SDQ is a screening tool widely used in mental health services across the country. It is expected that this tool will be used with all care-experienced children who have been in care for a year or longer; the expectation is that this tool is used once each year to assess the level of need that a child or young person might have. The benefits and weaknesses of this and other screening tools that are used widely in CAMHS are discussed. Again, this chapter is underpinned by my PhD research.

Chapter 4 also draws on my PhD research and presents social workers' views about mental health and the work they do with care-experienced children and young people in different settings. It shows the perspectives of social workers about their knowledge base, their direct work with children and young people, and their work with other agencies including education and CAMHS. The chapter also reports the gaps that social workers identify in their own skills and knowledge, and the availability (or not) of services to meet the mental health needs of care-experienced children. This includes: their own lack of training in this area which affects their confidence and competence to address mental health issues, a lack of confidence in the systems in place to support children, including CAMHS when waiting lists are long, and CAMHS refusing to see children who are not in 'permanent placements'.

Chapter 5 also utilises data from my PhD research about the role of CAMHS and highlights some of the strengths in working models that exist between CAMHS and social care as well as explores some of the tensions. I present three different typologies of social workers identified by CAMHS personnel:

1. social workers who refer most children on their caseloads;
2. social workers who never refer any children;
3. social workers who understand the remit of CAMHS and refer appropriately.

The chapter also looks at how CAMHS and local authorities can work effectively to support social workers as well as children and young people.

Chapter 6 outlines the role of different types of placements in supporting children and young people in care settings who have experienced significant trauma. This involves identifying the key factors within the literature that support 'stickability' in the relationship between foster child and foster family, as well as examine the impact of this for other forms of permanency for children. The secure base model developed by Schofield and Beek (2009, 2014a, 2014b) is also outlined.

Chapter 7 considers racism in mental health provision, with particular emphasis on the experiences of Black and minority ethnic children and young people within mental health and social care systems. This is important because Black people are over-represented in adult mental health services, and so this chapter examines the systemic influences on this. The chapter also looks at the Eurocentric approaches used to work with young people and their families (such as ACES) and addresses the impact that this has on Black and minority ethnic young people in accessing support that meets their cultural needs. There are significant cultural and religious stigmas for certain communities about accessing mental health support. In addition, racial trauma may be a significant experience for a young Black person (Black young people get stopped and searched by the police more often, they are described as 'aggressive', 'difficult', and so on, excluded from schools, and sectioned and medicated more heavily), which may result in mental health needs. This has an impact on the way that mental health is spoken about by young people and will affect the things that social workers may need to consider when trying to address this.

Chapter 8 looks at managing transitions into adulthood for care-experienced young people. This is the point where young people are moving on to independence, and it is a bumpy ride for most teenagers. However, for care-experienced young people, moving on to independence at 18 is early for such tremendous change to occur, especially as some of them continue to require considerable support throughout early adulthood. Although attention has been paid to improving services provided for young people leaving care via pathway plans and specialist leaving care services, a care leaver's journey to adulthood is steeper, quicker and occurs within a shorter timeframe than for young people not in care. Outcomes for many young people with care histories are not good, as just over half move regularly and 33 per cent experience homelessness in the two years after they leave care (House of Commons Education Committee, 2025). Young people with care experience have lower levels of educational attainment and lower post-16 further education participation rates; they have higher unemployment rates, more unstable career patterns and higher levels of dependency on welfare benefits; they enter parenthood earlier and they experience more mental health problems (House of Commons Education & Skills Committee, 2007).

Chapter 9 presents several service models for best practice in providing mental health support for care-experienced children and young people. This is another chapter that is based on my PhD research findings. There are three service models that I outline:

1. integrated/embedded into local authority;
2. co-located in local authority;
3. separate from local authority.

The key elements in each of these models are discussed, identifying their benefits for local authorities and other partners. I also provide a case study of one local authority that operated an integrated mental health service within a local authority and outline the strengths and weaknesses of this particular approach.

Conclusion

This book offers a commentary on the mental health of care-experienced children and young people from a social work perspective. In the 40 years I have spent as a social worker working with care-experienced children and young people, I am convinced of the need to keep a child/young person's mental health at the heart of everything we do. This means that social workers should raise their game and develop a comprehensive understanding of mental health issues and what it takes to make a difference in children and young people's lives. We are not mental health specialists (unless additional training is completed to enable us to become Approved Mental Health Professionals, psychotherapists or similarly qualified). However, we still have a duty to have a good amount of mental health literacy and legal literacy, particularly regarding duties and responsibilities defined in the Mental Health Act 1983, the Mental Health Act 2007 and the Mental Capacity Act 2005.

This work is complex and difficult. My wish is that the contents of this book will stimulate conversations and actions to enable social workers to feel more confident in the support they offer care-experienced children and young people. Relational practice is central to making a difference in these children and young people's lives. They deserve to have a social worker who can understand and support them and, where necessary, advocate for them to help them access the support they may need from specialist mental health professionals.

1

What do care-experienced children and young people want from mental health support?

Stephanie Tia, Leon Bumstead and Christine Cocker (supported by Tash Wightman[1])

Introduction

There is a lack of voices of care-experienced young people in the literature (Winter, 2006; Davies and Wright, 2008). This chapter, co-produced with care-experienced young people, counters this. It presents the views of young people who have recently left care on their experiences of the mental health support they received while in care and after leaving care. These young people are members of a support group for young people who are no longer in care facilitated by a county council based in the East of England. I obtained approval from the local authority research governance panel to speak with a number of their care leavers over 18 years old. I met with two young people and a personal adviser (PA), whose comments are cited in the chapter. Although the meeting I had with these young people touched on their personal experiences, this chapter does not focus on their individual stories. Rather, it identifies several issues relating to their broad experiences of mental health support and changes they think would help other care-experienced children and young people.

Material in the chapter is presented in a strengths-based way, following an approach that sets out young people's suggestions concerning how to improve services for them. Research with young people who have experienced safeguarding services has highlighted a number of key messages from them about their experiences of social work and health services:

> I don't like people looking down on me and I don't like people looking up at me like I'm an adult. I like people talking to me for my age.
>
> Kids aren't as naïve as you think. I think the reason that people don't listen to kids is that they're kids.
>
> You've got to trust [the social worker] and she's got to trust you. Otherwise, there's no point.
>
> (Cossar et al, 2011, p 4)

The aim of this chapter is to ensure that the voices of young people are central tenets that run throughout the book. It is important that social workers hear what young people who are care-experienced have to say about how social workers acknowledge, assess and support children and young people who have mental health issues. This chapter provides an opportunity to present their perspectives about the support they have received or would have liked to receive.

'Care' in the care system

There are many publications that outline what 'care' in the care system involves, particularly regarding the provision of support, nurture and opportunities for healing from trauma for children and young people (for example, Hunter, 2001; Golding, 2008; Schofield & Beek, 2014a; Treisman, 2017; Sen, 2018; Cocker & Allain, 2019). The use of the word 'love' has also been mentioned by academics when describing what is meaningful and necessary for young people in discussing the role of social work and the value of the relationships with social workers as representing corporate parents (Cocker & Allain, 2019; Forrester, 2024). It is also included in national policy reviews (Department for Education and Skills, 2007; MacAlister, 2022). Within the academic literature, further discussions highlight existing discourses around the use of 'love' in social work practice (Godden, 2017; Collins, 2024; Plowright, 2024), drawing on the work of bell hooks (hooks, 2001) and her writing on 'love ethics'. Why is this relevant? Because one of the core messages from the young people I spoke with is their belief that they did not matter to the majority of people with whom they had dealings. This did not apply to everyone who worked with them; both young people named some significant people in their lives who had made a difference, including some social workers, independent reviewing officers, foster carers and leaving care PAs. One young person had an extraordinarily high number of placements throughout their time in care and a very large number of social workers too and had found people within this number with whom they could connect. Their experiences show how valuable these connections were; however, they were the exception, not the norm.

The young people I interviewed were not positive about the systems and structures of the care system:

> As soon as you turn 18, it's, 'See you later, have fun!'
>
> We get fucked over in the nicest possible way. That's what I mean.

These comments reflect the lack of control young people feel that they have over their lives and the inequality in opportunity for them as care leavers, compared with other young people who still live with their families. The system also catapults young people, as soon as they turn 18, into having to take responsibility for so many areas of their lives, which can be stressful and demanding. Transition to adulthood is not a single event, and for most young people who are not in care, the responsibilities of adulthood do not immediately fall to them on their 18th birthday. Becoming an adult is a process rather than a single event (Cocker et al, 2024). Many care leavers have sole responsibility for rent, food, and other bills from this age, and have to engage with all the relevant systems and services with limited support. Is it any wonder that so many care leavers find themselves in temporary and unsuitable accommodation or become homeless?[2] The number of care-leaver households aged 18–20 assessed as homeless or threatened with homelessness rose by 33 per cent, from 2,790 in 2018–19 to 3,710 in 2022–23, compared with an 11 per cent rise in the general population over the same period.[3] These financial and other pressures are not always shared in the same way by other young people their age.

Young people's broad impressions of CAMHS and Adult Mental Health Services

Both young people I spoke with had used CAMHS and Adult Mental Health Services. Both had various diagnoses related to their mental health. When I asked them what had worked well with the mental health support they had individually received, both replied in unison, 'Nothing!' It is difficult to hear such negative views of mental health services being expressed, but it is important to understand the reasons why young people find engaging with services so difficult and do not always value the services they receive.

During our meeting I heard about the individual circumstances of both young people. What is common within their stories and with other young people I have spoken to over the past 40 years of my career is that young people are able to recognise when they need help and will seek help, but often this support is not available in a timely way and in a way that suits them. The additional hurdles that young people have had to grapple with over the past few years are the COVID-19 pandemic and accompanying lockdowns affecting their mental and emotional well-being, and the considerable impact this has had on access to and support from mental health services. Waiting lists for CAMHS, in particular, are long[4] and have remained so post-COVID. With these large waiting lists, young people report using drugs and alcohol to self-medicate. This is a public health concern, with long-term consequences for these young people and for health and mental health services.

> I turned 18 during COVID. So, when it came to me transferring over [to adult mental health services], they didn't transfer me over at all. I was just kind of left and then my medication stopped. And then I tried reaching out to help as well, like in that time I didn't get any help. So, I kind of suffered by myself and I relied on

> alcohol and drugs instead of getting the help I should have got.

The use of medication is controversial with young people; they are aware that medication has side effects, and some would rather use talking therapies, but these are not always made available to them, particularly when resources are scarce.

> But what really upset me and really annoyed me is that they just chucked antidepressants at me, put me on one of the highest doses of them, from like 13 up to 18, changed them constantly and just left me to it for six months to a year at a time.

One of the young people, who has experience of using specialist perinatal services, said that was the best NHS service she has received for her mental health support: 'What made it good? It was the worker that I had, ... she was absolutely lovely, very understanding, she actually treated me with respect ... pushed me out of my comfort zone ... she reassured me'.

The other young person discussed the challenges of being diagnosed with multiple mental health conditions and the lack of appropriate support and treatment they received, expressing frustration with mental health professionals who lacked an understanding of their struggles.

> Well, it is pointless talking to them, innit? Really ... They think they know everything just because they've been to school about it. But they don't. They don't know my life ...
>
> ... have a cup of tea, have a bath. Alright then. Go for a walk ... Thanks. Like I've not already tried that ... Yeah, and what if I drown myself.
>
> The amount of children and kids and even adults now that have said that they've had all of that and even worse stuff said to them is actually appalling. And that's from CAMHS. That's from Crisis line, Childline ...

The waiting times are also challenging, as the PA pointed out:

> You've been told that there's about a year wait. You've done the tool kit, they asked you all those questions, and the doctor said that you then wait for a psychologist or psychiatrist, which everyone needs to see, but it could take a year because they haven't got a psychiatrist or a psychologist in the IDT [Integrated Discharge Team] team at the time.

One of the young people also commented: 'I've had nothing.'

There are significant challenges when a young person has been diagnosed with multiple mental health conditions and they experience a lack of appropriate support and treatment, particularly on turning 18. 'It's just easier for them to give someone a label. They give you the label, but then don't give you the tools'.

This presents risks for young people, when they can potentially fall through a net without necessary support at a time in their life when everything is changing. Young people identified and emphasised the need for better crisis responses, more support groups, and advocates to represent their views and to help navigate the mental health system and ensure proper support. They acknowledged that funding and time constraints are key limiting issues but emphasised the importance of empathy and effective communication. The high cost of private therapy and the inaccessibility of this to them, because of a lack of funding for therapeutic support after turning 18, was also highlighted by young people.

In terms of accessing support in emergencies, they had strong views about NHS 111 Option 2 services: 'Option Two are the worst. 111, Option Two. Terrible.'

The young people were clear that their attempts to ask for help in emergencies when they felt unwell were not heard. Both talked about when they had turned up at Accident and Emergency services (A&E):

> You're just stuck with everyone else. You're also treated differently if you've like got there and you're treated as a nuisance … like if you've took an overdose then you're not treated the same as someone else waiting to see a doctor. They don't give two shits.

> There's been times that I went to the hospital even when I was younger. I used to run away from home when I was younger because of how bad I felt. And I used to run to the hospital when I was like, 13, 14, 15, walk all the way from where I was living, all the way to (name of local hospital). It would take about a good two, three hours, even longer to walk from where I was down. And I would go to the hospital. I will, and I will literally say, 'Look, I'm not happy where I am, I feel really unsafe or whatever.' They didn't help me at all. Didn't even bother.

Having had negative experiences when previously accessing health services can have the potential impact of creating barriers for future access and building mistrust and a suspicion of professionals.

Another issue that we discussed related to communication during those times when young people presented to services whilst in crisis.

> PA: But [name of young person] goes mute when they are really struggling. They won't talk to anybody. So, you take them to hospital, I've taken them to hospital and the hospital won't assess them. The hospital will just discharge them because they are not talking … because [in that moment of crisis] they're mute and they are an adult. They've got to be able to talk to [hospital staff assessing them]. But they go mute every time they are in crisis. They didn't speak once for about week, I think, one day, one; one time, easily, about week. And, I mean, didn't talk at all. They were on a section 136 [emergency powers under the Mental Health Act 1983 for police to detain someone and take them to a place of safety], put them in on a section 2 [voluntary admission to hospital under the Mental Health Act 1983 for assessment], wasn't it?
>
> YP: And a section 3 [compulsory admission for assessment and treatment under the Mental Health Act 1983].
>
> PA: Yeah, I went and saw them, and they were still mute. So, but that took a real crisis for you to get sectioned,

> wasn't it? Otherwise that would be, '... not talking to you, off you go.'

Both young people I spoke with shared with me that at various points in their lives, aged both under 18 and over 18, they had used in-patient services. Both commented that thresholds for this level of help were very high. The lack of preventative support had an impact on their use of crisis intervention services. However, their experiences of in-patient services were also poor, reflecting the pressures in this area of care and lack of resources across the sector. Further, both made comments about not being heard when they asked for support, and feeling unsafe living in the community. Again, they thought this was due to limited resources.

Personalisation of services and understanding the individual and their specific needs and circumstances is important in providing young people with appropriate levels of support when they become unwell. Not looking beyond the surface and not using professional curiosity to understand how mental ill health impacts on behaviour means there is a danger that behaviours are misunderstood. For example, someone who withdraws and becomes less responsive when they are unwell is misinterpreted as non-compliant or refusing services rather than this behaviour being framed as a survival mechanism.

Labels and personalisation

A psychiatric diagnosis can be useful for some young people as it can act as a conduit to access necessary services. Sometimes, however, the meaning of these diagnoses can be confusing for young people. This is often an issue when multiple diagnoses are identified, and explanations about the various symptoms that the young person experiences might not be forthcoming from mental health specialists:

> YP: When you get diagnosed with EUPD,[5] BPD,[6] you also get diagnosed with something alongside [like] separation anxiety as well as depression. ... But there was talks ... about the fact that, because I sometimes get hallucinations and stuff, they thought I was

psychotic, okay? And I'm just like, 'No, you can get hallucinations when you have BPD and stuff like that. It's pretty common'. But they're like, 'no, no, you're psychotic'. And then another person that tried to assess me before says, I'm bipolar. Okay, brilliant. Well, what? What am I then? And even the people that are in my life now, they find it generally so hard to deal with me and help me, because I don't know what's wrong with me. So how can I, how can I actually ask for help if I generally don't know what's actually wrong with me, because that label is so broad.

PA: But just by working with you guys, don't you also think this personality disorder is chucked out like smarties?

YP: Yes.

Helping young people understand their mental health diagnoses, including options for treatment, is important, as it can be frightening to understand the implications of these diagnoses, particularly when young people feel that obtaining support is a constant battle. The young people I spoke to thought that the way in which support is then delivered contributes to ongoing risks for many young people, particularly at the point when young people leave care:

> And with the people that I do know that's gone through the mental health services with NHS and whatever, it's corrupt, it's underfunded, we don't get the help that we need.
>
> You wonder why there's so many people that are getting, just like getting that [unwell], especially COVID as well, mental health skyrocketed from COVID. And then you wonder why there's so many people on the waiting list.

In terms of advocacy for young people who are care-experienced, one young person talked about situations where they had been detained in hospital under section 3 of the Mental Health Act 1983 and then not received section 117 aftercare when they left hospital, including proper care planning. This is an example of the risks for care leavers referred to earlier. The young people I spoke to thought that better advocacy would mean all services that should be provided to them actually are. It is not always possible to identify a family member as a nearest relative; a young person may be estranged from family members, so accessing advocacy to ensure that appropriate care planning is taking place can be challenging. This is something to be aware of when supporting care-experienced young people.

The role of social workers, including independent reviewing officers

Relationships with trusted adults, including social workers, are an important source of support for young people. I asked the young people what social workers could do better to support care-experienced young people. One young person highlighted the importance of having a social worker who genuinely cares and communicates effectively. They used examples of positive experiences with specific social workers to illustrate how they 'went the extra mile' to show that they cared. This discussion highlighted the importance of time, patience, good communication, and social workers having high expectations of the children and young people they work with. They also said that social workers should also provide age-appropriate support and guidance tailored for each young person. A lack of understanding and support from social workers and mental health services led to young people feeling dismissed and unheard.

> Without sounding like an absolute, utter twat or very rude, or whatever. Just have a fucking heart. Like, actually have sympathy, actually have compassion with people.

> Literally, like, don't come into social work … don't work with kids. Don't work with problematic teens. Don't work with, you know, really, like mentally unstable adults, if you can't hack it, if you don't have a good heart, if you don't have compassion and sympathy and actual general love and care for people.

> If you don't have any of those things, why are you in that line of work?

The relationships that young people form with independent reviewing officers (IROs) should not be underestimated. Often IROs are the 'constant' person in young people's lives. The two young people had both had many different social workers during their time in care, but only two IROs each, and both remembered each of their IROs warmly, commenting, 'They were kind, treated me with respect' and 'They nagged me … because they cared about me'.

The consistency and continuity of these relationships was valued by both young people. It models the importance of long-term relationships in the lives of care-experienced young people, recognising and evidencing the 'corporate parent' role of the local authority. It also positively impacts on young people's experiences of planning and preparation for leaving care. IROs oversee all the meetings at 16+ and a young person can choose to have an IRO involved in planning meetings post-18 for a limited period if they want to. This ensures that there is some effort around continuity so that potential risks are mitigated over the initial period when a young person turns 18 and leaves care, and there is oversight regarding how young people continue to be consulted and involved in decision-making about their lives. It replicates parental responsibilities, acknowledging that the young person does not immediately become an adult on their 18th birthday. This is a social construct. Most young people will continue to receive support from their families and communities long after they turn 18.

Leaving care services

As with IROs, some of the leaving care PAs were also praised by the young people for their endurance and dedication to working with young people and being a source of support for young people. Colleagues in the leaving care service offer a different service to that of an allocated social worker. This point of transition can be difficult – young people must get to know another person just when everything is changing around them. The important thing is that young people must be consulted about all plans and decisions that are made about them. The local authority must take young people's views into consideration.

> PA: We'll make a plan to see these guys every six to eight weeks, to see you monthly. I know we'll see you in here, but I also see you out of here. If I don't see you here, I'll seek you out. I'll come round and see you. And if they called me and said, 'I need you here', I'd be there … If I wasn't here, you would feel comfortable to speak to somebody else.
>
> YP: Yeah, I guess so. There'd be two other people that I would talk to in the leaving care service, that's all. … It's the relationship – innit!

At the point where young people begin their involvement with leaving care services, often other services change too. For example, many young people move school, from secondary to college/sixth form, and the people who provide mental health support may change from CAMHS to adult mental health services if a young person is eligible for adult services. Since May 2014, young people in foster care have the option to remain living with their foster carers under the 'staying put' arrangements, which is positive, but not all young people want this or are offered it. If young people are in other types of residential/supported living/hostel accommodation prior to leaving care, then other housing options post-18 should be discussed with them. PAs and support workers working in supported living accommodation help young people navigate the changes moving into adulthood alongside other risks and harms that young people may face, such as substance abuse issues. The multiplicity of people who may (or may not) be involved in a young person's life and the decisions that a young person navigates means that PAs could been seen to continue to offer them a parenting role, even though the local authority's legal duty towards them changes at 18. Because of the complexity of the eligibility requirements for mental health provision, PAs can also be the main link for young people, holding need and risk that ideally should be held by the multi-agency network. There are now a number of published Safeguarding Adult Reviews that explore these issues.[7]

The importance of relationships

There are many kinds of relationships that young people manage in their lives: with professional staff, extended family members, people in work and/or education settings, friends, romantic partners and peers in accommodation settings. All of these can be challenging, harmful and/or supportive; sometimes they are all of these things. Moving into adulthood means that the role of professional social services staff changes from 'corporate parent' to one of support and guidance for young people, should this be something that a young person wants. The young people I spoke with articulated clearly the benefits of good quality and longstanding relationships on them, for example: 'You care … like genuine people.'

We know that care-experienced young people are more likely to face additional hurdles in their lives regarding mental health, secure housing, addictions and not being in education or employment. The quality and stability of relationships between young people and professionals was a strong influencing factor on young people's experience of safety and their transition to adulthood. The importance of consistency in these relationships was a theme that constantly came through from the group conversations.

The 'magic wand' question: improving services for other children and young people in care

When I asked both young people about what they would change about their experiences of mental health services if they had a magic wand, the reply was: 'Not having trauma in the first place'.

This response says so much about the lived reality of the impact of trauma on young people's lives. Being aware of a young person's personal journey is important. This includes recognition that young people may be 'hard to help' at various points as a normal process of rebellion in adolescence. In hindsight, one young person was able to acknowledge that when they were younger, their behaviours were challenging and hard work for the people around them who were supporting them: 'That's because I was a little c★★t when I was younger!'

When I asked about what one thing to change that would make the most difference to other young people who are struggling with their mental health, the answer I received was 'more funding'. Given the experiences of these young people and the difficulties they have faced accessing services to meet their needs in a timely way, it is no wonder that funding is the top of the list for them. One of the other equally important changes that would make a difference to young people is employing people to work in the sector who can show compassion, understanding and sympathy towards children and young people who have emotional and behavioural difficulties and/or who are unwell due to mental illness. Giving them the time within their professional lives to form supportive and enabling relationships with the children and young people they work with is also important.

The young people also talked about their wishes for better mental health support, including having someone to talk to when they needed to and better crisis response services: 'That's the thing that would help is having a better crisis response, especially if you're feeling unwell.'

Young people being involved in the planning of mental health services in their communities is also critical and can lead to fantastic innovation (see Wallace and Cocker [2022], and Children's Society work in Birmingham and Newham offering a drop-in service for young people aged between 10–25[8]).

Thinking about options for peer support for young people with mental health problems was another idea that the young people raised, along with more voluntary support groups, better communication with mental health services and having advocates to help navigate the mental health system in lieu of family support. We also discussed the challenges of accessing private mental health services due to cost and the need for more affordable options for those on a low income, particularly with the NHS continuing to have such long waiting lists.

Conclusion

The conversation I had with these young people underscores the need for compassion and understanding in social work to effectively support care-experienced young people. The key message from the young people I spoke with is, 'treat me with respect', which seems a perfectly reasonable request.

How possible is it to take these views of young people and use them as a blueprint to improve services? As users of services, they have a different perspective from the professionals who deliver them. They have offered up insights and perspectives on their own journey. Some of the views expressed are hard hitting; others are contradictory. The perspectives shared in this chapter do not represent 'truth' to all young people who have experiences of care. Neither do they offer simple answers about what might be effective, although some of the problems that both young people highlighted relating to their experiences of mental health services are resolvable. The respect and compassion that these young people expect from staff working in mental health services should be easily deliverable. Other comments show that they do have a good understanding of the crisis within the NHS and the lack of funding available to improve services because they have directly experienced the fallout from this.

Both young people were motivated by wanting things to improve for the children and young people in the care system who are younger than they are and who will also have to navigate incredibly complex systems and structures with limited support. This altruism is to be commended. Ultimately, the young people co-authoring this chapter with me would like a mental health service that balances rights and risks and is person-centred. They want support from others to help them be and feel safe and both were tenacious enough to seek this from the adults in their lives with whom they had professional and trusting relationships, despite the obstacles they faced. Our challenge is to listen to what they have to say and to set about removing the remaining barriers.

2

What research tells us about the mental health of care-experienced children and young people

Introduction

This chapter presents the research evidence from a number of systematic and narrative literature reviews concerning what is known about the mental health of care-experienced children and what interventions are informed by this evidence base. Table 2.1 lists the systematic and narrative reviews included in this chapter.

To identify the systematic reviews, the following databases were searched: Social Care Online; Web of Knowledge; CINAHL; Psycinfo; EBSCOJournals; MEDLINE Ebsco; MEDLINE Ovid; MEDLINE Pub Med; Science Direct, Ingenta Connect; and SCOPUS. References were selected on the basis of title and keywords including the following:

- 'looked after child*' or 'child* in care' or 'out of home care' or 'public care' or 'state care' or 'care experience'; and
- 'mental health', 'mental disorder' or 'emotional and behavioural difficulty'; and
- foster care or residential care; and
- SDQ.

Table 2.1: List of systematic and narrative reviews

Reference	Systematic/Narrative
Turner et al (2005)	Systematic
Winter (2006)	Narrative
Davies and Wright (2008);	Narrative
Forrester et al (2009)	Narrative
Oswald et al (2010)	Systematic
Jones et al (2011)	Systematic
Everson-Hock et al (2012)	Systematic
Jones et al (2012)	Systematic
Pritchett et al (2013)	Systematic
Simkiss et al (2013)	Systematic
Luke et al (2014)	Systematic
Rock et al (2015)	Systematic
Smales et al (2020)	Systematic
Wilson and Barnett (2020)	Systematic
Bogen-Johnston et al (2024)	Systematic
Cummings and Shelton (2024)	Systematic
Evans et al (2024)	Systematic
Goulet et al (2024)	Systematic
Evans et al (2025)	Systematic

Despite the robust approach to this search for systematic reviews that I have outlined here, it is unlikely that every relevant literature review was included.

There is a lot of information already known about the mental health of care-experienced children and young people. The information found in these systematic and narrative reviews provides evidence about what factors are important in determining how well a child or young person may do in a foster or residential placement. There are several similar factors identified consistently in these reviews. These include key common variables: age at first placement; type and duration of abuse experienced prior to entry into care; behavioural problems of the child or young person in the placement; warmth in the relationship between the foster carer and care-experienced child or young person; and the boundary-setting abilities of the foster carer. Each review identifies key factors and points to the complex relationships between the factors intrinsic to the child and young person, and the skills and attributes of the foster carers, including their parenting approach. This is critical when thinking about the factor or factors that are most important for each child or young person, and placement. This goes some way toward helping us to think about how to actively support the mental health of care-experienced children in foster care, given the impact that mental health difficulties have on their functioning and their families in all aspects of everyday life.

The views of children and young people are largely missing from studies which have looked at mental health provision for care-experienced children and young people. What work does exist points to the importance of relationship building as a key part of an intervention strategy (Munford & Sanders, 2015; Sanders & Munford, 2017). This should be considered alongside the need to understand the different nature and context of the problems that care-experienced children and young people have, and the problems that affect timely assessments and referrals to specialist services (Cocker, 2019).

What do we know about the mental health of care-experienced children and young people?

One of the first papers to review the research needs relating to the health of care-experienced children in the UK (Bamford & Wolkind, 1988) highlighted gaps in existing knowledge about the mental health of this group of children and young people. Since that time the work of various other researchers (McCann et al, 1996; Dimigen et al, 1999) has provided seminal evidence about the high rates of mental disorders of children in care in England and Scotland. Concern has been raised about the amount of time it can take for social workers and other professionals not only to identify problems but also to seek appropriate help and treatment where this is necessary. However, this is not a difficulty that can be laid solely at the feet of the social work profession, as timely access to CAMHS has been problematic historically.

In 1999, the Audit Commission published a report that talked about a 'postcode lottery' concerning the length of time some children had to wait to see a CAMHS specialist. At that time, only 14 per cent of CAMHS referrals were from Social Services and Education, compared with much higher referral rates (66 per cent) from NHS clinicians such as GPs and paediatricians.

The Audit Commission suggested at that time, on the basis of anecdotal evidence, that the reasons why social workers did not refer children to CAMHS were due to concerns that children would have to wait for a considerable period of time for an appointment and that there was no flexibility concerning where the child or young person was seen (Audit Commission, 1999). This remains the case for mainstream CAMHS. At the time of the Audit Commission report, a number of other critical reports were also published about CAMHS, which made it increasingly apparent that care-experienced children and young people with emotional and behavioural difficulties were not getting the services they needed, and were a group with high levels of need that were not being met (NHS Advisory Services, 1995; Utting, 1997; Mental Health Foundation, 1999).

As CAMHS became more of a political priority in the UK, the government's 'Mental Illness Specific Grant', provided an opportunity for the development of 24 pilot projects for Local Authorities and Health Services in England to provide joint specialist CAMHS provision for care-experienced children (Richardson & Joughin, 2000; Kurtz & James, 2003). These projects paved the way for the development of specific jointly commissioned and funded mental health services for care-experienced children and young people across England, in the early 2000s (Cocker, 2003; Cocker & Scott, 2006; Kurtz & James, 2003).

Existing systematic and non-systematic reviews of the literature

In searching the research literature relevant to the mental health of care-experienced children, a number of systematic (n= 16) and non-systematic reviews (n=3) were identified. These reviews investigated three broad areas about the mental health of care-experienced children and young people that are related to this study. These comprise: the characteristics of individual children and young people that may contribute to their entry to and outcomes from care (n=8); the role of foster placements in supporting children and young people (n=4); and interventions that are effective with this client group, including improved access to services (n=3). In addition, the non-systematic literature reviews highlighted the views of children and young people receiving services (n=3), which the systematic reviews did not, and this is the main reason for including them in this summary. This section presents an overview of the findings from these literature reviews.

The characteristics of children and young people

There are several key characteristics that are known about children and are measured at entry into care, which can positively or negatively affect psychosocial and/or placement outcomes. These include: low birth-weight; prematurity; disability; injuries; and attendance at A&E; however, a number of reviews suggest that individually these factors are not predictive of outcome (Simkiss et al, 2013).

Several reviews (Jones et al, 2011; Pritchett et al, 2013) have found that at the point of entry into care, a child or young person's mental health is a key characteristic that can affect outcomes. One review identified an association between emotional problems and placement stability on the one hand, and risk factors and outcomes for children and young people on the other (Jones et al, 2011). The numbers of placements that children and young people have during their time in care can also affect outcomes, with children who come into care at a younger age having better placement outcomes in terms of permanency than do older children and young people (Pritchett et al, 2013). A number of characteristics are associated with placement problems, including externalising behaviours, older age of children and children's/young persons' experience of multiple social workers (Rock et al, 2015).

Rock et al (2015) found other characteristics were not so clear cut by way of influence on outcomes, although children or young people with a disability were more likely to have negative outcomes. There was no evidence that the gender of a child or young person affected their outcome, and the evidence in respect of education/cognition on outcomes was mixed. The evidence suggested that if a child or young person had problems in school or a learning disability at the point of entry into care then it was more likely to negatively affect placement outcomes, although the majority of studies identified in the Pritchett et al (2013) review reported no effect of education or cognition on placement outcome. Again, the authors specifically noted that causality was not implied.

A review by Oswald et al (2010) examined the relationship between a history of maltreatment and mental health problems in foster children and found that children in foster care had experienced high rates of abuse and neglect prior to coming into care. Oswald et al (2010) noted that many of the children and young people included in these studies presented with developmental delays as well as mental disorders. The authors champion assessments being undertaken on care-experienced children and young people that include considering their development, behavioural and emotional indicators as well as psychosocial functioning so that children and young people can be referred on to specialist services if required.

A review by Forrester et al (2009) investigated the impact of public care on the outcomes for care-experienced children and young people and identified 12 studies in the British literature that either compared children in care with children from similar backgrounds that had not entered care (three studies), or tracked children in care over time (nine studies). These studies consistently reported the serious emotional problems that care-experienced children and young people have when they enter care, likely because of their abusive and neglectful experiences, while living with parents who have drug or alcohol problems or mental illness, and showed that these problems improved for children and young people living in care over time (Forrester et al, 2009). This finding is consistent with the international literature.

A review by Cummings and Shelton (2024) reviewed the prevalence of mental health disorders among care-experienced children and young people in the UK in 39 studies. They found that prevalence rates varied across studies. The SDQ was the most frequent tool used to assess mental health (Goodman, 1997), but it is not a diagnostic tool. Over half of the 39 studies included in the review utilised prevalence information from a comparator group; this was most commonly young people in the general population, which may not be the best comparison group to use. Their results show that estimates of mental disorders among care-experienced young people in the UK vary considerably. There is a lot we still do not know about care-experienced children and young people's mental health, which is surprising given the state has responsibility to care for them and we have been routinely collecting data about mental health via the SDQ for many years. The authors suggest that further consideration should be given as to the measures that are used to assess mental health of care-experienced children and young people and how their support needs are assessed and supported.

Foster placements

Foster placements are seen as key to the outcomes that children and young people are able to achieve in public care. The warmth of the carers' parenting relationship with the child/young person, including their persistence or 'stickability' and ability to set boundaries is critical, as is the interplay between the two (Pritchett et al, 2013; see also Chapter 6). Rock et al's (2015) review also acknowledged a number of protective factors, including more experienced foster carers with strong parenting skills, older foster carers, and placements where foster carers enable children and young people's academic development. Common to both these systematic reviews is the 'concept of "fit" between the child and the foster family' (Rock et al, 2015, p 197), linked to the child/young person and the carers liking each other, and the child/young person being treated equally alongside other children/young people living with the foster carers with no rivalry within these relationships. The framework that Rock et al (2015) developed to explore this 'fit' between foster child/young person and foster carers divided up background and risk and protective factors related to the child/young person and foster carers, but it did not give any indication of how to weigh up and prioritise these elements. It is precisely this task that professionals struggle with.

Targeted training and support for foster carers may assist with strengthening the factors which are known to produce beneficial outcomes for children and young people. However, the systematic reviews that have evaluated evidence on this have found mixed results and limited impact of foster carer training or support on the behavioural problems of care-experienced children or young people, placement stability or mental health. In their review, Everson-Hock et al (2012) found that very few courses for foster carers had been evaluated using randomised controlled trials (RCTs) to ascertain the impact of the training on the child's within-placement behaviour and wellbeing, including problem behaviours and placement stability. Of the five studies discussed, three reported benefits from the training on the behaviour and wellbeing of the child or young person in placement (all of these were US studies), and the other two (both UK studies) reported that the training had no significant impact. Better child/young person outcomes are associated with foster carer training programmes that last for longer periods of time but have shorter follow-ups (Dozier et al, 2006; Chamberlain et al, 2008; Sprang, 2009). In their review, Turner et al (2005) also found that while the provision of training to foster carers increased their caring attitudes and skills and reduced behaviour problems in foster children, evidence for the efficacy of CBT-based training intervention for foster carers was inconclusive (Turner et al, 2005).

Interventions and improved access to services

Although there is no dispute about the higher rates of mental health problems within care-experienced children and young people compared to those in the general population (Meltzer et al, 2003), less is known about the issues care-experienced children and young people face accessing support services and the types of interventions available. A review by Jones et al (2012) found little evidence of interventions aimed at improving access to health and mental health services for care-experienced children and young people, commenting that such evidence was in its infancy and that methodological problems with the small number of studies included in the review affected the quality and generalisability of findings. However, several points were made about interconnected factors that are worth mentioning as relevant. Firstly, effective information sharing between agencies may not on its own be enough to guarantee appropriate and timely assessments and referrals to specialist services. Secondly, there were various factors affecting how care-experienced children and young people experienced services – such as the attitude of staff toward them, the length of the waiting list, opening times and location of the service, and the way they perceived and labelled such services – which may have impacted on whether they chose not to attend. Additionally, the nature and context of a care-experienced young person's problems did not always match the services available within local areas, as these were services designed for children and young people living in their birth families. By contrast, many care-experienced children have not lived with their foster carers for a long period of time, and community CAMHS might expect them to have lived in their current placement for at least two years before accepting a referral. This can further compound problems for care-experienced children and young people:

> it is acknowledged that the lack of timely and appropriate interventions from specialist mental health services can compound or create a circle of [care-experienced children and young people] with emotional and behavioural problems unable to receive appropriate treatment or help from services due to placement instability but continuing to experience placement disruption because of their unresolved or untreated emotional distress or behavioural difficulties. (Jones et al, 2012, p 82)

A review commissioned by the National Institute for Health and Clinical Excellence, examined empirical studies that investigated the identification, assessment and treatment for attachment difficulties in care-experienced children and young people. It provided clinical guidance for practitioners about evidence-based interventions for care-experienced children and young people with attachment difficulties (National Collaborating Centre for Mental Health, 2015). The two main factors identified as associated with poor attachment outcomes for care-experienced children and young people were: the birth mother's sensitivity/responsiveness to the child prior to care (this is causally related to the child's attachment); and placement instability, including numbers of placements and placement breakdowns the child or young person has experienced in care. Other associated areas of concern were the child or young person's poor emotional/behavioural functioning/wellbeing; poor foster carer attitude, knowledge and behaviour; criminal status of the child or young person; and their developmental status (National Collaborating Centre for Mental Health, 2015). This review identified several research-based interventions for care-experienced primary-school-aged children: intensive support to foster carers and adopters as required (including supervision via daily or weekly telephone contact, weekly support group meetings and a 24-hour crisis intervention service), alongside training using a behavioural management method; help with peer relationships; support with school; and help to defuse conflict. Other age-related service recommendations emerging from the reviewed research were listed for secondary-school-aged young people, including group-based sessions for adopters and foster carers, and individual sessions with young people to assist with developing self-confidence.

In a review of 106 studies, Luke et al (2014) raised issues with the overall low quality of the intervention research with care-experienced children and young people. Most studies had small sample sizes and very few were randomised. Taking this into account, the review found that several factors were associated with better outcomes for interventions offered to care-experienced children, young people and foster carers. Structured programmes that used attachment theory and social learning theory were best used in combination to address behavioural issues the foster carer might be experiencing. The most effective approaches concentrated on relationship-building between the child/young person and the foster carer and focussed on caregiver sensitivity and attunement, including helping the foster carer develop insight into the reasons for the child/young person's behaviour. Development of the child/young person's understanding of their own emotions and identity was helpful for maximising the success of any intervention. A high level of commitment by the child/young person and the foster carer to the programme also impacted on the success of the intervention. Some flexibility was needed to meet specific needs of children and young people, and follow-up support was advantageous (Luke et al, 2014).

Evans et al (2025) conducted a systematic review about the various programme theories used in mental health and wellbeing interventions offered to care-experienced children and young people in foster care, kinship care or residential care placements. These theories of change explain how interventions should bring about change, how they might be implemented, and how they are influenced by contextual factors. The review identified 13 interventions, with 24 study reports. Most interventions used either attachment theory, theories about Positive youth development, or social learning theory. The review identified a lack of theoretical clarity and coherency, scarce implementation and context theories, and minimal stakeholder involvement in theory development. The authors suggest that there is more to understand about how theories of change underpin interventions, and a need to utilise theories that strengthen relationships and relational practice to support structural changes (Evans et al, 2025).

Further, Evans et al (2024) found that most of the evidence base that examined intervention effectiveness is primarily from the US. They looked at what would be required to transport and adapt interventions to the UK. However, there is still a lot that is not known about mental health and interventions that work effectively with care-experienced children and young people. In some areas, such as wellbeing and suicide, very little empirical work exists. There are many contextual factors, that potentially inhibit delivery: 'These include: insufficient resources; time, emotional and cognitive burden; challenging interprofessional relationships; non-responsiveness to young people's needs; and discounting of carers' knowledge' (Evans et al, 2024, p 3590).

Bogen-Johnston et al (2024) undertook a systematic review investigating available programmes to support reproductive and mental health among care leavers. The authors found no programmes that included an assessment of mental health difficulties even though they found evidence of association between sexual health and mental health difficulties. They suggest that there should be better awareness of the interplay between good sexual health and mental health support and consider any specific support or services that care-experienced young people may need.

There are links between physical activity and mental health in children (Smith et al, 2024). A systematic literature review that examined physical health interventions for care-experienced children (Wilson & Barnett, 2020) found very little existing literature about specific interventions targeting them, which is surprising, as we know that care-experienced children also have more physical health problems than children not in care (Murray et al, 2020). Wilson and Barnett (2020) found that most interventions in the studies that met their inclusion criteria showed benefits with good 'evidence for rhythmic movement on visual motor integration and behaviour, yoga in relation to balance, flexibility and muscle strength, and initiative or general recreation activities for self-concept, self-efficacy and general psychological temperament.' (p 1). The authors caution against generalisation, noting 'particular gaps in relation to children and young people residing in foster or kinship care and for studies examining the effect of sports participation' (p 1).

Supporting care-experienced children and young people with their education is an important role for those that care for them. While not directly addressing mental health issues, Goulet et al (2024) found in their systematic review of interventions that help support academic achievement of care-experienced children and young people that supporting them directly with their education is effective in improving their academic skills when in out-of-home care. The most effective ways of doing this are via tutoring, individualised support, and distributing academic material. Often care-experienced children and young people face social difficulties within school environments and may also exhibit behavioural difficulties. Any intervention to support children and young people with their education should be holistic and not just concentrate on academic learning.

The views of care-experienced children and young people

One systematic review by Smales et al (2020) explored how the voices of care-experienced young people were represented in research examining their health. They found only three studies from 2005 to 2020 that directly involved interviewing young people about their perspectives on what health/mental health means to them.

Two non-systematic reviews have examined the literature on care-experienced children and young people's views of mental health services (Winter, 2006; Davies & Wright, 2008). Davies and Wright's review of 14 qualitative studies pointed to the ethical and consent complications around involving care-experienced children in research and the difficulties that professionals have in asking even less vulnerable children and young people their views about the services they receive. The authors were not able to identify any studies that solely addressed the views of care-experienced children about mental health services received. Rather, care-experienced children were included as part of a wider group of 'vulnerable' children, which also comprised adopted children and children with histories of abuse who were either living at home or with extended family. There were some differences between these groups and children in the general population. Children deemed 'vulnerable', including those in the care system, expressed a marked ambivalence about mental health services. The need for practitioners to pay close attention to building relationships with care-experienced children appeared to be as important in respect of the work done with the child as the techniques and theories used by the therapist. Care-experienced children also expressed an ambivalence toward talking, valuing the use of non-verbal communication as a way to access and connect with the therapy. However, the numbers of care-experienced children were small, and the authors cautioned against generalising these results, instead pointing to the need for further research, examining the views of care-experienced children where therapy had been effective, as well as when it had not been.

The participation of care-experienced children and young people in their health care was a key theme explored in Winter's (2006) review. She also highlighted the lack of research with care-experienced children that addresses their views or participatory experiences in relation to their health: 'Instead most research concerns either the level of need, contributory factors and/or the effectiveness of particular service interventions.' (Winter, 2006, p 78). What was missing was an in-depth investigation about the experiences and participation of young people and younger children in their health and mental health care. Winter highlighted the consequences of this needs-based discourse, which was concerned with identification of need, provision of services and review of effectiveness of such services, on which much research interest had been focussed. She pointed to theoretical approaches and models of development that were used by social workers, where children were the 'object' of study and, 'are presented as passive, with little focus on their own agency, capacities and capabilities' (Winter, 2006, p 88).

Research practices have changed, and there is now much more emphasis and expectation that children and young people will be involved in research conducted about them as co-researchers, or via consultation groups. 'Nothing about us without us', a phrase linked to the disability rights movement originally, has now become part of what is seen as 'good practice' in work undertaken to improve the public care system more broadly. For example, the UK government's independent review of children's social care (MacAlister, 2022) included a consultation group of people with lived experience. Care-experienced young people know the systems of public care very well, including its strengths and weaknesses, and can therefore offer a unique perspective on it.

Key features of reviews

The information found in these systematic and narrative reviews provides evidence about what factors are important in determining how well a child or young person may do in a foster placement or other type of placement, and there are several similarities in the factors that the existing reviews indicate are significant. These include:

- age at first placement;
- type and duration of abuse experienced prior to a child/young person's entry into care;
- numbers of previous placements;
- behavioural problems of the child/young person in the placement;

- warmth in the relationship between the foster carer and child/young person;
- boundary-setting abilities of the foster carer.

Each review points to the complex relationships between factors intrinsic to the child or young person and the skills and attributes of the foster carers, including their parenting approach. This is critical when thinking about the factor or factors that are most important for each child/young person and placement, and goes some way toward helping think about how to actively support the mental health of care-experienced children/young people in foster care, given the impact that mental health difficulties have on the functioning of children and their families in all aspects of everyday life. As highlighted in the previous section, the views of children and young people are largely missing from studies which have looked at mental health provision for care-experienced children and young people. What work does exist points to the importance of relationship building as a key part of an intervention strategy, alongside the need to understand the different nature and context of the problems that care-experienced children and young people have, and the problems that affect timely assessments, referrals to and support offered from specialist services.

Use of the SDQ

Despite the statutory use of the SDQ with care-experienced children and young people since 2009, only one review (Cummings and Shelton, 2024) addressed how the SDQ is used with this population. They recommended that further consideration should be given about the measures used to assess mental health for care-experienced children and young people, and the timing of these assessments. In the systematic review undertaken for my PhD (Cocker, 2019), which examined peer-reviewed literature about looked after children, mental health and the SDQ, I found that studies used the SDQ either as an outcome measure, a screening tool, or a combination of the two. There was relative agreement about the SDQ being an appropriate measure to use as a screening tool. Screening is accepted as a useful activity, and the SDQ has been successfully used by a good number of studies to assess mental health need with care-experienced children.

Similar issues were identified in my review about the usefulness or otherwise of screening care-experienced children and young people for mental health problems, since not all children and young people who had a high SDQ score received the services that they required. This issue of how the use of the SDQ as a screening tool affects access to the support indicated by the needs identified is an area that is less well researched. There are a variety of reasons that might affect access to the care and support that the SDQ screening indicates; however, there is limited research evidence around these critical factors. While the use of the SDQ as a screening tool may be an effective means of gathering information regarding the mental health of care-experienced children and young people, this information is not necessarily utilised to ensure that their mental health needs are met appropriately (Cocker, 2019).

Children and young people known to social services and their access to mental health care

One issue picked up by most, if not all, of the studies is the issue of care-experienced children and young people accessing services quickly. This is a long-standing problem, and one where a quick solution is not available because of very real resourcing pressures. In order for this issue to be addressed, change needs to happen at multiple levels and will take time to embed.

However, it would appear that children in need (and not in care) face even more difficulties accessing adequate CAMHS support. A study investigating the experiences of children known to social services found, through accessing more than 71,000 child health records, that despite evidence showing that these children are more likely to have mental health conditions, they are also more likely to be rejected from CAMHS support compared with peers who are not known to children's services (Mannes et al, 2024). This research also found that children from the most deprived areas are twice as likely to be rejected than those from the least deprived areas. This feels counter-intuitive to what should be the reality for these children, particularly as they will have faced adversity in their lives, and we know the likely impact of this for children and young people's mental health. Public health and care systems should be the backstop and able to redress some of the early hardships that children and young people experience. We now have clear evidence that our services are not meeting the needs of some of our young citizens who are most in need. It is time to address these shortfalls across the systems of support that are available, particularly as the impact on the public purse over time is considerable.

Conclusion

This chapter has provided an overview of research evidence from systematic reviews about what is known about mental health of care-experienced children and young people and what interventions are informed by this evidence base. There is agreement in the literature that care-experienced children and young people have higher rates of mental disorders than children in the general population. We also know, through the use of the SDQ as a screening tool, that where children and young people score highly, indicating concerns, that this does not automatically lead to children and young people being referred to mental health services or being seen by mental health specialists. This needs to be addressed.

Mental health support is not all about referrals to CAMHS. Relational work is important in creating nurturing environments for care-experienced children and young people to flourish. Supporting relationships between children and young people in care and their families and carers is important. Social workers have a role in this process. It is critical to be aware of the evidence base for what is effective in practice in supporting care-experienced children and young people's mental health, and this includes a holistic understanding of effective strategies to support children and young people's physical health and educational development.

3

The role of the Strengths and Difficulties Questionnaire and other screening tools

Introduction

This chapter provides an introduction and overview to the Strengths and Difficulties Questionnaire (SDQ) (Goodman, 1997) as an important screening tool available to social workers to help them understand the mental health needs of care-experienced children and young people. The SDQ is an internationally validated questionnaire used in clinical practice with individual children and in research as a measure of mental health across populations of children. Since 2009 it has been used in the UK as a population measure of care-experienced children's mental health in the annual statistical return for looked after children (see Table 3.1). I describe how the publication by the Department for Education of SDQ aggregated data for children in care in England can be helpful for practitioners and managers. I look at the different models used in local authorities to administer the SDQ process and integrate these data into the care plans for children and young people.

The SDQ: what it is and how to use it

The SDQ is designed for use with children aged between four and sixteen years, although it has been validated for use with children as young as two. It comprises 25 items, each scored 0, 1 or 2, with the higher score indicating raised levels of symptoms. The 25 items are broken down into five scales, covering:

- emotional symptoms
- conduct problems
- hyperactivity or inattention
- friendships and peer relationship problems
- prosocial or positive behaviour

A 'general difficulties' score is identified by adding together the scores from the 20 items comprising the first four categories.[1] The potential range of this overall 'general difficulties' score is between 0 and 40. The scoring of the SDQ enables classification of the general difficulties score into one of three categories:

- normal (score is between 0 and 13);
- borderline (score is between 14 and 16);
- abnormal (score is between 17 and 40).

There are three versions of the SDQ – one for the parent/carer, one for teachers and the self-report scale (for completion by 11- to 16-year-olds) – which provide the potential for triangulation of information about a child or young person across the different versions. An 'impact supplement' is available on an 'extended' version of the SDQ, which asks whether the respondent thinks that the child or young person has a problem and then asks further questions about 'chronicity', 'distress', 'social impairment' and 'burden to others'. This enables clinicians and researchers to gather additional information about the impact of any difficulties on the child or young person (Goodman, 1999).

Other screening tools used by CAMHS clinicians

In addition to the SDQ, there are other general screening tools and questionnaires commonly used in clinical practice in CAMHS in England with care-experienced children. These include the Child Behaviour Checklist (CBCL – developed in the US), the Development and Well-Being Assessment (DAWBA – developed in the UK) and the Assessment Checklist for Children (ACC – developed in Australia). These general tools are briefly outlined in this section, including the clinical advantages and disadvantages when compared with the SDQ.

Apart from the SDQ, the CBCL (Achenbach, 1991) is the measure used most widely in CAMHS. It is also used extensively in the US, has been evaluated alongside many other tools (Rosanbalm et al, 2016) and included in many research studies examining mental health issues in children and young people aged between four and eighteen years. As with the SDQ, it measures internalising and externalising problems and has the capacity to seek the views of multiple informants, with parent/carer, self-report and teacher versions. The CBCL has over 113 questions, compared with 25 for the SDQ, so is considerably lengthier for clinicians and others to administer and score, and for children and young people to complete.

The DAWBA (Goodman et al, 2000) is a diagnostic measure designed to assess ICD-11[2] and DSM-V[3] psychiatric disorders in children aged between five and seventeen years. Again, as with the SDQ, there are parent/carer, self-report and teacher versions; these can be completed as computer-administered interviews as well as face-to-face by an interviewer. It is a lengthy tool as the parent/carer questionnaire is 67 pages long and takes 50 minutes to complete.[4] The SDQ is part of its collection of 14 questionnaires. The DAWBA has been shown to have merit as an epidemiological measure and a clinical tool (Goodman et al, 2000) and has been used in all the British nationwide surveys of child and adolescent mental health completed since 1999.

Tarren-Sweeney has developed a range of screening tools specifically for care-experienced children. The ACC (ages four to eleven years – 125 items) and the Assessment Checklist for Adolescents (ACA) (ages 12 to 17 years – 105 items), developed by Tarren-Sweeney (2007; 2013), are screening tools that have been used in more than 20 studies with care-experienced and adopted children in the UK, Europe and Australia. Short versions (the ACC-SF is 44 items, and the ACA-SF is 37 items), and brief versions (BAC-C and BAC-A are both 20 items long) are also available. According to Tarren-Sweeney (2013), the ACC and ACA measures have similar screening accuracy (sensitivity and specificity) to the SDQ for identifying mental health problems for children in care. The full and short versions of the ACC and ACA have sub-scales that can be independently analysed, whereas the brief version, which has a similar number of questions as the SDQ, does not. There is some evidence that foster carers favour the BAC over the SDQ as it better captures the specific difficulties encountered by care-experienced children (Lewis, 2014).

The main benefit of the SDQ over other commonly used child mental health screening tools and questionnaires is that it is quick and relatively straightforward to use. It is also free to use, which many of the US equivalents, such as the CBCL, are not. Unlike the short form ACC, which is the SDQ's nearest equivalent in terms of brevity, it has sub-scales. The SDQ is used routinely in CAMHS in the UK (Jacobs, 2020) and is also used in many other countries, having been translated into more than 80 languages (Goodman, 1997, Goodman et al, 2004). It has become one of the most widely used and well-recognised child and adolescent screening tools internationally (Tarren-Sweeney, 2013). This means that both individual and population-level findings about care-experienced children can be easily compared with population norms.

The usefulness of the SDQ with care-experienced children and young people

Many CAMHS professionals use standardised assessment tools in their clinical work, as either screening aids or diagnostic tools. These are instruments used to measure data gathered through an interview, or self-completion with a child, young person or adult. These standardised tests have been through a rigorous process of development, including publication of data in peer-reviewed sources detailing their reliability and validity in respect of whatever they are specifically designed to measure. The test will have been used on different (large) samples of the population to create 'normative' data against which individual test scores can be compared. This process has taken place with the SDQ.

There is now therefore considerable research evidence which assesses the psychometric properties of the SDQ (reliability[5], validity[6], sensitivity[7] and specificity[8]) and supports its efficacy as a screening tool in the general population in the UK (Goodman,

1997; Goodman, 1999; Meltzer et al, 2000; Goodman, 2001), internationally (Woerner et al, 2004; Zakaria & Yaacob, 2008; Elhamid et al, 2009; Van Roy et al, 2009; Anselmi et al, 2010; Petermann et al, 2010; Amstadter et al, 2011; De Giacomo et al, 2012; Niclasen et al, 2012; Abbo et al, 2013; Bele et al, 2013; Gómez-Beneyto et al, 2013; Tanabe et al, 2013; Lai et al., 2014) and for care-experienced children (Goodman et al, 2004; Ford et al, 2007; Egelund & Lausten, 2009; Marquis & Flynn, 2009; Goodman & Goodman, 2012,).

The three versions of the SDQ (parent/carer, teacher and self-report versions) have been validated independently in community samples (Goodman et al, 2003; Becker et al, 2004a, 2004b; Pez, 2012), although some studies report limited agreement between the versions when used together in community samples (Meer et al, 2008; Stokes et al, 2014). When not used together, studies have shown that the parent/carer version has a good degree of reliability when used with care-experienced children (Goodman & Goodman, 2012). Additionally, Mason et al (2012) showed that the SDQ is sensitive to change over time and that there was also a high degree of association between the changes noted over time in SDQ and CBCL measures. The authors suggest on this basis that the SDQ is a cheaper and shorter alternative to longer measures, such as the CBCL.

In a national survey undertaken in England (Meltzer et al, 2003) (n=1,028), several instruments were used to assess the mental health functioning of care-experienced children, including the SDQ and the CBCL. In terms of its use with care-experienced children, Goodman et al (2004) found that comparison of responses by carers on the multi-informant SDQ for parent/carer, teacher, and older children aged 11–16 with other independent psychiatric questionnaires, such as the CBCL, resulted in a specificity for the SDQ of 80 per cent and a sensitivity of 85 per cent. Goodman et al (2004) suggested that the SDQ works best when versions have been completed by both carers and teachers, but both have roughly equal diagnostic predictive value, compared with the self-reports by 11- to 16-year-olds, where the diagnostic predictive value is lower.

There are a number of other research studies that have included the SDQ when examining levels of mental health problems in care-experienced children and young people; studies have large samples with comparison groups enabling population-based assessments to be made (Meltzer et al, 2003, 2004a, 2004b; Goodman et al, 2004; Ford et al, 2007; Egelund and Lausten, 2009; Lehmann et al, 2013). These are consistent in identifying significantly higher levels of mental health problems among care-experienced children compared with the general population. In several of the studies listed here, the SDQ was used as one of a number of tools, usually alongside diagnostic measures such as the DAWBA, CBCL and/or a clinical interview. Researchers were then able to comment on how useful the SDQ was at identifying serious mental health problems for children and young people in care. All the studies discussed here demonstrated that the SDQ was 'a genuinely dimensional measure of mental health need in care-experienced children' (Goodman & Goodman, 2012, p 427) and able to identify children at high risk of mental health difficulties.

Why was the SDQ introduced into social work?

Before 2009, mental health screening or assessment tools were not routinely used by local authority social workers in England working with care-experienced children. Due to a number of research studies outlining the high prevalence of mental disorders within the care-experienced children population (Dimigen et al, 1999; McCann et al, 1996; Meltzer et al, 2003), and the lack of national data available, the Care Matters White Paper (Department for Education and Skills, 2007) recommended that a new local government indicator (NI58), should focus on the emotional and behavioural difficulties of care-experienced children. The SDQ was the tool adopted and, since 2009, regular annual SDQ carer data collection has been undertaken across England as an administrative data exercise for the annual central government statistical returns required from local authorities about outcomes for care-experienced children. The government continues to collect and publish information on the psychological and emotional health of care-experienced children who have been in care for one year or longer and who are aged between four to sixteen years, using the SDQ carer report version only. Data are collected for each child after around one year, and then every subsequent year at some point within the year. These data are presented by the government in aggregated form in their annual statistical publications.

Department for Education aggregated SDQ data

We now have 15 years of aggregated SDQ data collected by the Department for Education (DfE) available on the DfE website.[9] These data show completion percentages for each local authority (n=152). Table 3.1 shows a summary of the aggregated English 2009–23 SDQ data on care-experienced children.

The data in Table 3.1 indicate that throughout these years the return rates have been relatively stable, with around two thirds of eligible children and young people included in the return each year. This means that, conversely, just under one third of eligible children and young people are consistently not included in these returns. This is a considerable amount of missing data that could be a source of systematic bias; for example, it would be useful to know if the children with the most challenging problems are more likely to be missing. We also know that some local authorities manage very good return rates, whereas others struggle to provide them.

The DfE aggregated data report also includes a mean of the overall SDQs received. The most recent (2023) mean SDQ score was 14.4, which is at the bottom end of the 'borderline' category, and the highest it has ever been. However, there is relative consistency across the 15 years of data, with a range of 13.7 to 14.4. Between 2009 to 2023, consistently around half of all care-experienced children had emotional and behavioural health that was within the 'normal' range on the SDQ, around one in ten were 'borderline' and around four in ten were within the 'abnormal' range.

While SDQ data provide an overview of the emotional and behavioural health of care-experienced children in England, there are some important points to observe that might affect the validity of the aggregated data and the conclusions which can be drawn. Firstly, local authorities have many different ways of obtaining these data. This includes via administrators based in Social Services or CAMHS, care-experienced children's health nurses, assistant psychologists, other CAMHS clinicians, Social

Table 3.1: SDQ scores, 2009–23

	2009	2010	2011	2012	2013	2014	2015	2016	2017	2018	2019	2020	2021	2022	2023
Number of valid SDQ returns	22,700	22,810	23,870	23,480	24,080	23,650	26,020	27,652	28,810	30,730	32,089	34,425	34,968	33,333	32,542
% of those eligible with SDQ returns	68%	68%	69%	71%	71%	68%	72%	75%	76%	78%	78%	81%	80%	77%	75%
Mean SDQ difficulties score*	13.9	14.2	13.9	13.9	14.0	13.9	13.9	14.0	14.1	14.2	14.2	14.1	13.7	13.8	14.4
% with 'normal' score*	50%	49%	51%	51%	50%	50%	50%	49%	49%	49%	49%	49%	51%	50%	47%
% with 'borderline' score*	12%	13%	13%	13%	12%	13%	13%	13%	12%	12%	13%	13%	12%	12%	13%
% with 'abnormal' score*	38%	38%	37%	37%	38%	37%	37%	38%	38%	39%	39%	38%	37%	37%	40%

Notes: 2009–11 sample stated as aged 4–16; 2012–15 sample stated as aged 5–16; * SDQ range 0–40, categorised as 0–13 = 'normal', 14–16 = 'borderline', 17–40 = 'abnormal' (Goodman, 1997).

Services staff and care-experienced children's designated GPs. A second potential issue in relation to the validity of SDQ data is that foster carers or residential care workers may either over- or under-report mental health issues (Ford et al, 2007; Goodman et al, 2004). A third issue is the one third of children from whom data have not been collected. Further investigation is needed to understand why this is the case.

Despite these issues, the SDQ data provide an opportunity for scrutiny and analysis on an unprecedented scale. The government requirement to collect the SDQ annually has been perceived by some as introducing a population screen for care-experienced children. The issue of when to use screening instruments in a population has been debated in the health literature for many years, and the next section discusses this in relation to the use of the SDQ as a population-based screening tool for care-experienced children.

The SDQ as a population-based screening tool for care-experienced children and young people

I have already presented an argument showing that the SDQ is an effective screening tool for care-experienced children at a population level as well as at an individual level (Ford et al, 2007; Goodman & Goodman, 2012; Goodman et al, 2004). However, is population screening of care-experienced children a justified use of resources? It takes considerable effort to collect these data every year. Given the results do not differ significantly from year to year, what is gained by repeating this exercise annually?

One way to answer this question is to apply the classic criteria previously used to consider whether to screen populations for non-infectious diseases (Wilson & Jungner, 1968; Public Health England, 2013, 2014). The following discussion takes this approach, using criteria suggested by Wilson and Jungner (1968).

The condition should be an important health problem

As noted earlier, prevalence studies show that mental disorder rates within the care-experienced population are high (Meltzer et al, 2003, 2004b). The DfE aggregated data show that of the children and young people with completed SDQs, half show levels of 'likely caseness', that is, scores within the 'borderline' or 'abnormal' categories. This has major implications for children and young people and their carers, as well as the services required to address needs.

The natural history of the condition should be understood

This is a little more complicated to define in terms of what is known about care-experienced children and mental health at an individual child level and population-based level. Historically, there is some evidence from studies that highlight the relative stability of the high level of mental health needs within the care-experienced children population, which suggests that high levels of mental health problems in this population of children have been known about (from studies) for a long time (Wolkind & Rutter, 1973; Rutter et al, 1976; Bamford & Wolkind, 1988). Until 2009 individual-level child data were not routinely available.

There should be a recognisable latent or early symptomatic stage

Meltzer et al's prevalence study (2003) and the smaller-scale studies which have screened children at entry into care (Dimigen et al, 1999; Sempik et al, 2008) would suggest that using a screening tool can be an effective way to identify children who are at 'high risk' of developing mental disorders but whose problems may not yet have become entrenched.

There should be a test that is easy to perform and interpret, acceptable, accurate, reliable, sensitive and specific

As outlined previously, there are several questionnaires that are effective at screening children and young people for mental health problems. The SDQ is used internationally and has several benefits, which have already been identified earlier. It is also the questionnaire that the DfE mandates for use (Department for Education & Department of Health, 2015a).

There should be an accepted treatment recognised for the disease

This is another more complicated area. Within the general population of children there are a few common child mental health problems where accepted effective treatments exist. There is an evidence base that guides interventions for many types of mental health problems faced by children (Luke et al, 2014). However, children within the general population are more usually faced with one problem, not multiple problems, which is the case for care-experienced children (Minnis, 2013; Cocker and Allain, 2019). Treatments are often more complex for care-experienced children because of the interplay of problems that affect them (Minnis, 2013). Although conduct problems are most common within this population of children (Meltzer et al, 2003), it can be difficult to know which mental health issue to address first when children present with a number of different problems. Knowledge about what treatments or interventions are effective with care-experienced children is limited because of the known co-morbidity and overlap of risk factors present for these children. However, some of the interventions for children who live in the community will be applicable to those who are care-experienced (Luke et al, 2014). Interventions may involve individual sessions with a child to address mental health issues, or consultation or training via parenting programmes for foster carers. However, systematic reviews offer mixed views on the efficacy of such programmes for foster carers (Turner et al, 2005).

Treatment should be more effective if started early

There is little evidence or research on the effectiveness of early intervention in addressing mental health problems of care-experienced children, but early intervention principles for general child psychiatric problems are likely to apply (National CAMHS Support Service, 2011).

There should be a policy on who should be treated

The statutory health guidance clearly sets out the expectations about which care-experienced children should expect to receive treatment by CAMHS, including children placed out of borough and children moving from children's services to adult social care services (Department for Education & Department of Health, 2015a; NICE 2021). However, providing these services in a financial context which includes severe staff shortages and significant local government and NHS funding pressures is problematic. For example, the 'Future in Mind' report on the work of the Children and Young People's Mental Health Taskforce was published in 2015 (Department of Health & NHS England, 2015) under a previous government. This set out the problems and issues in child mental health. Nothing has been implemented following the publication of this report. The Labour government from 2024 has announced the publication of a 10-year plan which, it is hoped, will address these issues.[10]

Diagnosis and treatment should be cost effective

There are a number of studies that provide information on the cost-effectiveness of child psychiatric interventions (Knapp, 1997; Beecham & Knapp, 2001; Knapp et al, 2015) and interventions for fostered children (Minnis et al, 2006). Knapp et al (2015) conclude that 'poor targeting, inequality and inefficiency in the way that mental health, education and social care systems respond to emotional and behavioural problems might explain some of the variation in costs' (p 667). A screening programme may therefore help with better targeting and use of resources. There is evidence to show that costs of support for care-experienced children who have additional support needs are significantly higher than for those children without such needs, and that these additional costs do not lead to better outcomes for children (Ward & Holmes, 2008). These authors suggest that a different configuration of services may be required to better meet the needs of children with complex difficulties. However economic analysis has its limitations, as costs for CAMHS only provide part of the picture as to how children with complex needs are supported and the full costs of that support (Beecham, 2014), and there is some evidence to suggest that even very expensive interventions could prove cost effective in the long term (Boyd et al, 2016).

Case-finding should be a continuous process

Given the resources available for promoting and monitoring children's health in the UK, identifying the needs of those children known to have higher levels of emotional and mental health difficulties should occur on a regular basis, not as a 'one-off' exercise (Wilson et al, 2009). The framework for the looked after children statistical returns provides an opportunity for routine data collection and continuous case-finding. However, case-finding must be accompanied by clear and effective strategies to identify and refer 'cases' to relevant treatment services.

Looking across these criteria, most are fulfilled except that: (a) there is a lack of knowledge about effectiveness of treatment; and (b) local authority teams may not have the systems in place to routinely refer cases for services once the SDQ has highlighted children as having difficulties. There are, therefore, crucial unanswered questions about treatment effectiveness and whether and how these systems work. So how do we address these concerns?

According to Luke et al (2014), there are several factors that make assessment instruments such as the SDQ useful, including how straightforward the tool is to use and whether it can 'predict mental health service need (when used by non-clinicians) or, for clinicians, whether they can help to select and direct the allocation of resources or further diagnostic assessments' (p 11). From their systematic review, Luke et al (2014) concluded that the SDQ provided a good approximation of mental health prevalence in care-experienced children, especially during annual health checks, where 'its use as a screening tool during routine health assessments for looked after children was shown to increase the detection rate of socio-emotional difficulties' (p 12). The study that Luke et al (2014) referred to which used the SDQ during routine health assessments was American (Jee et al, 2011). Outcome data are not collected about the routine use of the SDQ in annual health assessments in England. Further, Luke et al (2014) commented that the information gained from the SDQ could be better used: 'although a number of children's services managers currently make use of local data to identify children needing early interventions, there is further potential for this practice to be developed' (p 15). The next section of this chapter discusses how the English SDQ data regarding care-experienced children might be viewed and analysed.

Accounts in the literature suggest that the way in which screening is undertaken may affect results. For example, studies point to the need to link effective screening to effective treatment strategies (Chaudron & Wisner, 2014), with some acknowledgement of the complexities of the debates about evidence-based medicine and the implications for clinical work and practice (Miles et al, 2003). For care-experienced children, social workers and foster carers, there are no data available that evaluate the effectiveness of any screening/intervention approaches to improve the mental health of care-experienced children.

There can also be unintended consequences of screening and intervention. For example, one of the effects of some screening tools on individuals can be the Hawthorne effect[11] (McCambridge & Day, 2008), where positive changes are evident while there is an emphasis on a particular aspect of service provision, but with a quick return to previous levels once the focus is gone.

There is also evidence to suggest that screening programmes are not always useful. For example, in a related field, Sayal et al (2010), working in England, did not find evidence of long-term, generalisable benefits following a school-based universal screening program for ADHD introduced when children were five. Instead they concluded that there may be adverse effects associated with labelling children at a young age with ADHD, with none of the interventions associated with improved outcomes (Sayal et al, 2010). This again raises issues about how screening tools are used within populations of children. If there are no demonstrable benefits – or there are even harms – observed for the target population of children, the question needs to be asked whether their use should continue.

Potential approaches to the use, and analysis of the English care-experienced children SDQ data

There are several ways in which the aggregated SDQ data could be used. Firstly, it might serve as an indicator to examine geographical variation (local authorities can compare the average mental health of their care-experienced children population with other local authorities seen as statistically similar), or to analyse time-trends (Cocker et al, 2018).

Secondly, linking the datasets at the individual level could also enable longitudinal analysis to track changes in, and correlates of changes in, the SDQ scores of care-experienced children. The year-on-year data generated via this massive undertaking could be viewed and analysed from two perspectives. The first is that mass screening and availability of results might reasonably be expected to impact on the planning and commissioning practices of those involved to enable timely referrals to services that can address the levels of need identified. This could potentially impact on the mental health of care-experienced children. However, there are significant staffing vacancies in local government and NHS CAMHS that affect service delivery.

The other issue is that, as a common first step in evaluation of other screening programmes, population trends are examined (for example, trends in breast cancer mortality over time in order to assess the impact of mammographic screening) (Broeders et al, 2012). It could be possible to evaluate the impact of SDQ screening of care-experienced children by examining *aggregate*, population-level trends in SDQ scores over time. If screening had a positive impact on practice, the result might be expected to be a trend of reducing aggregate SDQ scores since 2009 (or, at least, that scores would be lower a few years after its introduction than they were at or immediately after its introduction), reflecting better mental health of care-experienced children following this 'intervention'. This trend is not seen in the SDQ data. What could be the reasons for this, and what other factors could be considered to explain the SDQ aggregate data trends?

A complementary, way of viewing and analysing these English SDQ data is at an *individual* level; linking the datasets from each year in order to conduct longitudinal analyses on individual children over time to examine changes, and, potentially, correlates or predictors of changes at the individual level. This is complicated or, potentially, precluded, by the considerable number, estimated at 40 per cent (Department for Education, 2015), of children who move in and out of the care system each year, thereby reducing the numbers of those with several years' data available for analysis and introducing the possibility that any such analysis might be conducted on a biased sample, since those who remain in the care system over an extended period are likely to differ from those who move out. Additionally, the SDQ data are not gathered either at entry into care or at regular, fixed times throughout the year so cannot be used to analyse child mental health 'before' and 'after' care. Finally, there are significant amounts of missing data, which is a factor that needs to be taken into account. Even with these shortcomings, this vast and annual increasing dataset has great research potential (Cocker et al, 2018).

However, gathering SDQ scores on care-experienced children with problems is only the first step. The next critically important stage involves understanding what is done with these data to address the difficulties many of these children and young people experience. The final section in this chapter describes the expectations of the existing statutory guidance (Department for Education & Department of Health, 2015a), which outlines how the SDQ can be used to improve mental health outcomes for care-experienced children.

Promoting the Health and Wellbeing of Looked-After Children: the English statutory guidance

The rate of local authority statutory SDQ returns over a period of time is only one factor to consider when judging whether a local authority's use of the SDQ in practice is of a 'good' standard. In addition to considering compliance with the central government's requirements, the second factor is the local authority procedures that detail how to collect and use the SDQ data in practice. I summarise next the process considered to be 'good practice' in using SDQ data as a tool to achieve better outcomes that is outlined in the statutory guidance (Department for Education & Department of Health, 2015a).

The statutory guidance sets out how the SDQ should be used in local authorities. It was issued under section 7 of the Local Authority Social Services Act 1970, which means that local authorities are required to implement the guidance unless the local authority has a compelling reason for not doing this.

The guidance states that 'mental health is as important as physical health' (p 4), and the use of the word 'health' in the document includes mental and physical health. The guidance sets out expectations that 'Local authorities are required to use the SDQ to assess the emotional well-being of individual looked after children' (p 10).

Regarding the processes that the statutory guidance outlines for social workers, it states the following:

> As an integral part of care planning, social workers must make arrangements to ensure that every looked after child has:
>
> - Their physical, emotional and mental health needs assessed
> - A health plan describing how those identified needs will be addressed to improve health outcomes
> - Their health plan reviewed in line with care planning requirements.'
>
> (Department for Education & Department of Health, 2015a, p 14)

In terms of the role of social workers, the statutory guidance summarises the purpose of the SDQ as providing social workers with information from a reputable tool which, alongside other information and observations that a social worker will make, helps them consider the emotional wellbeing of care-experienced children and young people. It states that the main benefit of the SDQ is that social workers do not require any training to administer or analyse the data produced from it.

The guidance requires that the SDQ is completed by the child's main carer, usually around the time of the child's health assessment. There is some advice in the guidance about the length of time the carer should have to complete the SDQ (one month), and that where children have recently moved placement, consideration should be given to which carer would be best placed to complete the SDQ, as the carer has to have some knowledge of the child. The guidance also suggests that the carer should be told that the questionnaire is about the child and not about the care being provided to the child or young person in the placement.

The guidance states that the local authority then collects the questionnaire, the child's score is calculated (presumably by the local authority– although this is not explicitly stated, the guidance (p 30) describes the SDQ as 'a simple questionnaire that does not require any training to interpret') and made available for the child's health assessment. The guidance recommends that where the carer SDQ total score is outside the 'normal' range, the social worker and Virtual School Head[12] should arrange for the teacher's version of the SDQ to be completed and, for children over 11, the young person's version should also be completed, to triangulate the data. If these additional questionnaires support the carer's view, then the guidance suggests that referral for a further/fuller diagnostic assessment of mental health should then be undertaken. 'The SDQ should be used as evidence to support a referral to local targeted or specialist mental health services where appropriate.' (Department for Education & Department of Health, 2015a, p 31). The guidance therefore suggests that the SDQ is used as an assessment tool by social workers with care-experienced children. These requirements also apply regardless of where a child lives, so social workers and health professionals should work together to assess and arrange for children to have access to the mental health support they need when they live out of area. This is also the case for children who are moving placements, including from foster care to adoption.

Different models used to collect SDQ data

There were as many different ways in which local authorities and CAMHS gathered the SDQ data as there were local authorities co-operating with this research. What was clear from the qualitative data was that most social workers interviewed were not routinely involved with the Department for Education collection processes, apart from being asked by administrators to supply addresses for foster carers. This extended to most social workers not being regularly informed of the SDQ scores for the children they were allocated. As an exception, a small proportion of social workers were informed and were expected to use this information in the care planning processes for the child.

There are broadly two different models used in local authorities to administer the SDQ and integrate the data into the care plans for children and young people. Figure 3.1 sets out these

Figure 3.1: The two methods used by local authority and CAMHS personnel to collect and disseminate the SDQ data

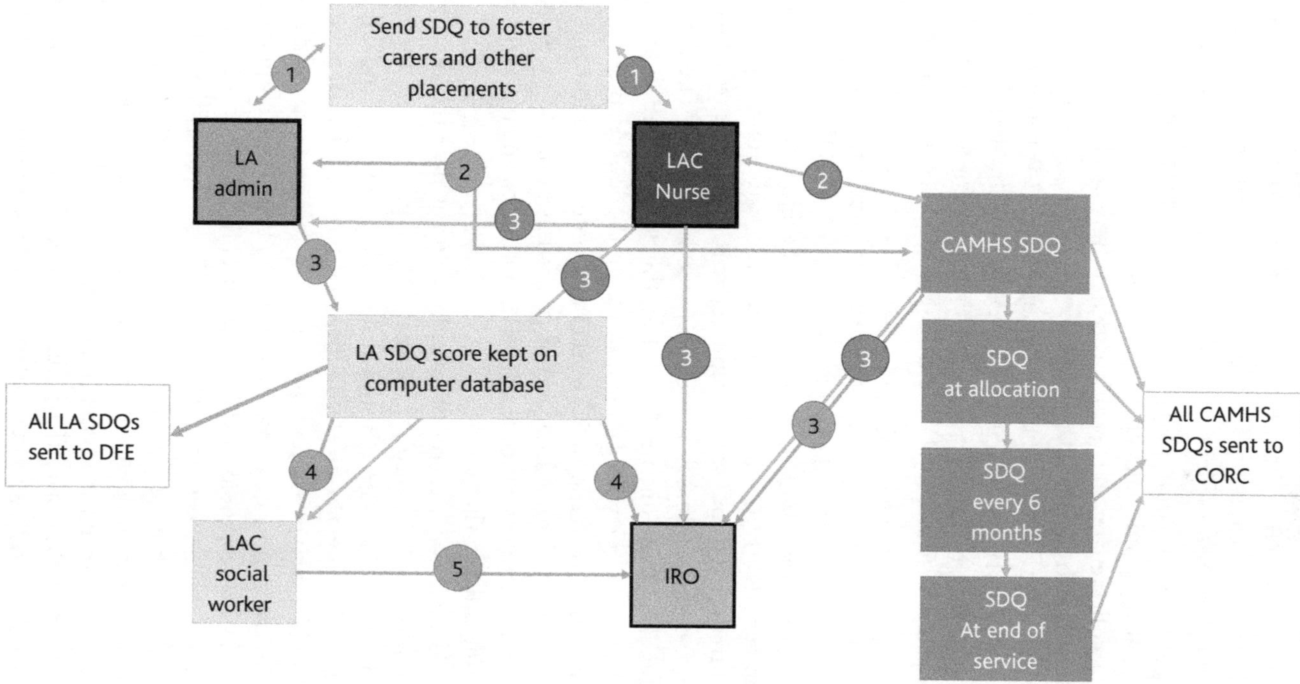

pathways. The numbers denote the order of events in the figure and the direction of the arrows indicates the direction of the information exchange. A double-headed arrow indicates that the information is sent out and returned to the originator. This figure sets out composite processes so each local authority would not always undertake all processes (for example, where the data are collected by the local authority, they would not always be shared with CAMHS).

The pathway with the numbers in black is the pathway that the local authority uses to gather SDQ data for the statistical returns. The administrator sends the SDQ to the foster carer or other placement provider (1), who then completes and returns it to the administrator (1). It is then sent to, and scored by a CAMHS clinician (2), who returns it to the administrator (2) who enters the score on the local authority database (3). A CAMHS clinician could also send the SDQ score directly to the independent reviewing officer (IRO) (3), in which case the IRO administrator enters it onto the local authority computer database (4). The social worker can access the score from the computer database (4). The IRO uses the SDQ score during the six-monthly looked after child review process to review the mental health of the looked after child, in discussion with the social worker and other professionals present at the review (5). A local authority administrator also prepares the annual statistical return for the local authority, and the SDQ score is included in that return.

The pathway with the numbers in white involves the looked after children's (LAC) nurse sending the SDQ paperwork to the carer and then collecting it at the annual medical for the looked after child or young person (1). The foster carer or residential placement provider brings the completed SDQ score to the medical, or the foster carer or residential placement provider completes the SDQ at the annual medical appointment (1). In most cases, the nurse either scores the SDQ themselves or passes the form to a CAMHS clinician to score (2), and the CAMHS clinician then passes the completed SDQ back to the nurse (2) or to the IRO (3). The nurse then returns the form to the social worker (3) or the Local Authority (LA) administrator (3). As before, the IRO uses the SDQ score during one of the six-monthly looked after child review processes to review the mental health of the looked after child. The local authority administrator enters the score on the local authority database and the social worker can access the score from this. A local authority administrator also prepares the annual statistical return for the local authority, and the SDQ score is included in that return.

The CAMHS SDQs (grey boxes to the right of the figure) which are completed at the beginning of, every six months during, and at the end of their work with children, are routinely sent to the Child Outcomes Research Consortium[13] (CORC). This is a separate arrangement from the local authority's SDQ returns.

Resources are required to introduce and use the SDQ as a screening tool within a local authority, to have the screening completed and then to implement any changes to practice that might occur as a result. Processes are bureaucratic. With the high 'likely caseness' rates among looked after children, there are resource implications for what should then happen to those whose scores are high. Five years prior to its introduction, Goodman et al (2004, p 30) suggested that: 'Routine SDQ screening of looked-after children would consume resources, not only in the administration and scoring of the questionnaires, but also in the subsequent assessment of screen-positive children to see if they really have problems that warrant specialist attention.'

When the SDQ annual return was set up in 2009, the principal aim was to collect data that would provide an annual national snapshot of the emotional and behavioural difficulties of those children and young people who had been looked after for a year or longer. This was seen as important because of the high rates of mental health problems that looked after children were known to have (Meltzer et al, 2003, Ford et al, 2007, Goodman & Goodman, 2012). It was also hoped that it would provide an opportunity for local authorities and clinical commissioning groups to use these data for strategic planning purposes within their local areas and for social workers to be able to use individual children's scores to assist with care planning for individual children.

The SDQ was considered by central government to be the appropriate tool to provide mental health data at a national, local and individual level that could then assist with resource allocation to meet local need (Department for Education & Department of Health, 2015a). However, resource data are not collected nationally so it is not possible to see how many more social work or CAMHS appointments are offered to looked after children and/or their carers than before the SDQ data collection began. Some CAMHS discussed the increase in demand for services:

> The actual volume, the demand for services which I think, certainly for looked after children and children on the cusp of care in [the area], are increasing quite dramatically. In [name of service] we have quite a tight contract in terms of number of cases which we provide services to. I'm aware the broader Tier 3 CAMHS service doesn't, and within the last year they've seen a 30 per cent increase in numbers of referrals broadly. That also includes looked after children so I think that's one of the biggest demands. (Systemic Family Therapist, 11)

In Chapter 9 I present a case study of one local authority whose specialist CAMHS for care-experienced children and young people worked well. This included an integrated approach to using the SDQ as a screening tool.

Conclusion

The SDQ is a questionnaire that has been robustly validated by several independent international studies as a tool for accurately screening the mental health of children aged between four and sixteen. It has been chosen as the focus for this book because it is the tool used by the DfE to collect data about care-experienced children who have been in care a year or longer. These collected data are available publicly in aggregated form.

Social workers have a corporate parenting role for care-experienced children and young people. As well as acting as de facto parent, they have a professional relationship with the child and a responsibility to be able to recognise mental health difficulties at an early stage, and work with children and young people and their carers to find the best way of managing these difficulties effectively. This may, in turn, result in referrals to specialist mental health services, because of the high level of emotional and behavioural problems that care-experienced children display. Knowledge of how to use the SDQ in practice does not replace the use of intuition and critical thinking, but it does go some way toward ensuring that rigorous assessments and referrals to specialist agencies occur in a timely manner. Given the challenges to local authority budgets and services, any recommendations to improve current practice must be mindful of resource implications. A multi-agency approach remains critical to establish the routinised usage of the SDQ. This has the potential to benefit all agencies and most importantly, care-experienced children and young people.

4

What do social workers need to know about mental health?

Introduction

This chapter draws directly on the research I completed that forms the basis of this book. The chapter begins with a summary of the perspectives of the 58 social workers from nine different local authorities across the country. I asked social workers for their views about care-experienced children and young people and mental health. I heard about their work with care-experienced children and young people in different settings, including adoption and fostering, children with disabilities services, leaving care services and care-experienced children's teams. They talked about mental health, including their direct work with children and young people, their work with CAMHS and their views about the SDQ. I also highlight the gaps that social workers identified in their own skills and knowledge as well as their frustrations with CAMHS services. The chapter concludes with recommendations for social workers about how to improve their knowledge and skills in this area.

Social workers and children's and young people's mental health

Social workers described their role in supporting children with mental health problems as monitoring, signposting and liaising with specialist services rather than working directly to address any mental health issues. This was largely because of time and caseload pressures. Most social workers were able to give a good account of the concepts of mental health, mental illness, emotional and behavioural difficulties and resilience and how this applied to their work, including the importance of their own role in working directly with children. Social workers also acknowledged the complexity of the caring role for foster carers and adopters, particularly where children and young people struggled with either mental health problems or emotional and behavioural difficulties.

Local specialist mental health teams for care-experienced children and young people were valued by social workers, where they were available. In the main, they were viewed as flexible and approachable and were able to see children reasonably quickly when compared with general CAMHS. However, long waiting times were an issue with some services. For example, general CAMHS had high thresholds or criteria for their services. Furthermore, many children were placed out of the area that they came from and so did not receive a service from that CAMHS provider, despite the existence of national statutory guidance on this issue.[1] This was an ongoing concern given the different moves that many children and young people experienced.

Consultation was used effectively in all CAMHS included in this study and was one way in which social workers and foster carers received a timely service about any child or young person where there were concerns about their mental health. Some social workers that I spoke to were critical of how they thought social work colleagues saw therapy as a 'cure-all' for care-experienced children, rather than part of a range of services to support children and young people to address trauma: 'One of the alarming trends I've noticed over the last couple of years is that a lot of people put therapeutic support or therapy as almost like the magic pill that going to fix somebody' (Adoption, SW2).

There were similarities in terms of how social workers described and understood their role with mental health. Because many social workers saw direct work with children as outside their role because of time pressures, referring a child to another service was an attractive option. Someone else would then work with the child, allowing the social worker to work with other urgent cases.

One of the areas of discussion among all social workers was the role of therapy:

> I think that's a tension when we're working with young people when we say 'and actually this is going to be really beneficial for you if you will engage with it I think that it will be good in the long term', but actually for a lot of our kids either they want to avoid that pain and they do not want to go there, or that they just won't engage at all and I think that's one of the difficult things. (Child, SW1)

One social worker referred to 'the great river of therapy', and the need to not expect CAMHS to 'fix' a child via therapy: 'very often the pressure is from people who want something done therapeutically about specific behaviours .... The distress, the sadness, the grief, the depression, all those enormous adult terms that we do and can apply in children, very often get subsumed into, "I wish he'd just stop doing this."' (Adoption, SW1).

Most social workers' discussions about mental health related to observed behavioural symptoms. A small number of social workers were able to distinguish the differences between behavioural problems that were due to social and environmental circumstances, and mental illness. Some social workers identified the following factors that could affect someone's mental health and emotional wellbeing: genetic influences; points of transition for children between placements and/or in and out of care. They articulated the importance of understanding the nature/nurture debate and issues around predicting future behaviours of young children, particularly in adoption in relation to current mental and emotional status. There was a good appreciation of the complexity of understanding about how to manage this: 'we haven't got a crystal ball and that's what we struggle with. I don't know about you, I struggle with it all the time' (Adoption SW2). The work that foster carers and other agencies, in particular schools, did with children to support their mental health was valued by social workers.

Some social workers showed an understanding of the link between a complex understanding of mental health and the skills required by foster carers and adopters when caring for care-experienced children.

> What we need to look at is adopters who have some understanding of mental health as a positive understanding of supporting it, rather than looking for adopters all the time who want somebody to come in, give people a bit of an MOT, get them over adolescence, define, 'this behaviour's due to adoption, this behaviour's due to temperament, this behaviour's due to nurture', which we do get. We have to accept that people can have highs and lows in their lives, can be affected in terms of their mental health in the same way as their physical health, and they survive it. But I do not feel we often believe that when we say it. We feel that they've got to be got better. (Adoption SW3)

One social work focus group discussed the characteristics of children who were referred to CAMHS. They questioned whether the confidence, experience and expertise of the social worker and foster carer had an influence on whether a child was referred to CAMHS, not just the characteristics and behaviours of the child. They thought that a social worker with low confidence might lead to more referrals to CAMHS (this is discussed further in Chapter 5). Social workers in another focus group did not think they had the correct skills to approach this area of work competently and confidently.

> I think there is a real level of panic around mental health, and wanting to try and fix it and make it better immediately, but not actually having as social workers the ability to do that because we are not trained mental health professionals and we're sort of the jack-of-all-trades and micro-managers in what we do more than we are a specialist in anything. (Child, SW2)

The role of social workers in supporting children and young people

Resilience is a concept often used in social work. It is defined as 'relative resistance to psychosocial risk experiences' (Rutter, 1999, p 120, cited in South et al, 2016, p 178). It is a strengths-based approach that uses attachment theory in its understanding of how children can overcome adversity in their lives (Schofield & Beek, 2005). Despite its widespread use, resilience occupies a contested space in terms of how social workers understand it and use it in practice (South et al, 2016). These differing perspectives have implications for how social workers use CAMHS, with a positive outlook about children's resilience noted as potentially incongruent with their emotional wellbeing (McMurray et al, 2008). These are not separate and opposing entities.

The relationship the social worker had with the child or young person was seen as crucial, with reliability, stability and dependability being the core components of this. 'Being there', 'going the extra mile', 'let the young person know you are making time for him or her' were frequent comments. Social workers saw this relationship with a child or young person as more important than information gathered from a questionnaire like the SDQ.

In my study, most social workers demonstrated an understanding of resilience as a multi-faceted construct. Social workers talked about their role in encouraging resilience by being able to identify the positive qualities of children and young people, and build on these, even if they were small. Some acknowledged that this could be hard to do for some children: 'Sometimes it's quite difficult to try and be positive about a child and to look for the resilience, to look for the positives, their strengths' (Adoption, SW2).

Participation in school and after-school activities, including sports clubs, music and cultural activities, could encourage children's and young people's confidence and self-esteem. However, some children and young people were not able to take advantage of these opportunities; 'some young people "kick-off" at every available opportunity' (care-experienced children, SW3), because of their experiences, their vulnerabilities and low self-esteem. Some children found socialising with peers difficult. Social workers commented that although they saw their role as important in working with and encouraging resilience, their high caseloads affected how much time was available for direct work or life story work.

Another issue emerging from a few focus group discussions concerned how a child or young person's temperament and IQ affected mental health and coping mechanisms: 'you have to know a child's temperament, and you have to assess that as much as their emotional wellbeing, and figure out how to build self-esteem' (Child, SW4).

Social workers identified the need to adjust parenting techniques to match the child's needs, so that the strengths and weaknesses of children were accounted for and nurtured. They suggested that assessing the resilience of placements was a task for social workers too. Placements were valued with carers who could offer positive attachment experiences, provide healthy developmental opportunities throughout the child's life, offer good health care, positive experiences of education and good social developmental opportunities with peers; these were the features of good-quality placements identified by social workers.

How did social workers use the SDQ?

The SDQ was routinely used by social workers in their practice with care-experienced children in only two of the nine local authorities included in this study, despite all nine local authorities returning data for the SSDA903 annual statistical returns to the Department for Education. The processes in place to complete the Department for Education performance indicator returns were either done by administrative staff within a local authority, who sent the SDQ to the foster carer to complete (a stand-alone system), or it was organised as part of the annual medical completed with each care-experienced child or young person. In these circumstances the nurse working with care-experienced children or young people sent the form to the foster carer to complete, along with an appointment time for the annual medical.

A mixed picture emerged regarding the availability of these results for social workers. Two local authorities provided the social workers with the SDQ results and expected them to use these results in their care planning for the child or young person, including referral on to other agencies. The other seven local authorities did not notify the social worker of the results of the SDQ, although in some places they were entered onto the child's electronic records on the local authority computer system independently of the social worker. In two of the local authorities where I conducted focus groups there was almost 100 per cent compliance with SDQ monitoring, but social workers did not look at the results; instead, the SDQ was seen as information that was collected for 'management'.

Independent Reviewing Officers

In all the local authorities, all social workers described how mental health issues were discussed in the Looked After Children Review[2] process. These meetings were chaired by IROs (who are qualified social workers).

Four IROs attended focus groups. The IROs reported a preference for discussing physical health issues in the review rather than mental health issues. Three out of the four IROs interviewed said that social workers did not independently raise issues about mental health in review meetings but did raise physical health concerns. General emotional and behavioural issues might be covered in the meeting, if foster carers or schools raised these about a child or young person. The fourth IRO had a different experience:

> I would say, yes, the child in terms of mental health as a whole is picked up as the standard agenda in terms of the review process and if there's any significant mental health issues or none, that will also get picked up by the LAC medical or via the strengths and difficulties questionnaires. I think that's what I like about them because even as a Chair you could have a view about the presentation of the child in terms of what mental health issues they might be struggling with. Sometimes it's important when you do get the SDQ and you think, 'Ah. see that's where I would've placed it as well for this child'. (IRO, SW4)

The IROs commented that there were now more referrals to CAMHS being made than ever before. One IRO questioned whether social workers should be more discerning with their referrals to CAMHS and pointed out that caseload pressure might be one of the reasons for this increase in referral rates rather than this having anything to do with SDQ scores. The IROs also thought that there was a danger that the current focus on speed in adoption, in court proceedings and in other timescales given for social workers to complete assessments, might be counterproductive; they were concerned that the need to be seen to 'do something', such as refer a child to CAMHS, dominated the social workers' responses.

Adoption social workers

One focus group was comprised of adoption social workers who worked in the same local authority. The SDQ was not directly used by social workers working with care-experienced children in that authority, and the age range of many of the children who were adopted (under four) meant that the SDQ was not used with these children. These adoption social workers commented that CAMHS sent SDQs to them to complete when children they were finding families for were over four years old and in therapy, but this occurred only when the child's social worker did not know the child well. The turnover of social work staff was a problem in that particular local authority: 'the social workers in the looked after teams change on such a rapid, almost weekly, basis that they don't actually know the children well enough to pick up any mental health problems or any trauma' (Adoption, SW2).

There was also an acknowledgement of the complexity of the caring role and the importance of supporting the foster carers and adopters in caring for children who were emotionally affected from many of their pre- and in-care experiences. In this regard, adoption social workers reported having a different role than their social work colleagues regarding their understanding of a child or young person's mental health. They were required to respond to adopters' questions about the future mental health needs for very young children, for example:

> one of our most difficult areas is trying to predict what the future may look like for a particular child depending on their age and obviously we're working with much younger children so we're having to try and guess really what that may look like in the future. In my experience, quite a lot of adopters have quite a high level of anxiety of the future because of their

> inexperience as parents and they want some kind of assurance from the authority or from the placement social workers as to what that behaviour may look like, how they may parent that behaviour and also what kind of support we can offer much further in the future. (Adoption, SW4)

Children with disabilities social workers

Two focus groups included social workers who worked with children with disabilities. They reported that they did not routinely use the SDQ with children and young people in care who had learning disabilities. This was because some children and young people's challenging behaviours might be linked to a learning disability rather than because of emotional problems, or there might be an interplay of a variety of factors. Discerning this was challenging and social workers said that this could cause problems for services working with these children and young people. However, when workers had concerns about the emotional health of their children and young people, they approached relevant services:

> If necessary, I would come and seek the advice of the specialist looked after children mental health team. However, we have such close ties to the medical community anyway, it makes life a lot easier for us because the community paediatrician will also be holding case management for them. So, if I was worried about someone, I would literally be just picking up a phone, and the process is much speedier and much easier to get into CAMHS because it's already coming from the medical side of things. It's nowhere near as difficult as I know it is for other teams. (Children with disabilities, SW1)

The use of the SDQ by social workers

Most social workers thought the role and impact of the SDQs on their own practice were minimal.

> Social workers don't use the SDQ routinely in their work at all ... (Care-experienced children, SW6)

> It's redundant... zilch impact. (Care-experienced children, SW7)

> I think it's a bit sad that it's literally being filed and no one's paying attending to it because you can get quite a lot of really relevant stuff out of it. (Care-experienced children, SW1)

> I guess it a good safety measure in case something's been missed but so far I haven't noticed that that's triggered anything for us. (Care-experienced children, SW8)

> It's a monitoring tool – a little snapshot of a child's life. (Care-experienced children, SW2)

Some social workers, who were not familiar with the SDQ, had limited knowledge about it, did not know its potential capability and had not been offered training on how to use it in practice. Social workers in two different local authorities said they were not aware that the SDQ was used in their borough.

> I'd like to be able to use them. I think they'd be useful, but no one's trained me and I'm not going to faff about with something when I don't really know how it works. (Care-experienced children, SW9)

> I'm aware it's done, because we get emails asking for addresses sometimes, saying that they need to do the SDQ, but I've never seen, I don't know where I'd get it. I don't know where the information goes, or I've never seen the outcomes. (Care-experienced children, SW10)

Of the social workers who were familiar with the SDQ, most said that the SDQ scores did not tell them anything about their young person that they did not already know through regular visiting.

> It just seems like another top-down process, where forms get cascaded down and collected. I mean, the point is, the admin staff send it out because if they left it to social workers, most of them wouldn't go out …. Nobody's shown us how the form could be used, you know, when you're thinking about mental health … because, you know, when I've got information back about particular children, the scores, it's not been a surprise. We're aware that they have got issues and that's because of the assessments that are done, independent of the form. (Care-experienced children, SW10)

A number of social workers spoke positively about their specialist CAMHS service and the way that the SDQ was used by that team.

> I think it's good that there is that net outside of the social worker because I think there's a tendency to try and say 'oh well, the social worker can do that because it would be good for the social worker to know'' and it's like 'well actually, sometimes we can't do everything' and we have to be quite realistic about what we can do. (Care-experienced children, SW11)

A few social workers questioned the science behind the development and use of screening tools and diagnostic tests, and of studies which had published high rates of mental disorder within the care-experienced children population. The rationale given for this by the social workers concerned was that labels were not helpful for children or young people and indicated a 'deficit' view of mental health.

> I do not think that it is in looked after children's interests to be having a label like that around them, unless that was really the case. You know I'd be trying to defend them from a label like that, if you like, because that kind of feeds into all sorts of ideas that already exist about looked after children being 'damaged goods' if you like. (Care-experienced children, SW13)

Social workers in half of the local authorities raised concerns in focus groups about how accurately foster carers completed the annual SDQ. Some social workers who saw the SDQ scores for their child or young person said they did not agree with the scores the foster carer had given. Some thought foster carers overstated the difficulties so that the child or young person would receive a service, whileothers thought the foster carers understated difficulties for children as they did not want to be judged or seen as incompetent.

> I worked on a particular case where when the referral did go across to children's mental health services and they sent the paperwork to the foster carers. And when they filled in the questionnaire, I didn't recognise the child and when the clinicians met the child, they recognised that this is not the child that's been described because the foster carers weren't attuned, and they didn't really understand what was going on for the child in their care. It did lead us to move that child because of it ... These foster carers felt that if they recorded the information more accurately, it would reflect badly on them, that they weren't doing a good job. (Adoption, SW1)

The relationship between CAMHS and social work: a social work perspective

The design and delivery of services varied enormously within the sample of local authorities and CAMHS included in this study, from more traditional social work teams with 'outpatient' CAMHS support, to specialist looked after CAMHS integrated into the local authority. The three service models of integration ('High', 'Moderate' and 'Non-') covered in more detail in Chapter 5 provide a summary of the approaches that local authorities and health trusts had for organising their services. Each borough organised its services differently, depending on resources, staffing and historical services.

Social workers spoke positively about having therapists in the same team:

> a massive difference is having them so that we don't have to do a referral, or we don't have to do paperwork. They can jump NOW! … we don't have to wait all that time, and in a way you've missed your moment more often than not, which used to be very frustrating – the old way of working. (Care-experienced children, SW14)

However, some of the other, more traditional services were also well regarded:

> I must say in terms of my experience of working with our CAMHS pathway, I would regard them as being pretty exceptional. Referral is a very fluid process. As I said, you can have conversations. They're very flexible. One particular difficulty I have is that often my young people won't engage at the beginning so we provide the opportunity for the team to go and gain advice and to see things differently, then often the young person will then join that process. To start on a positive, I think we're pretty blessed. (Care-experienced children, SW15)

> I think once they've been referred to a CAMHS service and the service has been provided, it's usually quite a good service … To me I think we've got a very good CAMHS service, and in adoption work I think they're absolutely excellent. (IRO, SW3)

Regardless of the level of integration between social work and CAMHS in an area, mental health issues were primarily viewed by social workers as the responsibility of their CAMHS. Social workers believed that access to specialist support for children, carers and social workers had improved over the past 10 years. Other social workers talked positively of the benefits of having CAMHS workers available for a quick consultation about a child, including for those children placed out of borough. Consultation was a highly valued service and was available in all the local authorities included in this study.

The social work focus group participants outlined a number of issues that affected their relationship with CAMHS. Firstly, there were still issues for some CAMHS about children needing to be in settled placements before long-term work would start. There were difficulties in getting a child seen by a clinician when the child was not in a permanent placement, but in transition, or where a child had not already been living in a placement for at least 18 months. Social workers thought that CAMHS were still reluctant to see children in these circumstances.

> We do have some conflict with CAMHS sometimes when they're refusing to become involved but all the professionals are feeling it's right for this child and we're the professionals that know the child, whereas they might be making a decision … we have rather a bun fight about it and it goes to and fro. In my experience, we have found compromises where CAMHS have agreed to work with the foster carer or birth relatives or even the prospective adopters once the child's in placement, to gain an understanding of what's going on for the child but in order not to load all the responsibility on the child to face their problems and maybe get better. (Adoption, SW3)

Two other practice issues were highlighted as problematic throughout all local authorities. The first was transitions between CAMHS and adult mental health services when a young person reaches 18. A small number of CAMHS saw young people up to the age of 21 or 24 years. This was also a problem for CAMHS clinicians:

> The problem we have is that we don't want to label children, and unless we label them, post-18 they don't actually have a service. The labels kind of carry the service along with them. They don't kind of, you know, we can try as hard as we can with looked after children not to diagnose them. However, when they are 18, if they haven't got a diagnosis then they won't get the service post-18, and then the child's problems

> become a lot worse, which is why I think a lot of us do refer to CAMHS, especially for the older children to ensure that they do get a service post-18. (Care-experienced children, SW16)

The second issue was poor CAMHS for children placed out of borough. This was also unanimously acknowledged as difficult for social workers and CAMHS clinicians because of problems with accessing CAMHS out of borough, with reports of long waiting lists in many community CAMHS. Social workers reported being told that many CAMHS did not see children who were the responsibility of another local authority as a priority for their services. There were also problems securing funding from the originating local authority to pay for children to be seen more quickly, including privately, where this was required. 'I think we've got 50 per cent of our kids out of borough and we can't engage CAMHS, it's hit and miss and we can't get our CAMHS on board to assist us with that really, you know' (Team Manager for care-experienced children and young people 1).
Additionally, some social workers raised issues about the inflexibility of CAMHS:

> I think the difficulty is that the service offers a one-hat-fits-all kind of service. It's not flexible. If the child doesn't want to go it doesn't think outside of how we could get the child to engage – it's left to us to do it. I think sometimes they need to maybe leave the offices, see them outside of the offices. Yeah, we're going to have a lot of young people who are going to be resistant, but as far as they're concerned if they resist they're not interested. There's got to be that trust, but we had to build trust. I think they should be having to do the same thing as well. (Care-experienced children, SW17)

Social workers who were part of focus groups said that they did not like the potential 13-week wait for children to be seen at CAMHS, which was a considerable wait-time, even though this was within national timescales.

> You can still access local services via local CAMHS, but there's a long waiting list. (Care-experienced children, SW3)

> it's another difficulty we find as well as the growing waiting list in some areas where adopters are waiting for a long time to see a specialist. That's also another difficulty. Obviously we can put in post-adoption support but it's not the same as CAMHS. (Adoption, SW3)

Social workers commented on some of the specialist care-experienced children services that were run like Tier 3 CAMHS:

> it can be a bit like, well, we only offer one service, you know, and you have to fit into the service, take it or leave it or, you know, as IRO1 has said, the CAMHS service is good, but for a lot of teenagers they might not feel that that's what they want and that's what works best for them. So then if that's the only service then we're kind of stuck … (IRO, SW2)

Some social workers and IROs noticed changes to this approach and thought that CAMHS were becoming more accountable for its work through holding regular meetings with social workers to review the progress of children they were seeing. For a small number of social workers, this did not result in CAMHS being any more open about sharing information about what they were doing.

> I don't want to be a killjoy but the CAMHS in my particular borough looks good on paper but I don't think serves their purpose. I had a family that I was working with and information doesn't seem to be two-way, do you know what I mean? I feel I get dragged in for a review – how's the child getting on, what's happening? I'm giving them all these things and I've got nothing back. I don't know if there's been any progress being made. They've been in review for long

> enough. How are you still highlighting the same thing? Clearly your service is not doing the child any good. I've got to the stage now where I can't even go for reviews because I think they're pointless. I've yet to meet a child who has actually said they've found the service helpful and that's where I am with that at the moment. (Care-experienced children, SW18)

Social workers and contested knowledge about mental health

Although many of the comments in the previous sections relate to the SDQ, social workers expressed views about a number of broader topics around mental health. Social workers had strong views about the labelling and stigmatising of children with mental health problems using formal DSM-V/ICD-11 diagnostic criteria. This was a significant issue for many of the social workers I talked to. They claimed it was also an issue for children and young people, to the extent that it stopped young people seeking help. Some social workers thought it might also stop their colleagues from referring children and young people to CAMHS. A minority of social workers said they would only refer a child or young person to CAMHS when everything else had been exhausted. This was explained as a conflict between the social models and medical models affecting mental health practice paradigms:

> I also think that mental health diagnoses … is a very medical way of viewing behaviour and people, and we as social workers try not to prescribe ourselves to look at it in a medical model way. So that's why we're much more into context, much more into relationships and I think that's why we shy away so much from labels and, because it does go down the 'white coat' avenue and you need a pill or you need a hospital wing, but really, we ask ourselves, 'what is that diagnosis going to do? What use is that going to have for this young person in their life right now? What service will it get them that we can't already get them?' (Care-experienced children, SW5)

So, if the paradigms are different, how can social workers find common ground with their health colleagues to support children and young people? This is important, particularly with the upturn in mental health problems for children being reported (Gregory, 2024) with long waiting lists ensuing, meaning that it is likely that children and young people will have to wait a considerable amount of time to be seen by CAMHS specialists. During this wait, children and young people still need support and social workers are part of the network that should be providing this. I heard from social workers that their own lack of training in this area sometimes affected their confidence and competence to address mental health issues. This was not necessarily linked to the number of years a social worker had been qualified. Many social workers who were at the beginning of their professional careers showed a good level of insight into the mental health needs of children and young people, understanding the importance of relational work in supporting children and young people through their experiences of trauma involving separation and loss.

There is an issue about how the differences between an emotional and behavioural issue, a mental health problem, a mental illness, and a psychiatric disorder are understood by social workers (please refer to Introduction for different terms and meanings, and see the discussion in Chapter 1). These terms are not all interchangeable, so understanding the language used to describe mental health is important. This is critical when considering whether a child or young person has a problem because of mental illness, or whether their behaviours are a trauma response they could be reasonably be expected to have because of their experiences. A social worker may not be able to discern this, but for a CAMHS psychologist or psychiatrist, there will be a fundamental difference in what is known about a particular disorder or a trauma response, its potential causes and possible ways of working with it based on evidence. This is where CAMHS specialists are incredibly skilled. Their work is evidence based and while social workers may criticise the medical model, it does have strengths and should not be rejected outright. Social workers should be able to discuss any reservations they have with CAMHS specialists, who will not give a child or young person a psychiatric diagnosis unless it is going to be helpful for that child or young person. This is further explored in Chapter 5.

In particular situations, psychiatrists will recommend that children and young people with specific conditions should be prescribed medication, to assist with some of the symptoms that they might experience. This would occur when medication is known to have a positive effect for the specific disorder the child or young person has. Medication can be a source of contention between social services and health colleagues, because social workers are concerned about inappropriately labelling and stigmatising children and young people as previously mentioned. This is a concern for CAMHS staff too. Discussion between professionals can help work through these tensions. Social workers should feel able to express their views and should request information from child and adolescent psychiatrists and psychologists about recommended treatment options for specific disorders and the implications of this (including side effects) in order that social workers can support children/young people in their role as corporate parent.

I have already mentioned that care-experienced children and young people have much higher rates of mental illness diagnoses than children and young people in the general population. For care-experienced children and young people one other major issue is comorbidity – that is, a child or young person may have more than one chronic or long-term condition. This is more likely to be something that affects children and young people in care than the general population of children and young people who are referred to CAMHS (Luke et al, 2014). The challenge is then how the interplay between the various problems or conditions is understood and which interventions will be effective given this constellation of issues for the individual child or young person. There is less research information available about effective interventions where multiple concurrent mental health problems and other conditions occur. Again, good communication among the professional network is important.

There is an ongoing debate within CAMHS about when a child or young person is most receptive to therapeutic support, with some CAMHS practitioners believing that children and young people who are in short-term placements that are not permanent should not receive therapy, whereas others do not support this view (Wilson, 2001, cited in Hunter, 2001). This was a common criticism expressed by social workers, as it excluded some children and young people from accessing support. It is an issue that is raised time and time again and links to the question of whether children whose inner (emotional) and outer (physical) worlds are in turmoil are able to make use of therapeutic experiences. Hunter (2001, p 1), herself a psychotherapist, believes that psychoanalytic work with deeply mistrustful, traumatised children requires modification of therapeutic practice. She argues that processes require adaptation in order to work with children and young people at various times, and she believes this work can be done with children and young people who are in short-term placements. Support for carers is important in this context, and many specialist CAMHS for care-experienced children and young people will also consider providing sessions for foster carers, recognising their needs.

Another added complication is that children may not always be able to accept and respond positively to support and therapy at the time it is offered. The results of a whole range of clinical and other interventions may only be seen over the course of time and with the developing maturity of the child or young person. This is called 'the sleeper effect' (Flückiger & Del Re, 2017) and is relevant for these children and young people. Archer (2003, p 91) suggests that:

> forming therapeutic relationships with looked after children who have experienced trauma is likely to be difficult because the foundations upon which relationships are based have the capacity to be rocky … the child may share few common perceptions of the world with the therapist: lacking fundamental self awareness and possessing distorted 'road maps' by which to negotiate his [her] healing journey.

Archer outlines some of the difficulties of children engaging in talking therapies, commenting that children's poorly developed reflective capacities will also interfere with the acquisition of appropriate insights through dialogue. In these circumstances there may be other appropriate activities that can be suggested and done with key adults in children's lives, including social workers, which may involve raising self-esteem (for example, engaging the child in some kind of sports activity), or practising key skills such as sharing, concentration and modelling behaviours through a range of everyday activities. Examples of this are: play; sand play; doing practical activities such as cooking and baking; and reading with the child. All of these activities should positively build on the relationship between the child and adult (Cocker & Allain, 2019).

Systemic challenges

Staff turnover and high levels of vacancies in social work teams is an ongoing and significant issue. This is also an issue for specialist mental health services for care-experienced children and young people and in general CAMHS services. Although various governments have promised additional funding to address this challenge, problems in recruitment and retention remain across many NHS and public sector services, which only adds to the complexity of response required to address this at a structural level. The Department of Health and Social Care target continues to be that all children should be seen within 18 weeks from referral (CQC, 2019). This shortage of qualified CAMHS practitioners and long waiting lists mean that it can be a considerable time before children access general CAMHS. Most local authorities have specialist mental health services for care-experienced children and young people, which means that timescales for children and young people to be seen should be a lot less than for mainstream CAMHS. When children are eventually seen, it is important that social workers understand the role and remit of the different mental health specialists and interventions on offer in order that they can effectively advocate for the child and discharge their corporate parental duties (Cocker & Allain, 2019).

Serious mental illnesses that require ongoing support in specialist residential care or admission to hospital can often see local authority colleagues struggling to find appropriate placements, with some children or young people ending up in secure accommodation to keep them safe. Since 2021 I have written a number of Safeguarding Adult Reviews (SARs) involving care-experienced young people who have died or been seriously injured as a result of abuse or neglect and who all experienced mental health issues (Bateman & Cocker, 2021; Williams & Cocker, 2023). The purpose of a SAR is to establish whether there are lessons to be learned from the circumstances of the case about the way in which local professionals and agencies work together to safeguard adults (Department of Health & Social Care, 2023). Problems with mental health services, particularly transitions between CAMHS and adult mental health services, have featured prominently in the SARs about care-experienced young people; there are many lessons to be learnt more broadly from SARs and Child Safeguarding Practice Reviews about the challenges and risks for these children and young people (for a summary of research results, see Chapter 8 of Cocker et al, 2024).

The evidence from reviews illustrates the many placement moves that care-experienced children and young people experience have a knock-on effect for the kind of support (including therapeutic support) offered to children and young people by the professional networks. 'Out of area' placements provide another ongoing challenge that affects young people's experiences of help and support. These can be foster placements, residential placements, specialist therapeutic residential placements or tier 4 in-patient mental health provision. The policy and service implications are complex in these circumstances. For clarity, the following apply:

- The local authority which looks after a child or young person will remain responsible for their care regardless of where they are placed under the Children Act 1989, as well as for providing leaving care support until the young person turns 25.
- Where young people are placed out of a local authority area, services such as CAMHS support and education services become the responsibility of the relevant organisations in the receiving area. There is often a 'postcode lottery' in terms of the response from 'receiving' health partners although there is existing guidance which states that the local authority must notify the Integrated Care Board for the area in which the child

is living in writing. However, there is currently no national protocol or procedure that determines the response in terms of waiting lists or parity of service from the NHS Trust where the placement is based. This is not a new issue.

- The local authority responsible for meeting a person's care and support needs under the Care Act 2014 is the one in which the person is ordinarily resident, unless they have no settled residence, when the test is physical presence, and the local authority carrying out the assessment is responsible for arranging a Care Act advocate to support the individual if they need this to engage with the assessment.
- Where a care-experienced (or any) child or young person requires an assessment of their mental health under the Mental Health Act (MHA) 1983 provisions, the local authority where the individual is physically present is responsible for organising an Approved Mental Health Practitioner (AMHP) to assess whether to make an application to detain a child or young person under section 2 or section 3 of the MHA 1983, although in limited circumstances, the AMHP can suggest that another area should do this if they consider this more appropriate.
- When an incident that needs to be looked into takes place, the local authority where the individual is physically present (including temporarily) is responsible for carrying out any safeguarding enquiry under section 47 of the Children Act 1989 or section 42 of the Care Act 2014, and will be responsible for arranging a Care Act advocate to support the individual if they need this to engage with the investigation.
- The local authority where the individual is ordinarily resident will be responsible for carrying out a Best Interest Assessment (BIA) and authorising a Deprivation of Liberty Safeguards (DoLS) application under the Mental Capacity Act 2005.

Finally, transition from CAMHS to adult mental health services is another area of practice that is fraught with difficulties. This is because the eligibility criteria for adult mental health services set out specific mental illness pathways. Many care-experienced young people do not meet these conditions and so do not receive a service once a CAMHS discharges them when they turn 18.

However, a young person's 18th birthday should not be a surprise to anyone working with that young person. In England there are clear legislative and social policy frameworks in place to assist with transitions planning for care-experienced young people who have enduring mental health difficulties:

- *National Institute for Health and Care Excellence (NICE) guidance*: NICE has produced two guidance documents that set out quality standards for transition from children's to adults' health and social care services and transition from children's to adults' services for young people using health or social care services (NICE, 2016a; 2016b). For all young people in receipt of mental health services, transition planning should start when the young person is 14, with an updated assessment of their needs to ensure a smooth transition to adult services. The guidance advocates a care planning approach to transfer between services in complex cases. This guidance also requires staff to receive training so that they know how to assess risk, provide individualised care and make adjustments or adaptations to health and social care processes to enable access, and that they have the skills to communicate with the young person. The expectation is that those providing care will anticipate and make adjustments to prevent behaviour that challenges, or offer psychosocial interventions as a first-line treatment for challenging behaviours.
- *Special Educational Needs and Disabilities (SEND) Code of Practice*: The Special Educational Needs and Disabilities Code of Practice (Department for Education & Department of Health, 2015b) describes the duty placed on education, health and social care to work together to plan and jointly commission services for young people with special educational needs and/or disabilities whether or not they have an education, health and care plan (EHCP). These duties are set out under the Children and Families Act 2014, the Care Act 2014 and the National Health Services Act 2006.
- *Care Act 2014 Care and Support Statutory Guidance* (Department of Health & Social Care, 2023): Section 58 of the Care Act 2014 places a duty on the local authority to carry out a child's needs assessment prior to their 18th birthday, to ensure that

careful planning is in place to meet their care and support needs as they transition to the adult legal framework. The Care and Support Statutory guidance sets out that an assessment should be carried out if a young person is 'likely to have needs', and not just those needs that will be deemed eligible under the adult statute. Such needs include care and support that arise from or are related to a physical or mental impairment or illness (including a condition as a result of physical, mental, sensory, learning or cognitive disabilities or illnesses, substance misuse or brain injury), but not needs caused by other circumstantial factors. The guidance also sets out the reciprocal duty for relevant partners to cooperate for the purposes of transitions, and paragraph 16.43 states: 'Local authorities should have a clear understanding of their responsibilities, including funding arrangements, for young people and carers who are moving from children's to adult services. Disputes between different departments within a local authority about who is responsible can be time consuming and can sometimes result in disruption to the young person or carer.' The ethos of the Care Act 2014 is that assessments should be needs-led and not restricted by available services. Diagnosis should not act as a barrier to support.

- *Specific guidance for care-experienced young people leaving care (*Department for Education, 2025*)*: Care-experienced young people are another group of young people for whom the state has statutory responsibilities to provide support tbeyond age 18, delivered by a range of agencies including local authorities. There are three principles for transition set out in the Children Act 1989 guidance for young people leaving care, which should govern practice when talking to the young person and when making any decision about them. These are:
  - Is this good enough for my own child?
  - Providing a second chance if things don't go as expected.
  - Is this tailored to their individual needs, particularly if they are more vulnerable than other young people? (Department for Education, 2022, p 9).The Children and Social Work Act 2017 states that personal adviser support can continue to age 25 for all care-experienced young people, not just those in education and employment. The duties on agencies

to cooperate to improve young people's wellbeing, and to safeguard and promote their welfare (Children Act 2004, sections 10 and 11), apply to young people aged 18 and 19 receiving 'leaving care' services.

Several generic CAMHS teams offer ongoing support to young people up to the age of 25, but this is not universal across all services.

Practice issues for social workers to consider

In considering the key tenets from this chapter for practice, there are a number of points to highlight.

Social workers should be able to recognise different kinds of mental health difficulties that care-experienced children and young people might have and consider what support would work best for that individual child or young person to address their identified needs. This might be support that social workers provide themselves or approach other agencies about, depending on the level of need and taking into consideration the views of the child/young person, their family and the professional network supporting the child. The care review process provides opportunities for plans to be reviewed regularly.

Social workers should consider their own relationship with the child or young person, and how that relationship could potentially become a catalyst for change for the child. Relational practice is essential here and social workers are best placed to establish strong and meaningful relationships with children and young people which can be used to support their wellbeing and journey to recovery from trauma and illness. This will not always be easy. Social workers also need support themselves while working with children and young people who have experienced trauma, so organisations need to make sure that this is in place.

There are several issues that could cause tensions between social services and CAMHS. These include: labelling and stigma of receiving diagnosis of a mental illness; the complex nature of care-experienced children's lives and the impact of this on assessment and interventions, including specialised placements; difficulty of children being seen quickly by specialists; understanding therapeutic work – what it can do and what it cannot do; the effect of transition for young people leaving care; and how to support foster carers in their caring responsibilities. These are not issues that can be resolved quickly, so having realistic expectations is important.

Improving social workers' legal literacy is important, particularly around ongoing support for children and young people experiencing serious mental illness, including multiple chronic or long-term conditions, or those who are placed out of area, and young people who are preparing to leave care where there are enduring mental health concerns.

Despite what we know about the emotional and mental health problems that care-experienced children and young people face, there are still gaps in our knowledge about what is effective. Efforts need to continue collectively to concentrate on filling some of the gaps in our knowledge. This includes supporting research that examines specific interventions that embrace medical and social perspectives, making better use of the evaluations of current services to inform future development. Promoting evidence-based interventions and providing good quality opportunities for continuing professional development to social workers would improve their knowledge and skills in this area of practice.

Conclusion

Social workers can use the SDQ data about the children and young people they work with, but very few do this. I found that their understanding and insights into the mental health issues of the children and young people they work with was variable although their access to specialist mental health service support was generally proactive and positive. There are contextual and structural challenges when trying to identify and meet the mental health needs of care-experienced children and young people; navigating the mental health system to obtain help from services under extreme pressures is a challenge for many social workers. Improvements in knowledge and skills would enable social workers both to advocate for children and young people, as well as to recognise how they can contribute support through their direct work with them and their carers. There are also differences in theoretical approaches used by social workers and CAMHS specialists, and while this can create tensions, both approaches are valid. CAMHS specialists provide focussed mental health support. The next chapter discusses how CAMHS specialists view social workers' knowledge and skills in mental health.

5

The role of Child and Adolescent Mental Health Services in supporting care-experienced children and young people

Introduction

CAMHS are important partners in providing mental health services to care-experienced children and young people. This chapter uses data collected from 24 CAMHS specialists from 11 health trusts about their professional relationships with social workers. I was particularly interested in the way in which CAMHS professionals articulated the knowledge and skills social workers need to work effectively with mental health issues for care-experienced children and young people. This is important because social workers should be able to identify and refer appropriately when specialist support is required.

In addition, this chapter explores the relationship between CAMHS and social care. It highlights strengths of some working models between CAMHS and social care, as well as some of the tensions. I review how CAMHS and local authorities use the SDQ data and also how CAMHS clinicians work effectively to support social workers, as well as children and young people. I present three different typologies of social workers identified by CAMHS practitioners: social workers who refer most children on their caseloads; social workers who never refer children; and social workers who understand the remit of CAMHS and refer appropriately. Implications for practice are then discussed.

What is CAMHS (or CYPMHS)?

CAMHS and Children and Young People's Mental Health Services (CYPMHS) both refer to the same services. I have used CAMHS throughout this chapter and book as it remains the term most commonly used. CAMHS include specialist NHS child and young people's mental health services at tiers 1, 2, 3 and 4 (see Table 5.1); specialist social care, and educational, voluntary and independent provision for children and young people with mental health problems. Specialist services for care-experienced children and young people provided through local authorities are part of CAMHS provision. This is provided through the NHS or via a jointly commissioned arrangement. The primary function of CAMHS is to provide mental health care to children and young people. A multi-disciplinary workforce is required to deliver CAMHS provision, which includes psychiatrists, psychologists, psychotherapists, specialist nurses, specialist social workers, and family therapists, among others (Department for Education and Skills & Department of Health, 2004).

Over the past 20 years, the demand for CAMHS has increased significantly (Smith, 2017) and various governments have failed to address the shortfall in funding required to redress this balance (Rainer & Abdinasir, 2023).

The relationship between CAMHS and social work: a CAMHS perspective

Many of the descriptions of mental health services provided by CAMHS clinicians in the focus groups included comments about the degree of flexibility and bureaucracy in each service. Commissioning constraints were raised by several CAMHS clinicians as affecting the work they were able to do. One CAMHS clinician stated that the service that their team had been commissioned to provide included specific numbers of referrals and they were not able to go above this.

> We have had 20 per cent of funding altogether that was lost and at that point, we were able with the commissioners to renegotiate a reduction in terms

Table 5.1: The four-tier strategic framework, from the National Service Framework for Children

Tier	Professionals providing the service	Function/service
Tier 1: A primary level of care	• GPs • Health visitors • School nurses • Social workers • Teachers • Youth justice workers • Voluntary agencies	CAMHS at this level are provided by professionals working in universal services who are in a position: • to identify mental health problems early in their development • to offer general advice • to pursue opportunities for mental health promotion and prevention
Tier 2: A specialised primary care service provided by professionals	• Clinical child psychologists • Paediatricians (especially community) • Educational psychologists • Child and adolescent psychiatrists • Child and adolescent psychotherapists • Community nurses/ nurse specialists • Family therapy	CAMHS professionals should be able to offer: • training and consultation to other professionals (who might be within Tier 1) • consultation to professionals and families • outreach • assessment
Tier 3: A specialised community-based service for more severe, complex or persistent disorders	• Child and adolescent psychiatrists • Clinical child psychologists • Nurses (community or in-patient) • Child psychotherapists • Occupational therapists • Speech and language therapists • Art, music and drama therapists • Family therapy	Services offered: • assessment and treatment • assessment for referrals to Tier 4 • contributions to the services, consultation and training at Tier 1 and Tier 2
Tier 4: Highly specialised in-patient and day-patient units, including specialised eating disorder services, for young people with severe and complex mental health conditions		Child and adolescent in-patient units: • secure forensic units • eating disorders unit • specialist teams (e.g. for sexual abuse) • specialist teams for neuro-psychiatric problems

Source: Department for Education and Skills & Department of Health (2004, pp 46–7)

> of activity. But, like I say, we're still aware that the demand is there. We're also going out for tender next year and we don't know whether the financial envelope will be the same size as it is now. It could be even less. (Systemic family therapist, non-integrated service)

Another spoke about the SDQs not returning the level of need that the commissioners were expecting:

> It was quite interesting to then present that back to the commissioners to say, well, actually it's maybe about the identification of mental health difficulties … and it's how that information is used. You'd expect a higher number of people with higher SDQ scores based on the evidence, the literature about mental health needs in looked after children. But it was falling around maybe, say, 20% rather than 45%–50% that you'd maybe expect in terms of mental health need. So, either the SDQ isn't picking up on that or people aren't identifying it. (Clinical psychologist, highly integrated service)

CAMHS clinicians also identified difficulties with services for children and young people placed out of area, and for young people with mental health problems leaving care at 18 and still requiring mental health services. For children and young people placed out of area:

> There's often a lot of argument about who's providing the funding. Some of the different services won't – either they say they've not got the skills or it's not within their provision to be offering looked after work, so sometimes it's access to CAMHS. Sometimes it's the border as to which CAMHS. … We do have, even within neighbouring boroughs, lots of tensions actually about CAMHS support to our children so there will be differences across boroughs. (Clinical psychologist, highly integrated service)

For young people with mental health problems leaving care:

> transition is very difficult because we don't necessarily know what the provision is in the adult services for young people that have got very high mental health needs because we know we can't put them in our mainstream semi-independent units because there isn't enough support for them. (Clinical psychologist 2, highly integrated service)

In addition, many of the CAMHS and local authority services were in transition themselves, with reorganisations and staffing shortages. New guidelines for referrals were often introduced as part of this process.

> Everything started changing – let's say a foster carer wants a referral to a service. They used to be able to ring up and do it. Now they have to ask their supervising social worker, who has to ask the caseholding social worker, who has to have a meeting. Before this meeting they have to get themselves an SDQ, fill in a consent to treatment form, email it all over to us, then there'll be a phone call to fit in the slot and it's a massive and bigger process. And the consequence of that is that the number booking them has dropped off. (Family therapist, non-integrated service)

One focus group comprised three clinicians in one local authority who were each based in a social work team. The clinicians reported that the integration of clinicians with social workers was highly valued by the social workers as conversations about the mental health of children were part of everyday practice. The borough in question had also invested heavily in systemic training for members of social work staff:

> One of the bonuses of working here in a unit is that you have the opportunity to have that therapeutic lens all of the time, as opposed to occasionally, if you could get a referral. Here, that is our focus, so I think

> it makes the work therapeutic in itself, as opposed to, 'you do therapy with a therapist'. It just makes all of our work more therapeutic all of the time, as opposed to not. (Psychotherapist, highly integrated service)

However, another CAMHS clinician in another area spoke about changes in the local authority structure where social work units had been created based on the 'reclaiming social work' model,[1] but the therapeutic role was different from the 0.5 FTE (full-time equivalent) therapist located in the team in the original model: 'We've been allocated three hours per unit over the next six months, so that's how much they're probably going to get from me' (Family therapist, non-integrated service).'

Many of the CAMHS clinicians referred to the organisational circumstances in which social workers worked, including high workloads and high staff turnover, as affecting their ability to undertake direct work with care-experienced children.

> I think it's not so much about the skill set but the organisational structure around them. Certainly in [area outside London] one of the reasons in terms of the special measures was around caseloads and the supervision and people really not having the reflective space to actually think about the challenge of working through such a vast number. So trying to actually get it to a manageable level so that then you can hold the children in mind and you can be thinking and that you've got supervision which then enables and facilitates that, is important … (Clinical psychologist, highly integrated service)

CAMHS views about social workers' mental health knowledge and skills

Many CAMHS clinicians did not think that social workers had the correct skills and knowledge about child and adolescent mental health to identify and respond to many of the problems that care-experienced children might have because of their pre-care experiences. This also included being able to use the SDQ in practice. Consequently, some of the social work referrals they received were not viewed as appropriate by CAMHS. CAMHS practitioners were divided regarding whether these referrals came from more experienced social workers who understood the importance of mental health in the lives of care-experienced children, or whether it was newly qualified social workers, who had received better training on this issue and were thus more responsive to the mental health needs of care-experienced children and young people.

In the focus groups and individual interviews, CAMHS clinicians identified the skills and knowledge that they thought social workers should identify and use in response to a variety of mental health difficulties that care-experienced children might exhibit. They highlighted a broad range of factors, including the need for in-depth knowledge of questionnaires and how they worked. One psychiatrist had strong views about the ability of social workers to understand questionnaires and how they worked in practice.

> The thing about SDQs is that it's not just about giving a child, parent or teacher a questionnaire. It implies a degree of knowledge about the psychometric properties of any questionnaire, an understanding that this is an assessment tool, it's a screening tool. What does it mean for people to score above and below threshold? So, to just put a questionnaire in the hands of a social worker without knowing that they have a degree of familiarity with those concepts means that they're just not going to know what to do with it … It's not indicative of a situation where social workers have the skills to use screening questionnaires which could be extremely helpful if used in the right way. (Psychiatrist, non-integrated service)

In addition, others identified shortcomings in social work knowledge in the following areas: knowledge of child development; knowledge of developmental trauma and attachment; some general knowledge about the early symptoms of mental health difficulties; and mental health promotion. CAMHS clinicians perceived themselves as readily able to distinguish between children who were mentally ill and those children whose adverse experiences affected their behaviour, and they would expect a social worker also to be able to understand this. However, they recognised a wide variation in social work knowledge about mental health, with some social workers not having suitable knowledge about child development, never mind mental health.

> I'm a little bit disheartened by the lack of social workers' knowledge about things like children's development, for example ... it seems in practice, often part of the thing we've got to do is almost educate the social worker about, 'Look, this would be sort of roughly normal development, this really isn't,' and things like that ... and we have had children with very severe mental health problems including psychotic children, children who are hearing voices and were giving very clear symptoms of mental health disorders that just weren't picked up. (Psychiatrist, non-integrated service)

Clinicians also suggested that social workers should develop a number of skills, in particular: skills in talking to children; skills in talking with foster carers to identify issues that might be going on when the foster carer had concerns about the mental health of the child they were fostering; skills to be able to assess and know the difference between behaviours or difficulties that required CAMHS interventions and those that did not; and having enough skills to directly address some issues with the child and foster carer and to work in and with the child's current environment. Finally, clinicians identified the need for time to think and reflect about the information that had been gathered and to consider the degree to which it might be a normal reaction to an abnormal situation. In this regard, clinicians thought that social workers needed to be able to formulate and 'hold in mind' the children on their caseloads. They suggested that the social workers that struggled more were those who were overly focussed on practical outcomes for children rather than thinking about emotional concerns that children had.

Clinicians in some CAMHS commented that social workers referred many cases to them that did not meet their criteria or where the social worker could provide some support to the child or young person instead of a CAMHS clinician. Some children displayed a range of behaviours because of their experiences of abuse, neglect, separation and loss, and CAMHS did not necessarily see their role as providing support to these children where their responses were understandable given their experiences.

> I think there is something about social workers being able to differentiate between abnormal and normal psychological reactions to difficult times. (Clinical psychologist, highly integrated service)

> One would hope that understanding would be part of the social worker's skill set because sometimes that's the sort of job that we have to do, to say within the range of experience this child has had, you would expect them to have this particular type of behaviour, in which case maybe the CAMHS intervention isn't the best thing. (Psychiatrist, non-integrated service)

Some clinicians identified characteristics for social workers that they thought made a difference to social workers displaying a better understanding of mental ill health and its effect on children and young people in care: 'I think in terms of the ones that "get it", quite often they have quite a good understanding of developmental trauma and attachment, and that they look beyond the symptom. They do not just look at the behaviour' (Systemic family therapist/nurse, non-integrated service).

There was some debate about whether more experienced social workers or newly qualified social workers were more knowledgeable around mental health issues.

> But the other thing I notice is that what I'd see as the 'good social workers who get it' are the ones that perhaps have enough experience that they've got to the point where they can let go of their certainty a little bit. (Psychotherapist, non-integrated service)

> I think sometimes it's the newly qualified social workers who are a lot more up on what the psychological needs are of the children because they have fairly recently qualified. (Care-experienced children nurse, highly integrated service)

> I wonder if the newer ones, part of their training must cover some aspect of it, because they seem to know – I'm assuming that, I don't know that. (Clinical psychologist, highly integrated service)

A number of CAMHS practitioners referred to the social worker as 'a well-attuned parent' or knowing 'as much as a lay person'.

> Generally, they are the referrer so they are like the parent, so you talk to them like you would a parent and say, 'These are my thoughts about a child, and this is what I am doing, this is who I am going to talk to, and this is what my thoughts are'. (Clinical psychologist, highly integrated service)

Maintaining close links between social workers and CAMHS was valued by both social workers and CAMHS clinicians, and although the integration of the specialist CAMHS teams has helped with this, CAMHS focus group members also spoke about the benefits of establishing relationships with individual social workers through their work and saw these relationships as essential. CAMHS practitioners talked about the educative nature of this relationship, to ensure that they receive the 'right kind of referrals' from social workers. Some also spoke of the training they provided for social workers on mental health.

> We do a lot of training, so there's like the primary intervention team that I mentioned, every year they've got a yearly sort of running programme, things like you know – basic things about what is mental health, and then it briefly sort of covers main areas like depression, anxiety, psychosis, those kind of areas. So social workers are always invited to those kind of training …

> I do get asked to do bits of SDQ training, just a very basic this is what it is, this is what it does, this is what it catches, but it's not mandatory for social workers to attend that and it's not something that rolls out every year. (Clinical psychologist, highly integrated service)

Although this training offer was well received, a small number of CAMHS clinicians spoke about some negative effects of social workers receiving limited training about mental health:

> sometimes there are some social workers who have obviously had a little bit of training in mental health and have heard certain words and then start bandying them around very enthusiastically, which are actually quite severe, like kind of asking whether a child is schizophrenic or has a split personality, or something like that, and I'm kind of in horrors that they have got some, dare I say it, false confidence about some of those things. (Clinical psychologist, highly integrated service)

> I've got a repeating difficulty with social workers and other professionals telling carers that children have an attachment disorder, to the point where sometimes children have then not found an adoptive placement because there's labels been used. … And the longer-term impact of that can be really massive. A little bit of knowledge is quite dangerous in that context and that's happened again and again. Once that label's been used, that carries through, even though it's not based on an assessment. (Clinical psychologist, non-integrated service)

Additionally, some CAMHS clinicians spoke about the social workers they never hear from: 'There are some social workers we don't see. It seems impossible that the caseloads are divided so neatly' (Psychotherapist, non-integrated service).

The concern expressed by clinicians was that access to specialist mental health services depended on a social worker's knowledge about mental health rather than the needs of a child. 'Experience', 'confidence' and 'understanding' are the three words that clinicians in different CAMHS used to describe social workers who were more able around mental health issues.

The working relationship between CAMHS and social work: medical and social models

As touched on in Chapter 4, there are a number of barriers to collaborative work between health and social services. These include the different medical and social models used in practice by health and social work practitioners and disagreements about definitions of when a mental health difficulty becomes a problem requiring CAMHS intervention. Further, there are differences in commissioning and funding, eligibility, and legal frameworks which affect interrelationships, working practices and culture.

While there is some overlap, broadly speaking, a medical model involves medical and other health professionals acquiring specialist knowledge about the physical and biological causes of illness and disease through their training, involvement in ongoing research and practice experience. Health is viewed as 'a state of complete physical, mental and social well-being and not merely the absence of disease or infirmity' (World Health Organization, 1946), and health practitioners undertake interventions that use their expert knowledge, in order to relieve symptoms and/or 'cure' the patient (Shah & Mountain, 2007). The social model of health concentrates on environmental and social causes of ill health and focuses on the interplay of these factors (Yuill et al, 2010). Both models are interested in prevention and consider factors such as stress and lifestyle. However, social work practitioners who favour social models highlight social, economic and political influences on health, such as housing, employment, ethnicity and poverty (among a range of factors) as crucially important and are more likely to consider these in formulating interventions. While acknowledging public health approaches that look at the wider social determinants of health (Marmot, 2010; Marmot & Bell, 2012), the medical model tends to focus on biological/physiological understandings of illness, disease and treatment.

Language and terminologies used by the various professional groups working in health, social care and education to describe mental health, mental health problems and emotional and behavioural difficulties differ (Cocker & Allain, 2019; Richardson & Joughin, 2000; Richardson & Lelliott, 2003). These reflect the different theoretical approaches adopted by each profession (Cocker & Allain, 2019). Many of these terms are used interchangeably and so the intended meaning becomes unclear. Alongside this, although there is some crossover in understanding, the roles of various agencies also affect the way in which the mental health of care-experienced children and young people is understood in practice. Although there are many benefits in agencies working together, and a broad range of literature suggests that this is essential for care-experienced children and young people and their mental health, (Blower et al, 2004; Broad, 1999; Department for Education & Department of Health, 2015a; Rao et al, 2010), there can also be tensions:

> the core business of each agency is (and should be) different, although an effective service interface is essential in meeting the needs of vulnerable groups. Most mental health problems inevitably transcend these boundaries, in relation to the child's behaviour, attachment and other relationships, and emotional functioning, and this is where interagency tensions and service fragmentation are most likely to occur. (Rao et al, 2010, p 67)

In exploring these difficulties further, some medical assessments can involve diagnostic processes. In the social work practice recounted by the social work participants in my research, this was not generally favoured, because social workers did not want to label children with diagnosable mental disorders, given their young age and the ongoing significance of this information for children throughout their lives. For a social worker, more emphasis was given to environmental factors (for example, chaotic and/or chronic neglectful parenting) affecting the development of a child, and many social workers believed that by changing factors associated with this, or physically removing the child from significantly harmful experiences and introducing parenting that met a child's physical and emotional needs, there was a strong likelihood that observed distress in a child would dissipate over time. For a significant number of children, this was the case, but not for all children. When examining the mental health difficulties of adopted children, after children had been in adoptive placements for a number of years, there were still ongoing mental health problems for a significant number (Dance et al, 2002; Rushton et al, 1993; Selwyn et al, 2015). This kind of social work thinking also assumed that CAMHS practitioners were unaware of these wider issues.

Issues of professional hierarchies between social care and health, 'labelling' and ontology (how we classify and understand what it is we are examining) for social workers in terms of mental health are not new. Pearce (1999), a child and adolescent psychiatrist, highlighted the contrast in approaches and philosophies between the NHS and social services and provided a useful summary of the medical model:

> This is an approach that aims to be objective, analytical and, as far as possible, scientific. The philosophy of the medical model is based on the Hippocratic oath and is focussed on individual patients where there is a duty to do one's best for that patient, considering their needs above all else and maintaining confidentiality in all but the most extreme circumstances. Perhaps most important of all is the overriding imperative to do no harm. (Pearce, 1999, p 151)

Although many social workers found the medical model limiting in its scope, it could be helpful in structuring and understanding information and knowledge about illnesses and disorders. Pearce suggested that the social models favoured by social workers, such as systems theory, political theory, humanistic and psychoanalytic theories, did not lend themselves to scientific study. While Pearce highlighted many of the polarised positions which could make collaboration between health staff and social services staff difficult, he was careful to avoid proffering simplistic solutions. He cited personality issues, power struggles and misperceptions as frequently hampering effective multi-disciplinary collaboration (Pearce, 1999).

These theoretical differences between health and social services also create differences in generation and use of research knowledge. Although Pearce was careful to acknowledge the importance of both approaches, it was clear that the health approach is generally seen as more robust by virtue of the significant difference in research funding allocated to health and social care (Marsh & Fisher, 2005; Forrester et al, 2009). Pearce suggested that this also had an impact on the way in which social workers practise, in terms of concentrating on 'risk assessment' in their work, whereas health-related approaches embraced 'risk management', which was understood within a broader child development approach.

> Social work interventions are more often a response to a crisis, rather than a measured reaction to a developing problem. Many of these interactions are time limited … social work interventions have to take into account the needs of society just as much as the individual. At the same time, most social work intervention strategies are driven by bureaucratic processes to a much greater extent than within the NHS. (Pearce. 1999, p 151)

Given these criticisms by Pearce, it seems appropriate to probe the critical views of CAMHS practitioners as to the skills and knowledge that social workers have about child and adolescent mental health, including theoretical differences. This affects the way in which CAMHS and social workers work together at micro, meso and macro levels. Where there are professional differences in knowledge and skills, this can create tensions regarding how the work is understood.

Social workers and CAMHS working together

The majority of staff interviewed acknowledged that effective interagency working was key to successful delivery of mental health services to care-experienced children and young people. However, there were several concerns about how this can be achieved. A number of small-scale studies have pointed to difficulties in CAMHS and local authorities working together, including the remit of CAMHS and referral pathways not being well defined, and poor communication (Hill & Mather, 2003), with little evidence of multi-agency working (Stanley et al, 2005). These studies stressed the importance of mental health and social care services putting into practice joint mental health services for care-experienced children (Rao et al, 2010).

There have been some significant changes in the local service landscape for local authorities over the past quarter century. Since 1999, there has been a rise in specialist mental health services for care-experienced children, following the Labour government's use of the Mental Illness Specific Grant to fund the first pilot mental health multi-agency services for looked after children (Kurtz & James, 2003). These became the 'CAMHS innovation projects' and were well received. Most local authorities and CAMHS jointly commission specialist looked after children's services, and there are many different models for service delivery (see Chapter 9). In addition, 14 years of austerity have impacted significantly on funding levels for public sector services, alongside the numbers of under-18s referred to CAMHS having risen significantly since 2019 (Gregory, 2024).

A paradigm for practice

In analysing the data from the qualitative interviews from my research, I identified three groups of social workers by reference to their approach to mental health. While these groups represented broad typologies, they give an indication of three general approaches that social workers took toward recognising and dealing with mental health issues in their practice. Alongside providing information about social workers' theoretical approaches to mental health (including social workers' lack of knowledge), these typologies helped categorise three potential referral patterns from social workers to CAMHS, namely: social workers who refer most children on their caseloads to CAMHS; social workers who rarely refer children to CAMHS; and social workers who understand the remit of CAMHS and refer appropriately.

CAMHS clinicians also had views about the mental health knowledge of social workers and the effect that this had on referrals. Again, these views divided social workers into three groups, which I have named:

- Group one – 'Anxious'
- Group two – 'Anti-labelling'
- Group three – 'Partnership'

Group one – Anxious (SW perspective)

Mental health makes these social workers scared and anxious. They did not think they had the expertise to deal with mental health problems.

> As soon as I hear the word 'mental health' and I'm working with anyone with a mental health problem, straight away, I am, should I say, I'm scared, I'm anxious, you know, what am I going to come up against? (Care-experienced children social worker 3, highly integrated service)

> ... based on my own experience I know that sometimes working with young people with mental health problems, or anyone with mental health can be quite scary for social workers. (Care-experienced children social worker 4, highly integrated service)

For this group of social workers, the medical model was dominant. CAMHS clinicians were seen as 'the experts'. Referrals were made to CAMHS primarily because of behavioural issues, which social workers felt impotent in managing. CAMHS clinicians thought that this group was likely to make many referrals.

Group one – Anxious (CAMHS perspective)

According to CAMHS staff, some of these referrals were made at inappropriate times as the child did not have mental health problems but, rather, CAMHS clinicians thought the child was distressed.

> I think they [some social workers] have quite a lot of worries about what mental illness might be. They don't

> have information about the range of mental illnesses, so I think they're even more worried about having that conversation and the tendency is just do a referral to CAMHS and hope they'll sort it out. (Family therapist, non-integrated service)

> Sometimes we get referrals for children that are upset, but actually they are upset for good reason, and they don't need to see a therapist at that stage. i.e. they've had a bereavement or they've only just moved into a placement, they've been separated from their parents; things that you think, 'OK, this is a natural distressing psychological reaction', but it hasn't yet got to the stage where you think, 'oh dear, we need some professional input'. What they need is someone to do what we all need when we are upset, you know. We just need people to be with us and to support us, and something about that differentiating the normal from the abnormal, that there is definitely a kind of theme about, 'Oops they're upset, I'll send for the psychologist.' and there is actually a difference. We are not just here to see people that are upset for any reason. (Clinical psychologist, highly integrated service)

In contrast, CAMHS tended to view these children as most appropriately supported by the foster carer and social worker, without direct CAMHS intervention.

Group two – Anti-labelling (SW perspective)

Mental health was understood as emotional and behavioural problems in a child or young person. The social model was dominant, and these social workers were wary of labelling children by involving CAMHS.

> [W]hat I'm struggling with in particular with one particular case is when you kind of get a sense that the young person actually would like to have that label, you know, put on them, whereas you, the social

> worker, your views are that it's … they can actually kind of come through this difficult, through other means, rather than kind of maybe a label and having to kind of go on medication. (Care-experienced children social worker 6, highly integrated service)

This affected whether referrals were made to CAMHS and the value that was then attached to the CAMHS role. Often the reason for referral was because of behavioural problems frequently judged by the foster carer or social worker to be 'risky'. Some social workers in this group did not make referrals, because of the difficulties they perceived with labelling children and young people.

> As someone who sees himself as a champion of looked after children, I don't think that I would be thinking that it was in looked after children's interests to be having a label like that around them, unless that was really the case. (Care-experienced children social worker 1, highly integrated service)

Group two – Anti-labelling (CAMHS perspective)

This group of social workers rarely referred children to CAMHS. Several CAMHS focus groups commented on this and said it was highly unlikely that the children allocated to these social workers would not have any mental health problems. 'I think you get the same social workers who refer in children and you get some social workers who won't, even though we've got two psychologists in the building' (CAMHS specialist nurse, highly integrated service).

Group three – Partnership (SW perspective)

These social workers integrated mental health into their everyday practice with a child or young person. They actively sought to develop their knowledge and understanding of mental health, knowing that it contributed to their overall assessment of a child or young person. Both the medical and social models were used. The working relationship between them and CAMHS clinicians was a partnership, and social workers valued this relationship. These social workers were most likely to make appropriate referrals and not solely because of behavioural concerns.

> I think it's quite difficult to separate out behavioural difficulties that come from very traumatic and emotionally deprived backgrounds and a diagnosed mental health problem, because I think it's a very blurred line between the two and I think we often try not to label children too quickly. But at the same time you need to recognise sometimes there is an underlying disorder that can be hereditary disorders that can run in the family line, so I think you have to be quite sensitive in thinking with other professionals, with your colleagues, about 'is it a mental health diagnosis there that is needed, or is it actually trauma or emotional stuff from many placements being, you know, disordering with regards to attachments, that maybe not need diagnosis and treatment in the mental health field'. So I think it's quite a difficult call for us because our children come from such difficult backgrounds so it's actually not mental health per se, it's just having a really difficult, crap life and it's quite a reasonable reaction to that life. (Care-experienced children social worker 2, highly integrated service)

> I would say that we're about trying to keep an open communication with young people – keep them connected as far as is safely possible – with their networks, and to keep talking with them really and to maintain an open dialogue about what is going on in their lives, and what has happened, rather than seeing it as our job as soon as there is a sort of box that gets ticked that says 'mental health problem' – refer them on to another professional! Within our context we do have therapists who work within the units so we have a mental health professional working with

> us and there's a lot of close co-working around this. (Care-experienced children social worker 3, highly integrated service)

Group three – Partnership (CAMHS perspective)

According to several different CAMHS, the final group of social workers 'got it'; they used a trauma-informed psychosocial perspective in their work and understood the benefit of the CAMHS role in the life of a care-experienced child or young person. The working relationship between the two organisations was based on a mutual dialogue.

> In terms of our relationship with social workers, I think there's probably a pattern … there's certain workers who, once they become involved with us, they get it and we maintain a relationship with them. (Psychotherapist, non-integrated service)

> Some are really skilled, and in tune and sensitive to picking up cues from the children and young people they work with, and others are more blind or blunt in their approach. They just see behaviours. (Psychotherapist, highly integrated service)

While these typologies were general categories, they provided a way of understanding and reflecting on the patterns of referrals and underlying culture of interagency working between social workers and CAMHS. CAMHS clinicians and social workers recognised similar issues relating to the strengths and weaknesses of the knowledge and skills of social workers and how this was evidenced in the referral practices of social workers to CAMHS.

Implications for practice

A number of CAMHS clinicians adhered to a medical model: if a child or young person did not have a mental health diagnosis then their problems were social rather than health related. According to these clinicians, some children and young people

Table 5.2: CAMHS practitioners' views of appropriateness of social worker referrals to CAMHS

		Social worker identification of concerning (clinical) emotional/behavioural problem	
		Yes	**No**
CAMHS identification of psychiatric diagnosis	**Yes**	(Y/Y) Viewed by CAMHS practitioners as appropriate referral	(Y/N) Inappropriately not referred
	No	(N/Y) Viewed by CAMHS practitioners as inappropriate referral	(N/N) Appropriately not referred

were inappropriately referred to CAMHS when social workers should have been working with them directly, alongside foster carers (Group one). Some CAMHS staff commented that they should not be expected to work with 'upset' children, and children who had recently come into care could reasonably be expected to be distressed by the separation and loss they had experienced.

Given this, and some of the other comments made by social workers and CAMHS clinicians about the knowledge and skills of social workers in relation to mental health, Table 5.2 explores the relationship between social workers' responses to the behaviours and emotional states of care-experienced children and how this affected their CAMHS referral activities. Reviewing the mental health of a care-experienced child is a routine part of a social worker's role that is monitored in the child's review. Given that the SDQ was not routinely used by social workers in their practice, social workers said that they based their assessment of a child's mental health on their behaviour. Therefore, social workers' ability to synthesise children's behavioural and emotional problems was important in determining which children were referred to CAMHS. Table 5.2 shows the possible mental health and behavioural problem combinations that need to be considered when making referrals to CAMHS, alongside the expectation from many CAMHS clinicians that the children who are referred by social workers should show signs of mental illness.

In this table, only children exhibiting concerning behaviour with an emotional or behavioural element leading to psychiatric diagnosis (Y/Y) would be seen as an appropriate referral by CAMHS clinicians. It is CAMHS's ability to identify a psychiatric diagnosis that determines whether or not they see the social worker as having made an appropriate referral – therefore for the social worker to get this right all the time, they would need to have as much skill in diagnosis as the CAMHS clinician, which is not possible given the differences in professional education and training.

The other cells can be characterised as:

Y/N = Cases inappropriately not referred by social workers to CAMHS, where psychiatric diagnosis was present, but the social worker did not recognise emotional or behavioural problems as concerning.

N/Y = Cases that social workers appropriately referred to CAMHS, where a child or young person's emotional problems or behaviour were recognised as problematic by the social worker, but there was no psychiatric diagnosis, so they did not meet the criteria for a service, or thresholds were so high for services that this referral would be a low priority for allocation.

N/N = Cases appropriately not referred by a social worker, because there was no concerning behavioural or emotional element present and the child did not have a psychiatric diagnosis.

Social workers base a lot of their assessments about children on the behaviours they observe. For most social workers, a child's behaviour was the main criterion used to decide whether to refer a child to CAMHS: 'Their presenting behaviour; their social presentation; maybe information received from other professionals; concerns, referrals or by an incident that may have happened that brought themselves to the attention of social services; referral by the GP at times' (Care-experienced children social worker, non-integrated service).

CAMHS clinicians thought that social workers required advanced knowledge and understanding of child development to know when the behaviour they observed in children was because of trauma or neglect and could therefore be considered an appropriate response to distress and adversity given the circumstances a child had been through, rather than due to the child having a mental disorder. Additionally, several CAMHS clinicians thought that social workers prioritised 'acting out' behaviour in their referrals, which might explain why more boys were referred to CAMHS than girls.

> Where there's externalising behaviour, referrals come very fast so boys just starting high school would be one of our picks. I think underrepresented is then, when you ask about other siblings in placement, would be the children who've been really good and compliant, the quiet girls. So sometimes we have to seek out with further questioning whether other family members need referrals so that leads me to think there's lots of kids out there internalising that we don't see. (Psychotherapist, non-integrated service)

This identifies training and development needs for social workers, to help them distinguish between children with mental illnesses compared with children who show distress in response to environmental and social situations. However, some social workers did achieve thoughtful and effective practice and understood the implications of making statements about mental health that they were not qualified to make.

> And, more importantly, in terms of how we're recording it – so, for instance, when I suspect a young person may have mental health issues, I will put 'in my opinion, I suspect the young person has mental health problems or concerns' because until I know that that's been diagnosed by a health professional, I've got to bear in mind 'this young person can still read his/her file at any time', and one of the hardest things is, and I've seen it myself, where professionals have said 'this person has mental health' and they're not in a position to make that statement, so I'm very wary about that for a young person. (Care-experienced children social worker, non- integrated service)

CAMHS practitioners thought that this effective practice could be because of social workers' experience, including positive working relationships with CAMHS.

> … there are some who work closely with us and seem to be able to pick up, monitor and work with mental health difficulties really well and seek out consultation advice whenever necessary and it works really lovely. (Clinical psychologist, non-integrated service)

> I think in terms of the ones that get it, quite often they have quite a good understanding of developmental trauma and attachment, and that they look beyond the symptom. They don't just look at the behaviour, they think what's going on for this young person, and to have that holistic view about this behaviour that might need X, Y, Z, or they've been too quiet, 'I wonder what that's about'. So they have that broader understanding. (Systemic family therapist; non-integrated service)

Some social workers were good at holding children in mind and advocating for them.

> … and just keep the child in mind and not necessarily the label, but also it's just as important to share the information and, increasingly it seems, to fight for the child to get access to CAHMS and mental health services – because sometimes we need to be more creative in how we access the appropriate support. (Care-experienced children social worker, non-integrated service)

There were many points of agreement between social workers and CAMHS clinicians about whether an increase of referrals to CAMHS was a good thing (because social workers recognised problems earlier), or whether it was a response to other problems in child and family social work currently with high caseloads and diminishing resources, so social workers almost automatically referred children to CAMHS as part of a prevention strategy, because of the high numbers of care-experienced children who are reported to have mental health problems. 'Our job is the case management of it, to feed it out to where it needs to go and to be communicating that to everybody. ... I always thought my role was a case manager because I couldn't do all the tasks.' (Care-experienced children social worker, highly integrated service)

The role and meaning of the SDQ for CAMHS

CAMHS clinicians had mixed views about the efficacy of the SDQ for work with care-experienced children. All the clinicians participating in the research knew about the use of the SDQ in the annual return for the Department for Education (DfE). This was undertaken separately from its use within CAMHS, except for one highly integrated CAMHS service that I discuss further in Chapter 9. The DfE SDQ return was not a joined-up process for CAMHS either, as it was not linked to either social work files or CAMHS clinician files and was not used in CAMHS returns to the Child Outcomes Research Consortium (CORC).[2] One clinical psychologist of a highly integrated service described the process of organisation for the DfE return between the local authority and the NHS trust as 'a nightmare'.

> And that also then confirms a social worker's worst suspicions that this product is .... a tick box exercise and what was the point in doing that! (Psychotherapist; non-integrated service)

> I think the problem is, I think to be honest and I can see their point, social workers, they've got so many things to do, doing SDQs that they do not see any particular value in and nothing hugely happens with it, I could well – I think they think what's the point, and I can see where they are coming from. (Clinical psychologist, highly-integrated service)

One specialist team performed a different role from the other teams and identified itself as 'assuming the role of the gatekeeper for mental health for children in care' (Clinical social worker, highly integrated service). This had an impact on the social worker for care-experienced children and young people; the mental health needs of care-experienced children were most likely to be addressed. The team was based on the same floor as the looked after children's team, and the CAMHS practitioners were known to all the social workers for care-experienced children and young people, who approached them to ask for advice. All the carer SDQs were sent out by the specialist team and returned to the team. The team provided social workers with a brief overview report on the results of the SDQ, including an action list for the social worker, highlighting any areas of concern. The specialist team also routinely collected teacher SDQs for all eligible looked after children, to triangulate the carer SDQ data. These SDQ data were directly used in clinical practice and were also compiled for the annual DfE return. The IROs were sent SDQ reports from the team prior to every looked after child's review. The team manager's view was: 'I'm not sure social workers can do that (SDQ) with all their cases, you know, I don't think they could do that. They're smart enough, but it's just the workload.' (Please see Chapter 9 for further information about this specific service.)

With regard to the SDQ's usefulness in work with care-experienced children across all services included in the research, clinicians noted benefits, including that it was quick and easy to use, it did not cost money, it worked best as an initial screening tool and it could be scored easily.

> So, for screening, I think still it's useful though it's probably best for population screening than for high-risk screening which is the group we're dealing with. It has probably been taken a bit out of context in terms of what it is best for, but the thing is, it's cheap, it doesn't cost any money, it is very easy to score. So, I think those are real advantages because I do not think we've got anything any better, that's the problem, there is nothing that is better than it. So, for what it does, I think it's good. (Psychiatrist; non-integrated service)

However, most clinicians also expressed concerns about the use of the SDQ with care-experienced children, because of the variability and context-dependent nature of behaviours:

> ... the SDQ never points to the real strengths of the child or the foster carer. I mean, looking at, for

> example, 'often lies and cheats' – we know that these children will lie and cheat, etc., and we know the underlying drivers to it. So that's always going to be a 'yes', or the child might strike it as 'not true' and there'll be a discrepancy and, to me and the rest of our team will say 'actually those are not pointers to mental health or to attachment', because we know that their search is for something much deeper. (Clinical nurse specialist, non-integrated service)

Using the SDQ as a threshold for access to services

Clinicians also raised the possibility of foster carers or social workers consciously or unconsciously 'fixing' the SDQ score, which was a downside of using this scale as a threshold for access to treatment. This was an issue raised by social workers as well.

Despite these reservations, all but one specialist CAMHS service used the SDQ regularly in their work. This included at the point of beginning work with a care-experienced child, every six months while work continued, and at the end of the work. These scores were not regularly fed back to social workers. However, one CAMHS worker who was responsible for scoring the SDQs for the local authority DfE return, who worked in a highly integrated service, did feed back high scores to clinicians (not social workers) who were based in social work teams, as her manager strongly believed that to do nothing with these scores was unethical.

For some referrals to CAMHS, an additional SDQ completed by the social worker or foster carer was required at the point of referral. Some CAMHS used the SDQ score as a threshold for service eligibility. In one of the NHS trusts, no child with a score under 17 received a service from the specialist CAMHS service. The CAMHS clinician said this was done to limit service eligibility.

> Now they have to hit an SDQ score of 17 or more, or they have to be at risk of placement breakdown for them to be eligible. (Family therapist; non-integrated service)

> … a lot of other services are using 17 as a cut-off point in terms of clinical indicator. (Clinical psychologist, highly integrated service)

This is not what the SDQ was designed for.

Longstanding problems with CAMHS accepting referrals: care proceedings, out-of-area placements and transitions

The availability of CAMHS staff for consultation with social workers has improved generally since specialist mental health services for care-experienced children and young people were established. A specific issue raised by a number of different CAMHS in my study (referred to briefly in Chapter 4), was the timing of referrals to CAMHS, with CAMHS not wanting to see children during court proceedings or immediately after a placement move, as the view was that at that point children needed to experience consistent and caring parenting, rather than be seen by CAMHS.

> You do sometimes, unfortunately, have therapists saying, you know, we're not going to do anything with this referral because this child has not been in placement long enough. Although they still should be working with the carers, so you know, maybe a specific type of therapy isn't advised, because the child is not settled, but they still should be doing something. But social workers are still getting that feedback somewhere along the line, so that is still happening, but I can't quite find out where. It's very difficult to try and track it down. (Clinical psychologist; highly integrated service)

This is not a new issue (Hunter, 2001; Cocker & Allain, 2019). The advice provided in the statutory guidance to social workers and others regarding health and mental health assessments (Department for Education & Department of Health, 2015a), suggests CAMHS are wrong not to see children at this time: 'Looked after children should never be refused a service, including for mental health, on the grounds of their placement being short term or unplanned' (Department for Education & Department of Health, 2015a, p 6).

Another issue consistently raised by all (social worker and CAMHS) participants as being highly problematic was children accessing CAMHS when they were placed out of area.

> I think there's also an issue with commissioning and who actually pays for it, because although the commissioning guidance is very, very clear about who is to pay for tier 2 services, interpretation can sometimes be different and also depends where they were on a specific date; this is the key to who commissions the service. So trying to get someone to pay for it is really difficult. (Care-experienced children nurse, highly integrated service)

> It was out of borough in another part of the country which makes it difficult because the health authority didn't see him as belonging to their area. They saw him as belonging to our borough. Anyway eventually we did get CAMHS involved through a referral to some other team in that area, I can't remember now. There was a lot of assessments and a lot of back and forth before we got the help that he needed. (Care-experienced children social worker, moderately integrated service)

Even after such problems had been identified, services had not been able to change procedures and arrangements with NHS trusts to overcome these practice difficulties. Advice from central government also included arrangements for those children placed out of area who required access to mental health services and for children leaving care.

> Where the child will require specialist health services such as child and adolescent mental health services (CAMHS) the [commissioning service] that

> commissions secondary healthcare in the area authority should be consulted, so that the responsible authority can establish whether the placement is appropriate and able to meet the child's needs. ... The needs of the child should be the first consideration. (Department for Education & Department of Health, 2015a, p 23)

At a strategic level, at least, these clear directions indicate a willingness to unblock structural processes which could enable care-experienced children and young people to access services quickly. However, the experiences of social workers and CAMHS clinicians included in my research indicated that this remained a problematic area in practice. The wording of the guidance could mean that services for looked after children placed out of area were linked to mainstream CAMHS, and not specialist looked after children services, in the borough in question, so children would wait longer, and not necessarily access the specialist services they needed.

> I wanted to highlight that when the child lives out of borough it does most definitely become more complicated and very frustrating for the social worker to get the right level of support, because in the health service I know they've got a different threshold of what meets their criteria for having a mental health presenting issue. Whereas within our specialist looked after CAMHS our threshold is lower because we know they're vulnerable and they need support early on. Unless that child can access our borough's looked after CAMHS, and they can't if they live halfway across the country, it's so hard to get that same level of commitment, passion. and what have you, from the CAMHS in your local area. Then you get a lot of to-ing and fro-ing about who should be responsible to pay and it is definitely just a question of funding it. Then I think they twist – I think CAMHS in the other places twist their interpretation so that they don't take the referral. I've had them coming back, saying, 'No, that person doesn't want to engage so we're not

> offering it', when I know very well that person would engage if they only made an effort to engage them. (Care-experienced children social worker, moderately integrated service)

Young people turning 18 were not always eligible for support because the eligibility criteria for adult mental health services were different from CAMHS'. This is further explored in Chapter 8. One of the ways of addressing this was for CAMHS to continue to see young people up to the age of 24, which is the agelimit for leaving care services to apply, and some of the CAMHS teams interviewed worked to this arrangement. Those teams who did see children over the age of 18 argued the need for this with health/ local authority commissioners.

> … everything always says that LAC should, you know, extend, the children's services should extend up to 25 at least and in health, 18 is the cut off. We managed to get to 19, which doesn't sound like much of a victory, but it really feels like a victory, that one year that we got. (Clinical psychologist, highly integrated service)

> Our service offers up to age 24. (Clinical psychologist, highly integrated service)

> We've worked very hard and I think our counterparts in the adult teams also are beginning to realise that it is much more efficient to work with us rather than let it fester and then pick it up later. But I think there's still problems there. The children who don't meet threshold are left a bit neither here nor there, so that's a problem. (Psychiatrist, non-integrated service)

Conclusion

This chapter has examined the role of CAMHS specialists in supporting care-experienced children. Central to this is the relationships that CAMHS workers have with social workers who work closely with care-experienced children and young people. These are not without stresses and tensions. There are a great many barriers to achieving an integrated service that is flexible, responsive, cost effective and well regarded by its users, including children and young people. I presented three typologies that described individual social worker attitudes toward mental health issues and referrals to CAMHS. Linked to this, the chapter also explored how social workers' responses to the behaviours and emotional states of care-experienced children and psychiatric diagnoses affected their CAMHS referrals. Social workers appeared to base their assessment of a child's mental health on the child's behaviour rather than on the results from the use of an assessment tool like the SDQ. Therefore, social workers' ability to identify and synthesise children's behavioural and emotional problems was what then determined which children they thought should be referred to CAMHS.

There is acknowledgement of the effect on service provision for children and young people of austerity and significant cuts in services. Some recurring problems in social work referrals to CAMHS were highlighted, but overall CAMHS practitioners are well regarded by social workers – where this relationship works well, it is viewed as supportive and productive.

6

Supporting care-experienced children and young people in placements

Introduction

This chapter outlines the role of foster carers, adopters, special guardians, kinship carers and residential care providers in supporting children and young people who have experienced significant trauma, in care settings. This will involve identifying the key factors within the literature that support 'stickability' – the ability to remain connected and supportive in the face of challenge in the relationship between foster child and foster family, as well as examining the impact of this for other forms of permanency for children. Evidence regarding the use of the SDQ is referenced where appropriate.

Impacts of placements on mental health: what does the literature say?

Studies have investigated associations between children's mental health (as measured by the SDQ) and placements, including the impact of placements on children's mental health and the impact of children's mental health on placements. In Chapter 3 we examined the role of the SDQ as a screening tool. This section explores what we know from how the SDQ is used in practice.

Sinclair & Wilson (2003) found that where foster carers felt committed to the child or young person they are caring for, a high 'total difficulties' score or low pro-social score was not linked to outcome. However, when foster carers achieved a high 'rejection' score, defined as 'the degree to which the carer was fond of the child and perceived her or him as impossible' (p 879), which was rare, placement outcome was strongly associated with a child or young person's 'total difficulties' and pro-social behaviour scores, 'so it is likely that difficult children produce rejection as well as suffer from it' (p 880).

Ford et al (2007) found that placement type, history of placement disruption and educational attainment are all independently associated with all types of mental health difficulties. 'The care related variables and educational disadvantage may be markers of abuse, trauma and attachment difficulties that might explain both the increased prevalence of psychiatric disorder and the poor educational attainment and care history in these children' (Ford et al, 2007, p 324). They found that care-experienced children with serious mental health problems are more likely to be placed in residential care and have a larger number of placement changes compared to care-experienced children without such problems.

Cousins et al (2010) also found that the SDQ mean scores of children and young people were higher for those in residential care as opposed to foster care in relation to conduct problems, hyperactivity, peer problems and 'total difficulties' score, but the same in both placement areas for emotional problems. Identifying strategies to support children and young people exhibiting such behaviours is important. Again, these types of behaviours are not going to change immediately, but with the right kind of support centred on the needs of the child and young person, behaviours can shift.

Impacts of children and young people's mental health on placements: what does the literature say?

Sinclair and Wilson (2003) used data collected by questionnaires, including the SDQ, sent to foster carers, family placement workers, social workers and children and young people in care (n = 472), to investigate reasons for placement success and disruption. A follow-up occurred after 14 months, making this study one of the very few longitudinal studies undertaken in the UK with the care-experienced community at that time. They identified a model comprising of three elements that were key in determining placement success. The first element concerned the behaviours exhibited by a child or young person in the placement along with other factors intrinsic to them, such as motivation of that child or young person to stay in the placement and their having personal qualities that the foster carer viewed as attractive. The second element concerned a number of features that were seen as important for carers, including their 'warmth', persistence and ability to 'set limits' with care-experienced children and young people. Carers' ability to offer children and young people stability, care and love, along with liking and respecting them, were seen by foster children as important attributes determining the success of the placement. The third element concerned the interaction between the first and second elements (Sinclair & Wilson, 2003). When considering the characteristics of the child or young person and placement success/disruption, Sinclair and Wilson used three measures, including the pro-social score from the SDQ and the 'total difficulties score'. Unsurprisingly, placements were likely to be more successful when children and young people wanted to stay in the placement, had high pro-social scores and low SDQ 'total difficulties' scores.

Beck (2006) found that young people who moved placement frequently were more likely to have mental health difficulties and less likely to access mental health services. This might be because they are placed out of the local authority area where children and young people would ordinarily be resident, which changes arrangements for eligibility for CAMHS. Some residential placements will have CAMHS support; however, Ford et al (2007) comment that often it is residential social workers who work with children and young people with serious mental health difficulties, and they have little training to assist with the identification and management of this task.

Foster carers and residential workers identifying children and young people with mental health problems: what does the literature say?

In terms of whether foster carers are able to identify children and young people with mental health disorders, Meltzer et al

(2003) found that only 12 per cent of children and young people assessed as having a disorder were not reported by their carer via the SDQ to have emotional, behavioural or hyperactivity problems. However, 43 per cent of the children who did not have a disorder were viewed by their carers as having problems. Based on comparison of foster-carer and youth self-completion SDQs, Mount et al (2004) found that foster carers (n = 50) were four times as likely as the care-experienced young people placed with them (n = 50) to identify mental health needs in these young people. When comparing foster carers' 'intuitive' responses to the SDQ scores (that is, what the foster carer thought prior to completing the SDQ), two thirds of carers were intuitively accurate in identifying mental health needs of young people in their care, with just under a quarter of foster carers not identifying needs that were then picked up by the SDQ. The worrying issue is that less than half of young people assessed as having a need were then seen by specialists (Mount et al, 2004). This trend has continued, with many care-experienced children and young people not being seen quickly enough once problems have been identified (Hiller et al, 2025; Samuel, 2025).

Bonfield et al (2010) investigated factors that influenced when foster carers sought support for care-experienced children and young people placed with them (n = 113 foster carers; n = 108 care-experienced children).They found that foster carers' education, mental health literacy, and their attitude toward help-seeking, in combination with the presence and impact of a mental health problem identified via the carer-report SDQ in the care-experienced child or young person, were significant predictors of foster carers seeking support.

Another study found foster-carer SDQ-reported conduct problems were the main predictor of whether foster carers felt 'burdened'. This suggests a need for foster carers to have access to good levels of support in caring for these children and young people because of the link between conduct problems and placement breakdowns (McCarthy et al, 2003). This study found that 59 per cent of the care-experienced children (n = 70) were scored by their foster carer on the SDQ as having an impact factor of 2+, indicating the likelihood of a psychiatric disorder being present. Additionally, because many care-experienced children and young people experience multiple emotional and behavioural problems, effective care planning is required for them, as well as support for the foster carer, as 'it seems likely that these children will require multiple strategies of treatment targeted at a range of developmental domains' (McCarthy et al, 2003, p 17).

Wilson and Barnett (2020) believe that physical activity could be an effective intervention to address health concerns for care-experienced children and young people. Policies and practice that determine good care in foster care and residential care should therefore integrate physical activity, including sports, dance, yoga, swimming and any other activity children and young people are interested in taking up as part of supporting their development. This should be picked up in their six-monthly reviews. For the most part this will be happening, but it is worth underlining its importance.

Galvin et al (2022) undertook a systematic review of interventions and practice models for improving health and psychosocial outcomes for care-experienced children and young people in residential care. They found only four studies, which evaluated four different projects in Australia, the US and Canada. Despite the paucity of studies, the authors believe that there are a number of interventions and practice models that do have the potential to have positive impacts on the health and wellbeing of care-experienced young people in residential care. However, we urgently need robust evaluations of more projects to add to this very limited evidence base.

There is also evidence to suggest that residential care workers highlight different issues and concerns than young people in residential care. Martín et al (2020) found that residential care workers were more likely to highlight externalising problems, and young people reported more internalising problems. According to the authors, this highlights the importance of multi-informant practices when assessing mental health problems in order for a range of perspectives to be gathered, including the young person's where possible.

There were some similarities noted in the studies comparing the SDQ scores of children in residential placements versus those in foster care, with children and young people in residential placements having higher scores across all SDQ subscales than those in foster care. Some studies used SDQ scores to examine associations between scores and specific child characteristics, such as sex, age and ethnicity. Many of these reported findings concur with what is already known about risk factors and children's mental health. For example, the SDQ studies consistently showed boys scoring higher on subscales which record 'acting out' behaviour, and girls showing higher results for emotionality sub scales, or 'acting in' behaviours. However, among boys and girls who score very highly on SDQ 'total difficulties' scores and experience multiple placement disruptions, the differences between their subscale scores lessen (Ford et al, 2007).

Using the SDQ as a screening tool at point of entry or while in care

The argument for screening at the point of entry into care is twofold: firstly, it provides an opportunity to assess a child or young person, in order to refer them on to services geared toward meeting their specific mental health needs. Given this is a group of children and young people who are known to have high rates of mental health problems, early identification is considered by many to offer benefits. But it is not without problems, as service recommendations made as a result of screening are not always available. The second reason for screening at the point of entry into care is that it provides a baseline measure, where a child or young person's needs can be assessed before the processes of care and care planning begin to have an impact, in order to ascertain whether the care provided to the child or young person has a positive or negative effect on their mental health.

In England most local authorities now have specialist multi-disciplinary mental health services for care-experienced children and young people that are jointly commissioned and funded with health services, which has increased the numbers of children, young people, foster carers, residential carers and social workers who have dedicated input from mental health specialists. This has considerably altered the availability, timescales and delivery method of mental health services for care-experienced children and young people, with many projects and services evaluating the results of their interventions (Minnis & Del Priore, 2001;

Newlove-Delgado et al, 2012; Herrman et al, 2016). The SDQ is routinely used in the delivery of these services and many of these different projects have provided a growing evidence base about the different ways that services can be directed toward the specific needs of care-experienced children and young people.

Routine mental health screening using the SDQ occurs in England for care-experienced children and young people who have been in care for longer than one year, although problems have been noted regarding whether these needs are then responded to locally in a timely manner by the professional network and whether specialist services exist that can meet identified needs (Goodman et al, 2004; Mount et al, 2004; Goodman & Goodman, 2012). There are also considerable missing data (Cocker et al, 2018), as most local authorities do not manage a full return.

Additional research is required to investigate the care planning pathways after children and young people are identified as having mental health difficulties that require professional interventions. A few studies have identified gaps in the availability of appropriate services and a need for further research, including longitudinal research, to examine the reality of care-experienced children and young people's experiences accessing and receiving mental health services from CAMHS, especially for those who are known to have acute needs, such as those who move placement frequently. Further research is also required to understand the complexity of children and young people's characteristics, including the direction of causality between their pre-care experiences, their mental health, and placement disruption (Ford et al, 2007).

Social workers' use of the SDQ

Whyte & Campbell (2008) conducted several focus groups with social workers and managers (n = 76) regarding their use of the SDQ. They found that, despite initial reluctance because of social workers' lack of knowledge about the SDQ and of mental health issues generally, participants recommended its routine use as a screening tool, and that using the SDQ had increased the number of care plans that recommended further referrals for assessment and treatment. However, participants raised issues about a number of children identified using the SDQ not being referred on for further services because of waiting lists, fears of swamping service providers and not being able to access appropriate services (Whyte & Campbell, 2008).

Cousins et al (2010) found, in their study of care-experienced children in Northern Ireland (n = 165), that despite high rates of emotional, social and behavioural problems, with 72 per cent of young people scoring 'borderline' or 'abnormal' on the SDQ, social workers rated 92 per cent of the young people's health as being 'as good as' or 'better than' other young people their age, indicating that social workers are missing signs and symptoms that would indicate otherwise. Cousins et al (2010) show how complex this is by highlighting barriers that they think prevent social workers gaining access to this knowledge. Firstly, a social worker's understanding of health is generally limited to physical health, rather than also including mental and social health. Secondly, children and young people in care often face discrimination because of their care status, and the authors suggest that mental health is one such area where social workers make judgements about them; some of these judgements will be discriminatory because of their own lack of knowledge about mental health. Finally, existing cultural expectations of high-risk behaviour from young people within care, coupled with both social workers' and carers' low expectations of young people in care, impact on how children and young people are supported and helped.

Derluyn and Broekaert (2007) report 'relatively good agreement' (p 156) between social workers and children and young people who were unaccompanied refugees about the emotional and behavioural problems they face, but a few adolescents reported 'severe' emotional and peer problems, and social workers are not identifying these needs (p 149). Social workers identified more conduct problems and hyperactivity issues than children and young people did on the SDQ self-reports.

However, not all such studies have concluded that social workers have poor skills in identifying mental health difficulties in care-experienced children and young people. Although a small study (n = 23), Newlove-Delgado et al (2012) comment that 'One of the messages of this study is that the social workers taking part had a justifiable level of concern for the mental health of the young people in their care' (p 219). It would appear that it is not as straightforward as suggesting that social workers are unable to identify mental health problems, but rather that there are a number of other issues that impact on a social worker's decision whether or not to refer. The authors raise the problems of offering screening to identify those children or young people with difficulties if this need is not then met with a relevant service (p 222). The danger is that it raises the expectations of social workers and service users, and the authors suggest that this might negatively affect referrals to CAMHS by social workers if services are not then available. The study showed that over half of social workers' referrals were accepted, with only one child on a waiting list, but numbers were small. The specialist CAMHS service for care-experienced children and young people was co-located in the local authority, which made referrals straightforward, and the service was not overwhelmed with 'novel referrals' (p 221).

Role of the placement environment

There is evidence to show that the type of placement a child or young person has during their time in care is of significant importance for their wellbeing after they leave care (Sacker et al, 2021). We know that the numbers of placements that a child or young person has while in care is also of profound importance (Beck, 2006; Ford et al, 2007; Sinclair & Wilson, 2003).

Foster care and kinship care

The secure base model (Schofield & Beek, 2014a, 2014b) offers an attachment-based and relational approach to providing day-to-day caregiving to children and young people in foster care, kinship care and residential care (see Figure 6.1). It deals with the ordinary and everyday alongside the more challenging and nurturing behaviours and responses required from caregivers working with care-experienced children and young people who have all experienced separation and loss of some sort (Cocker & Allain, 2019). Attachment theory helps us understand caregiving relationships within families, in the main. However, residential care placements also involve the use of relationships to create an environment to foster change. Schofield and Beek (2024a) have therefore broadened out the application of their work to include group-based settings such as residential care, schools and teams.

The five caregiving dimensions that are part of this model are associated with developmental benefits for the child or young person, using positive caregiving characteristics that are important to emphasise in foster care and other environments where care-experienced children and young people are living. It is through experiencing positive relationships and interactions with caregivers that children and young people can build their own confidence in dealing with their outside world (Schofield & Beek, 2024a). It also helps us understand what matters in relationships between carers and children/young people that helps with 'stickability' – the continued commitment to a child/young person despite challenges experienced when parenting (Pritchett et al, 2013). These five approaches are briefly outlined below (Schofield & Beek, 2024b).

- **Availability:** caregiving that helps children and young people build connections and trust. This includes developing everyday routines, creating choices for children and young people to encourage efficacy, responding to signs of stress or anxiety, and holding them 'in mind'. Schofield and Beek (2024b) list a range of interactive activities that can be undertaken with small children, some of which are adapted from theraplay[1] (Norris & Lender, 2019). For young people, developing a sense of trust between the caregiver and young person can be complex, and while some of the same relational aspects of caregiving may be similar, they will also depend on the needs of each young person (Schofield & Beek, 2009).
- **Sensitivity:** supporting children and young people to manage their feelings and behaviours as this is central to mental health (Schofield & Beek, 2009). This means getting to know the child or young person and how they express their feelings in everyday situations and supporting them with feelings that arise from circumstances they may find difficult. This might also involve encouraging children and young people to think about and be aware of the impact of their behaviour on others. This is not to blame the child or young person, but to support their reflection and response.

- **Acceptance:** building the self-esteem of a child or young person and accepting them for who they are. There are many ways in which this can be modelled through caregiving that is supportive, reflective, responsive and strengths-focussed. Finding out what children and young people are interested in or what they are good at is important as this can lead to them experiencing positive feedback from caregivers and other community members, including peers.
- **Cooperation:** helping to nurture a child or young person's ability to make decisions within their day-to-day life. This can involve children having small choices. The age of the child or young person will determine the parameters of choices and decisions offered to them. There may be specific areas that caregivers want to focus on in terms of skill development or behaviour management. Agreements made in tandem with the child or young person, along with rewards for achievements, can support behavioural change. Again, age and developmental stage are important here, as boundaries and expectations for young people begin to change with preparation for independence, intimate relationships and experimentation with drugs and alcohol.
- **Family membership:** helping the child or young person feel part of a family and support their sense of belonging. This is important as moving to any new care situation, whether foster care, kinship care or residential care, involves children and young people moving from what is familiar to them, to something quite different. Sights, sounds and smells within their new environment will be different from what they are used to, and family practices, norms, cultural experiences are also all new and will take a while to adapt to. Alongside this, most children and young people will want to continue their connection to their birth family, even if they have limited contact with family members. Being able to have upfront and honest conversations about children and young people's contradictory feelings toward belonging to more than one family, is important.

At the point where it becomes necessary to remove a child or young person from his or her immediate family, kinship care, or family

Figure 6.1: The secure base model

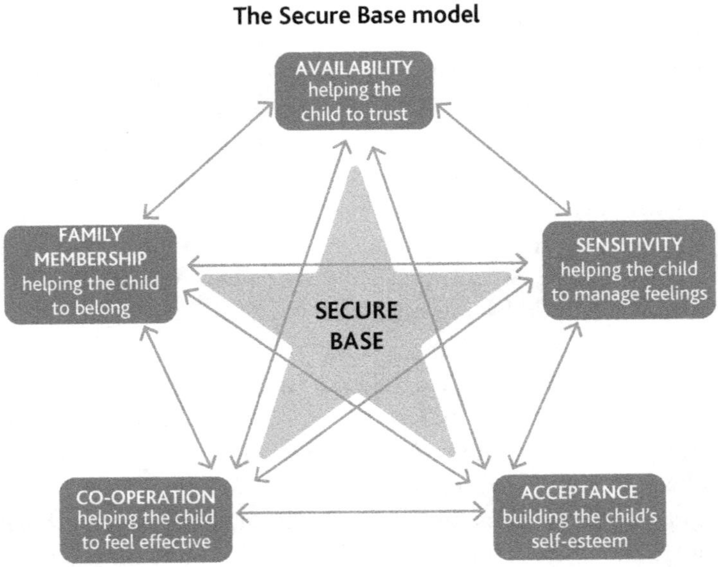

Source: Schofield and Beek (2014a, 2014b)

and friends foster care, should always be considered. The variety of cultural practices within many communities throughout the world demonstrate that children and young people are routinely placed within extended family placements during times of crisis as well as other circumstances without necessarily involving state services. Fahlberg (2012) highlights the value of this kind of placement for the child, in terms of continuity of care, supporting identity, continuing attachments, and maintaining ongoing contact with significant people in a child or young person's life.

When making arrangements for children or young people to be cared for away from birth parents, the local authority has a responsibility under section 22 of the Children Act 1989 to make arrangements wherever possible for them to live with a member of their family. In so doing, local authorities will assess the viability of family and friends to act as foster carers for a child or young person. In order for this to occur, the friend or relative must be recognised as a 'connected person', defined as a 'relative, friend or other person connected with a child'. A relative, for the purposes of family and friends foster care, is defined in section 105 of the Children Act 1989 as a 'grandparent, brother, sister, uncle or aunt (whether full blood or half blood or by marriage or civil partnership) or step-parent'. In this situation a child or young person is 'looked after' by the local authority: that is, whether under a care order, or accommodated under a section 20 agreement, the local authority has specific duties toward the child or young person. They are entitled to all the usual support that a child in care living with 'stranger' foster carers would receive. This includes mental health support, which applies regardless of placement type. If a relative or other connected person has a child or young person placed with them by a local authority, the local authority must assess the relative or connected person as a foster carer under regulation 24 of the Care Planning, Placement and Case Review (England) Regulations 2010 (Cocker & Allain, 2019). Kinship foster carers are also entitled to support from the local authority while undertaking this role.

Local authorities do not have a general duty to assess all arrangements where children or young people are living with their wider family or friends network rather than with their parents, as there will be occasions where private arrangements have been made between parents and relatives to care for them, and it is not necessary for the local authority to be involved. The local authority has a duty to assess where it appears that services may be necessary to safeguard or promote the welfare of a child in need (section 17 of the Children Act 1989). Children in need can live with extended family members or friends in a variety of different arrangements, some of which have been formalised legally via court orders and some of which are informal. Where arrangements involve the local authority in placing the child, but the child is *not* looked after, the local authority has a duty to assess and may then provide support under section 17 of the Children Act 1989 (Cocker & Allain, 2019). This may involve support for a referral to CAMHS.

Residential care

Residential care is most often used as a placement option for children and young people who are in crisis, have complex needs and who have had several placements. It is more expensive than foster care, and so local authorities are likely to use it only when necessary. That is not to say that residential care is always a second choice. However, some children and young people find it difficult to live in family environments because of their own experiences, and residential care offers a different experience. In England there are several well-established therapeutic communities such as Childhood First[2] and the Caldecott Foundation.[3] Both are charities, non-profit, and have psychotherapeutic or psychosocial approaches that underpin their method of caring for children and young people who have experienced trauma in their young lives. This includes providing education and therapy within their communities.

Working with children or young people who have high levels of behavioural problems, where there are mental health concerns, a history of poor educational experiences and sometimes ongoing health needs can be challenging. Residential care is a valuable placement option for some care-experienced children and young people (Scottish Institute for Residential Child Care, 2006; Smith, 2009). Many of the ideas presented in the previous section in relation to the secure base model will also apply within a residential care context. Relational, strengths-based work has its place within residential care too.

Unfortunately, residential care suffers from its past, with many high-profile inquiries and investigations into abuse and neglect having taken place in England since the mid-1990's. An example of this is the Waterhouse Inquiry, which investigated abuse in Welsh children's homes in the 1970s and 1980s (Waterhouse, 2000). Since 2015, concerns have been expressed across the sector about the number of residential care providers that are run for profit and where the standard of care is not always good (Holt et al, 2025). However, change is possible. On 24 March 2025, Wales passed the Health and Social Care (Wales) Act 2025. This legislation seeks to eliminate profit from caring for children and young people in public care, so that residential, secure accommodation and foster care for looked after children can only be provided by not-for-profit organisations, such as those in the public sector or charitable organisations.

Placement support for children and young people's mental health

There are behaviours that care-experienced children and young people may exhibit which will immediately be of concern to foster, adoptive or residential carers, and social workers (such as, for example, uncontrollable anger and outbursts; self-harming behaviours and physically hurting other children). Care-experienced children and young people may also be traumatised, upset or angry because of their experiences but present these feelings in different ways (for example, not being able to make and/or sustain friendships at school; lack of concentration at school affecting their ability to learn; being very quiet and withdrawn; not engaging/connecting with foster carers, adopters, family carers, residential care providers, teachers, or friends; sleeping and eating problems). Not all care-experienced children and young people will require specialist CAMHS intervention to be able to process their experiences. Further, with the current waiting lists, not all children and young people who need additional support and mental health services will receive them. All care-experienced children and young people require good experiences of care and that is where models such as the secure base (Schofield & Beek, 2014b) can be effective as they deal with the ordinary and everyday, alongside the specific behaviours and situations that are unique to each child or young person regardless of placement.

Reflections

It can be challenging to provide therapeutic care to many of our children and young people who have experienced a range of early adversities and ongoing protection concerns that have led to their coming into care. Does the placement environment cause poor mental health in children or are there specific mental health issues for children that cause difficulties in placements? Or is there an interplay where both play a role? What do we know makes a difference? There are some aspects and co-relationships that we know already. The literature (see Chapter 2) is clear that placement instability is not good for children and young people (Maguire et al, 2024). We know that children who are in residential care are more likely to have serious mental health problems than others (McCann et al, 1996), although this is an issue that can affect all care-experienced children and young people. The literature helps us to understand a little more about the interaction between placements and children's mental health.

Government and industry bodies also provide evidence-based guidance which is useful to understand what can help. The National Institute for Health and Care practice guidelines recommend a select range of approaches (NICE, 2021), including building positive relationships training for carers. There is a growing body of evidence evaluating a range of different training programmes for foster carers with varying results, see Minnis et al (2001), Turner et al (2005), Midgley et al (2019) and Moody et al. (2020). Generating better expertise in attachment and trauma-informed approaches among a range of practitioners and carers (Trubey et al, 2024) has positive impact. The work of Foster et al (2025) provides information about attachment theory and its importance for social work education and practice in general, which is applicable here.

However, there are disagreements between professionals too, with many CAMHS professionals insistent that children/young people are in permanent placements before therapeutic work can begin. This is not always possible. Foster carers and residential carers need support in undertaking their roles well, and where this support is offered to the professional network by CAMHS professionals regularly, it is valued enormously (Swann & York, 2011), especially when the professional network is supporting young people in particularly challenging circumstances (Jacob et al, 2024). Where this is not offered, the placement will not always survive, even with strong relationships between foster carer and the child/young person (York & Jones, 2017). How foster carers understand challenging behaviours that children exhibit, the support that they receive to address this and the ease of access to CAMHS and other support mechanisms are important in this process (York & Jones, 2017).

Conclusion

This chapter has outlined what we know about the role of the placement in supporting the mental health of care-experienced children and young people. The literature tells us about the way in which children's characteristics play a role in relationship building with carers in placements. We also know that the way in which carers undertake their caregiving role also determines the warmth within the relationship between the child/young person and carer and is then linked to 'stickability'. This is where placements endure, despite testing and challenges, because the relationship between carer and child/young person is strong. This intersection between factors that increase placement instability (such as externalising behaviours, numbers of placements in care, and multiple social workers), and those that protect placements, (such as experienced carers that value education and offer appropriately boundaried parenting) are key to understanding what is effective when supporting children and young people who have experienced adversity in their lives.

7

Racism, mental health and care-experienced children and young people

Introduction

In the long history of racism, the Black Lives Matter movement reminds us about the importance of understanding and acknowledging the effects of systemic racism experienced by all people of colour. This chapter considers racism in mental health provision (Bignall et al, 2019), with particular emphasis on the experiences of Black and minoritised children and young people within the mental health and social care systems. This is important because Black people are over-represented in adult mental health services and so this chapter will examine the systemic influences on this and investigate what we know about the mental health of children from minoritised communities. Throughout the chapter I will use the term 'minoritised' to refer to children and young people who are Black or from other racial minority communities in the UK.

The chapter also addresses the way in which social workers think about racism in their work with care-experienced children and young people from minoritised communities. It looks at the Eurocentric approaches used to work with children, young people and their families and addresses the impact that this has on Black and minority ethnic children and young people in accessing support that meets their cultural needs. For example, there are significant cultural and religious stigmas in certain communities about accessing mental health support (Bignall et al, 2019). This will have an impact on the way that mental health is spoken about by children and young people and will affect the things that social workers may need to consider when trying to tackle this. In addition, racial trauma may be a significant experience for a young Black person. We know that Black young people get stopped and searched by the police more often than their white counterparts. They are more likely to be described as 'aggressive' or 'difficult'. Young Black women experience adultification, which is when they are perceived and treated as older or more mature than they actually are, and are therefore too often held responsible for their harms (Davis & Marsh, 2020). Minoritised children and young people are disproportionally excluded from schools (Department for Education, 2024) and minoritised adults are more likely to be detailed under the Mental Health Act 1983 (NHS Digital, 2024). The responsibility for knowing about the effects of these structural biases is something that rests with all social workers. It is incumbent on each of us professionally and ethically to address the pernicious effects of racism and other types of discrimination in our work with care-experienced children and young people and understand how this might affect mental health.

What do we know about the interface between racism and mental health?

Existing data exploring the intersection between mental health and racism relies heavily on US-based studies, as the UK evidence base is limited. This means that our understanding about areas in the UK context such as internalised racism, systemic and institutional racism, and intersectionality is largely unexplored (Ghezae et al, 2025). Most of the prevailing work examines racism and mental health as it relates to adults, not children and young people, which again limits our understanding about when and how global majority people's experiences of racism as children affects their lives (Ghezae et al, 2025).

Models of early childhood adversity do not address the complex effect of racism on the mental health of Black children and young people. Some scholars refer to Black children's experiences of racism as an Adverse Childhood Experience (ACE) (Ayodeji et al, 2021; Bernard et al, 2021), as they believe they explain some of the mental health disparities between Black children and young people and white children and young people (Bernard et al, 2021). Although there are good reasons for wanting to acknowledge and understand the impact of racism and prejudice on children individually and structurally, and ACEs can potentially provide a framework for this via the culturally informed ACE (C-ACE) (Bernard et al, 2021), there is a danger that children and young people will be problematised because they have experienced racism without contextual factors being considered (White et al, 2019). In other words, 'According to the ACE model, problems reside in the quality of the individual rather than the lack of resources available to them' (White et al, 2019, pp 462–463). Additionally, the strength of the child or young person's family and the influence of community, including school experiences, friendship networks, formal and informal support, and even the broader sociopolitical context, should be taken into account when considering the effect of racism and discrimination on children and young people (Petrieet al, 2018 cited in White et al, 2019, p 458).

Ethnicity is an intrinsic characteristic to a child or young person, whereas racism is extrinsic, albeit endemic within our society. Unfortunately, it is a case of 'when' and not 'if' minoritised children and young people experience racism and discrimination, although every person's experiences will be different, as will the impact. However, while the experience of racism and vicarious trauma can mean that minoritised children and young people have an increased risk of mental health problems (Bignall et al, 2019), the pathologising of the response to this for all minoritised children and young people via ACEs is not always helpful. This is an argument made in the US-based literature since the 1980s, with Comer and Hill (1985) suggesting a sociopolitical approach to enhance the mental health of Black children on a large scale. This acknowledges the role of prevention and is based on the premise that much of the aetiology (the cause or understanding of the reason for something) of mental illnesses and emotional behaviours is rooted in social conditions rather than in individual defects (Clark, 1981; Comer & Hill, 1985). In addition, White et al (2019) comment that children and young people's voices are notably absent from being included in how ACEs are understood

> Instead they are monitored for 'markers of risk', measured, diagnosed and subjected to interventions. There is a clear danger of further demoralising already struggling sections of the population. Such a view of people as bodies and brains to be managed and treated, rather than citizens who should be represented and engaged, further excludes often marginalised people from democratic decision-making. (p 464)

The terms 'minority stress' and 'weathering' are used to describe the long-term effect of experiencing racism, homophobia and other types of discrimination (Geronimus, 2023). These are useful concepts to help understand how young people's journeys to adulthood can be described both in terms of the trauma they experience from exclusion and discrimination (minority stress) as well as their responses to it (weathering). In adults there are adverse physiological outcomes associated with long-term exposure to discrimination, including high blood pressure, obesity, Type 2 diabetes, and mental health difficulties such as depression (Geronimus et al, 2006).

So, what do we know about the rates of mental ill health for minoritised children and young people? The mental health of children and young people has generally been a subject of political interest for more than a decade, but particularly since the COVID-19 pandemic. Table 7.1 shows the landscape of government innovations between 2011 and 2023. Even with these changes, the sector has criticised the government's response as not radical enough, with an under-investment in required resources (England & Mughal, 2019).

Even with this considerable list of policy initiatives, mental health services for children and young people, 'have long been described as the "Cinderella of Cinderella services" with young people facing delays in access to support, a postcode lottery in provision and disjointed care' (Rainer & Abdinasir, 2023, p 10). The policy initiatives listed in Table 7.1 have spearheaded a series of measures introduced to improve mental health outcomes for children and young people. However, waiting lists remain long,

Table 7.1: Timeline of children and young people's mental health policy (2011–23)

Year	Policy/Strategy	Responsible Departments
2011	No Health without Mental Health Strategy	Department of Health and Social Care (DHSC)
2012	The National Suicide Prevention Strategy The Health and Social Care Act	DHSC DHSC
2014	Closing the Gap: Priorities for Essential Change in Mental Health The Children and Families Act	DHSC Department for Education (DfE)
2015	Future in Mind Mental Health and School's Link Pilot launched	DHSC and NHS England DfE
2016	The Five Year Forward View for Mental Health NHS Health and Justice Specialised Commissioning Workstream established	NHS England NHS England
2017	The Children and Social Work Act Prevention Concordat for Better Mental Health established	DfE Office for Health Improvement and Disparities
2018	The Transforming Children and Young People's Mental Health Provision: A Green Paper Independent Review of Mental Health Act 1983 published	DfE DHSC
2019	The NHS Long Term Plan Introduction of statutory relationships and sex education and health education Mental health assessments pilots for looked after-children launched Every Mind Matters campaign and online platform launched	NHS England DfE DfE Office for Health Improvement and Disparities
2020	Wellbeing for Education Return and Recovery programme launched	DfE
2021	Covid-19 Mental Health and Wellbeing Recovery Action plan Mental Health Clinically Led Review of Standards Consultation Reforming the Mental Health Act: White Paper published	Cross-departmental NHS England DHSC

Table 7.1: Timeline of children and young people's mental health policy (2011–23) (continued)

Year	Policy/Strategy	Responsible Departments
2022	Independent Review of Children's Social Care published	DfE
	Draft Mental Health Bill published	DHSC
	Youth Review published	Department for Culture, Media and Sport
	National Youth Guarantee	Department for Culture, Media and Sport
	Best Start for Life and Family Hubs programme launched	DfE and DHSC
	SEND Review: Right Support, Right Place, Right Time published	DfE
	Health and Care Act	DHSC
	Ten Year Mental Health Plan announced, and consultation published	DHSC
2023	Major Conditions Strategy announced	DHSC
	Stable Homes Built on Love Strategy	DfE
	Rapid Review of Data on Inpatient Settings	DHSC

Source: Rainer and Abdinasir (2023, pp 8–9)

with many services not meeting statutory minimum standards. Many of the policies and strategies published over recent years have focused on broadening support through education settings and NHS CAMHS. But there is still more demand than can be met by existing services, with children and young peoplefrom minoritised backgrounds or with multiple or complex needs often experiencing greater barriers to receiving timely care (Rainer & Abdinasir, 2023). Further, undiagnosed mental health concerns/ low referrals from specific minoritised groups and the impact of delays for minoritised children and young people being seen by specialists are concerning.

English et al (2024) state that 'racism pervades the UK health system, and urgent action to combat it must be prioritised' (p 1535). They note that

> racism in the UK health system is present in the delivery of care, as shown by unequal care outcomes, lack of access to translators, and overt interpersonal racism. Children's experiences of racism in the UK

> health system are compounded by their families' and caregivers' experiences, exacerbating racism's health impacts on children. (English et al, 2024, p 1535)

When looking at the demographic profile of young people who access services, a complex picture emerges. Edbrooke-Childs and Patalay (2019) found in their study of 15,000 young people accessing mental health services, that minoritised young people were more likely to be referred to mental health services through youth justice and social services than through community-based routes like education or primary care. Boys from African and Caribbean communities in the UK have lower levels of mental health problems at age 11 compared to white or mixed heritage boys (Khan et al, 2017). This is somewhat contradicted by other data available that suggest that boys from Black, Asian and other minoritised communities are at higher risk of developing a mental health problem in adulthood. They are also less likely to receive support for their mental health (NHS Digital, 2016), which might explain the low numbers of Black boys receiving services at age 11. Black men are more likely to experience symptoms of psychosis than other ethnic groups (3.2 per cent compared to 0.3 per cent of white men and 1.3 per cent of Asian men, using combined 2007 and 2014 data) (NHS Digital 2016). There is no significant variation by ethnicity among women.

Data show that Black people with mental health problems are over three times as likely to be detained under the Mental Health Act 1983 than white people (NHS Digital, 2024). However, more white people than people from Black and other minoritised backgrounds receive treatment for mental health issues and they have better outcomes (Cabinet Office, 2018). Some of the reasons offered as to why there are different rates of mental illness for people from Black and other minoritised backgrounds have been: inequalities in wealth and living standards; bias, discrimination and racism; stigma about mental health; and a higher likelihood of having mental health issues identified in the criminal justice system (Mental Health Foundation, 2024). This raises concerns about whether there is an inherent bias in the approach to working with minoritised individuals which leads to over-criminalisation and over-institutionalisation.

A welfare-oriented approach might see different outcomes, as support could be offered earlier as prevention, rather than accessed as crisis care (Bignall et al, 2019).

Racism and safeguarding

We know that racism is also endemic throughout child welfare systems in many parts of the world (Cornish, 2025). A number of social work scholars in the UK have written about the way in which this manifests within the UK context (Bernard & Gupta, 2008; Okpokiri, 2020; Cornish, 2024; Weekes & Ward, 2025), particularly within safeguarding paradigms used in practice, where deficit narratives about Black parenting continue to thrive (Bernard & Gupta, 2008). There are some models now in development which identify the challenges of parenting Black children through a whole systems approach. One such model is Requisite Parenting (Okpokiri, 2024). This model acknowledges the significant structural inequalities that exist within multi-racial societies, which Black parents navigate every day in order to parent their children. The Requisite Parenting approach centres those challenges, and its six principles – of selfless love, pride, adaptability, resourcefulness, courage, and spirituality (SPARCS) – provide a basis by which social workers and other professions can better understand the style of parenting practices used by Black parents (Okpokiri, 2024).

Another approach to work with minoritised communities is the SAWUBONA practice model (Cornish, 2025). This approach acknowledges the power imbalances, including white privilege, within statutory social work practices that are present for Black families in most, if not all, child safeguarding encounters. This approach seeks to challenge this by moving away from a Eurocentric, white hegemonic and colonialist intervention, to the use of a model that is culturally sensitive and prioritises human relationships.

> The SAWUBONA model advocates that social workers SEE the whole person within their socio-cultural context, ACKNOWLEDGE the shock and sensitivity of the situation. See the individual's

> WORTH, their UNIQUE qualities, uncertainties and BEAR with the person. Creating OPPORTUNITIES for the individual's voice to be heard on a consistent basis. To NEGOIATE, ensuring mutual care planning and keeping professional power in check. Be AVAILABLE and make available quality resources. (Cornish, 2024, p 860)

Cornish and others point to the over-representation of Black and other minoritsed children in public care systems in many parts of the Western world, including the UK. Studies show these children are in care for longer (Edney et al, 2023), with reduced opportunities for reunification in many previously colonised countries such as Canada (Adjei & Minka, 2018). The UK's rates of reunification for minoritised children differ, particularly if children were younger, had a longer period in care, and had fewer changes of placement (Neil et al, 2020). The support offered to families over the first six months after reunification was also significant (Goldacre et al, 2022). These critiques and models for positive practice with Black families offer insight into how we can work better with them when their young people experience mental ill health, including those in the care system, especially foster families.

Mental health services for care-experienced children and young people

Since the late 1990s when the Department of Health used the Mental Illness Specific Grant to invest in specific services for children in care across England, children and young people in care have had access to a range of mental health services developed for their needs (Jezzard, 1999; Kurtz & James, 2003). It was around this time that the Strengths and Difficulties Questionnaire began being used annually for all children who had been in care for a year or longer. However, there have been long-standing concerns about the number of 'missing' cases in the annual data collection processes. Up to one third of these questionnaires are not collected routinely by different local authorities and it appears that these missing data include a disproportion number of minoritised children (Cocker et al, 2018). There are also issues about what individual local authorities do with these data following collection. What the data does tell is that there are high levels of need within the population of children in care in England. Although these children have been able to access additional specific CAMHS services, the quality of services has been affected by staffing shortages for NHS CAMHS staff and by funding pressures in local authorities. There are also ongoing issues about how mental health support is provided to children and young people placed out of their local area, and whether they are eligible for support from the local authority that has responsibility for them or whether they need to be referred to services local to their placement address. This can cause intense frustrations and delays in service provision that could have devastating consequences for care-experienced children and young people. This situation is further exacerbated for Black and ethnic minoritised care-experienced children and young people, especially given the predominance of structural inequalities and racism potentially constricting access to essential mental health services. Consequently, the tensions in referring children and young people to CAMHS outside of a local area are likely to disproportionally affect Black and minoritised children and young people. Another major area of concern is the ongoing mental health support that care leavers receive, particularly where they have had significant CAMHS involvement prior to leaving care (Cocker et al, 2024).

There is now increased access to evidence-informed mental health service provision for children in care in England (Hiller et al, 2023), although waiting lists indicate that it still is insufficient. A NIHR study led by Professor Rachel Hiller at University College London on 'Increasing access to evidence-informed mental health service provision for children in care in England' has produced a number of national recommendations for change (Hiller et al, 2025). These include:

- All local areas to develop a joint service delivery plan and new KPIs, between CAMHS and children's social care, to increase knowledge and accountability.
- Introduction of an initial mental health and wellbeing assessment, 4–6 months after entry to care.

- All local areas to have a co-located mental health service between children's social care and CAMHS, which is commissioned to provide direct and indirect evidence-based support.
- The development of a new children's social care mental health practitioner (CSCMP) training programme, to upskill the children's social-care based mental health workforce on evidence-based therapies.
- Update to the NICE guidelines for Looked After Children.

(Hiller et al, 2025, p 5)

This report is worth reading. It is a robust piece of research, and it brings together exemplary thinking about what it is that care-experienced children and young people need from mental health services and where the problems are with current provision. It is unsurprising that many of the 'top 5' recommendations, or indeed the 20 recommendations contained in the report, echo previous reports and/or documents that have examined mental health provision for care-experienced children and young people. This shows that the complexity of the problems needing to be addressed to achieve change make them challenging to resolve.

Hillier et al's work has contributed to the growing evidence base for effective practice. However, even with our knowledge base about 'what works' continuing to develop (Luke et al, 2014; Davis et al, 2025; McGuire et al, 2025), current services remain highly Eurocentric in design. The challenge is how to ensure researchers investigate the specific needs of Black and minoritised care-experienced children and young people (Javed et al, 2025), and to then think differently about solutions, which may involve using resources from Black communities (Ejegi-Memeh et al, 2025).

Racism and the public care system

The Department for Education statistical data in England tells us that of the roughly 80,000 children and young people in care on 31 March 2023, 29 per cent were from non-white British ethnic groups (Javed et al, 2025). Javed et al (2025) completed a systematic review of ethnic representation in UK research involving care-experienced children and young people. They found that over half the studies they identified in their search (from 2012 to 2024) *did not* report ethnicity data. They explore the reasons for low rates of ethnicity reporting among studies, highlight the practices of specific studies that tried to understand ethnic disparities in their methods and conclude that it is vital to be able to use research evidence to identify commonalities and differences in children and young people's experiences of services, taking into account their ethnic backgrounds to avoid cultural and ethnic biases in practice (Javed et al, 2025, see Table 7.2).

This limited research investigating differences in outcomes for children in care of different ethnicities requires urgent attention in terms of further research, operational delivery and practice.

Research undertaken by Barnardo's (2023) sheds some light on what is known about the experiences of Black children and young people in care who were also in contact with youth justice services and where there were concerns about these young people's mental health. However, the sample size in this study was small (n = 22), so it is not possible to apply these findings generally. However, the study showed that: firstly, nearly all young people interviewed reported experiencing micro and macro racist aggressions and/or prejudice. Black care-experienced young people reported being treated differently by many of the services they came into contact with, in comparison with their white peers, for example being placed in white majority areas where often they were the only Black person, which highlights issues of racial visibility, feelings of not belonging and isolation. Secondly, young people's experience of being in care was rarely considered as a factor that impacted on their experience of the criminal justice system. Finally, these young people often had mental health issues because of past experiences, but were not able to access the support they needed. While previous research has shown that children in care are more likely to have a mental health issue and often struggle to access the support they need (Ford et al, 2007), this report highlighted that, based on the experience of the young people who were part of the study, this was an even greater issue for Black young people. The study authors attributed this to experiences of systemic racism and prejudice (Barnardo's, 2023).

Table 7.2: Javed et al's (2025) systematic literature review reports of outcomes for care-experienced children and young people by ethnicity

'Of the ninety-six studies that reported participant ethnicity, 10.4 percent (n = 10) reported subgroup analyses by ethnicity. Given the few studies reporting ethnicity with shared quantitative child outcomes, it was not possible to synthesize these outcomes using meta-analysis. A descriptive view of study findings by ethnicity revealed limited insights into patterns of need between children in care with different ethnicities.

Some studies found significant differences in outcomes related to ethnicity. For example, White and Mixed ethnicity children were more likely to re-enter care compared to Black and Asian children (Goldacre et al 2022; *Mc Grath-Lone et al 2017) and rates of new-born entry into care were higher for children of Other and Mixed ethnicities, followed by White and then Black children (Pearson et al 2020). Children of a minoritized ethnicity had lower odds of being able to identify a trusted adult in their lives compared with White majority children (Suh and Selwyn 2023). Ethnicity was also found to impact the educational trajectories of children living in care (Sutcliffe, Gardiner, and Melhuish 2017). Furthermore, Eisen, Williams, and Cohen (2023) found some differences between the country of origin of Unaccompanied Asylum-Seeking Children and rates of positive tuberculosis testing.*

Regarding mental health outcomes, mixed findings were identified concerning the ethnicity of children living in care. Children classified by the study as BAME ethnicity were over-represented in the general population amongst children with high PTSD symptomology but not amongst children in care specifically (Hitchcock et al 2021). Contrastingly, White children living in care were found to have higher reported peer problems and hyperactivity compared to non-White children (Hiller et al 2023).

Further studies were unable to find significant differences in outcomes between children of different ethnicities. For example, there were no ethnic differences found in predicted fixed school exclusions (suspensions) using White and non-White categorization (Melkman 2022). Joseph and colleagues (2014) found no significant relationship between the child's ethnicity and the formation of new secure attachments by adolescents in foster care.'

There are recommendations in the Barnardo's (2023) report that speak to the importance of improving services for Black children and young people in care, including mental health support (see Table 7.3).

Intersectionality and mental health for care-experienced children and young people

Intersectionality describes the connections between every aspect of a child or young person's multi-faceted identity, such as ethnicity, class, gender, sexuality, disability, religion and so on. These are unique to each person, as are the effects these factors can/will have on an individual's experience of life. Intersectionality was originally intended to highlight the compounding experiences of racism and sexism faced by Black women and how this creates new sites of oppression (Crenshaw, 1991). It is now used in a broader way to describe the interplay between facets of identity and forms of oppression, not just at an individual level, but also alongside broader structural discrimination and institutional oppression. As well as the 'protected characteristics' included in the Equality Act 2010, other identities and experiences such as class, experience of care, and homelessness provide further dimensions of social exclusion and intersectionality (Cocker et al, 2026).

Children and young people who are care-experienced face additional intersectional hurdles. Colleagues at Barnardo's (2023, p 5) comment that '[i]nequalities are exacerbated for those who are Black, care-experienced and in the criminal justice system'. They also highlight the whole-systems nature of the intersectional-relationship: 'aspects of identity are interconnected and can mutually influence one another, shaping experiences and opportunities in society, from an interpersonal, structural, and institutional level' (Barnardo's, 2023, p 5).

Figure 7.1 identifies four interrelated domains that describe the interface between intersectionality and care-experience. Any care-experienced child or young person will have experienced public care or being 'looked after' in ways that are influenced by their own intersectional identities (1). For many Black young people, their experiences are additionally affected by structural discrimination and institutional oppression (2). There are also challenges for professionals acknowledging their own biases when supporting Black children and young people, as well as their own intersectional experiences (3). This can have a profound effect on how children and young people experience the support given to them (4). This figure is adapted from a model used to discuss aspects of intersectionality and transitional safeguarding (Cocker et al, 2026). It is helpful because it provides a structure to understand the complexity and provides insight into what we can affect and change at practice, policy and social levels.

Domain 1 relates to how the intersectional identities of care-experienced children and young people impact on their experience of care and being 'looked after'. There is considerable information available, particularly from the sociology of childhood literature, that explores general identity formation and maturation in children (Corsaro, 2018). There are some differences in how children and young people who have experienced adversity, including state care, develop their personal and social identities (Munford & Sanders, 2015; Sanders & Munford, 2017). This domain expects professionals working with children to have a good understanding of the way in which care-experienced children and young people's histories might affect their maturation, their journey to independence, and their experience of universal services, such as mental health services, because of intersectional issues.

Domain 2 highlights how children and young people's intersectional identities influence their experience of risk and harm. For example, we know that care-experienced children

Figure 7.1: Intersectionality domains for care-experienced children and young people

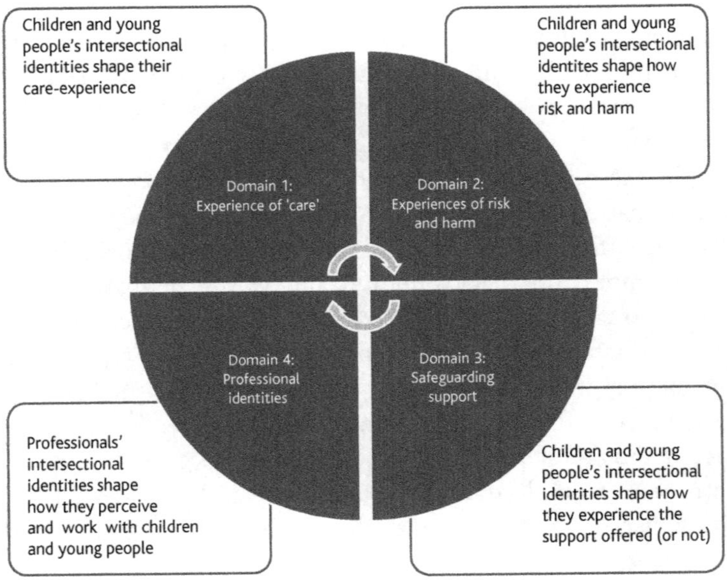

Table 7.3: Barnardo's project on 'Double discrimination: Black care-experienced young adults navigating the criminal justice system' – recommendations for change

1. *'Improve the experience of Black children in foster care*
2. *Improve access to mental health support for Black children in care.*
3. *Take action to reduce the over-criminalisation of children in the care system.*
4. *Improve understanding across agencies of the needs of children in care and care-experienced young people as well as providing training on how to better address these needs.*
5. *There must be a renewed emphasis on implementing reform aimed at tackling institutional racism within the criminal justice system.'*

Source: Barnardos 2023, p 7

and young people are more likely to experience risk and harms because of their life circumstances: care-experienced young people are over-represented in the homelessness statistics (Ministry of Housing, Communities and Local Government., 2024) and are also over-represented in the criminal justice system (Office for National Statistics, 2022). When combined with the discrimination, disproportionality and adultification that minoritised young people face, this can have a compounding effect on children and young people, with far-reaching consequences.

Domain 3 explores how the intersectional identities of care-experienced children and young people affect how they experience support offered to them. Those providing services to care-experienced children and young people should have a comprehensive understanding of the concept of intersectionality, engage deeply with understanding children and young person's experience of the world and actively challenge structural inequalities arising from their own services (Cocker et al, 2024). This is particularly important for children and young people from minoritised communities, given the impact of racism and the wider systemic and structural issues that impact on their lives.

Domain 4 addresses how professionals' own identities mean that they will also experience intersectionality, which is shaped by their individual life experiences, faith, gender, ethnicity, age, culture, sexuality class ability and so on. The 'use of self' in relational practice is important here (Munford and Sanders, 2015).

Professionals should think critically about how their identity and perspective shapes their practice. To support young people making sense of the world, professionals must understand themselves, and an intersectional lens is key to this.

Professionals working with Black and minoritised children and young people who are care-experienced should develop their cultural competence, or 'cultural humility', and not make assumptions about any child or young person based on skin colour. This work is highly relational, so it is important at all stages to get to know a child or young person. Young people tell us that this is important (Hiller et al, 2025). At the beginning of building any relationship it is important to ask, who is it that knows the child or young person best? Who and what do they say is important in their life? Build on that and include other important people/relationship(s) (for example extended family, teacher, youth worker) in this work.

There are several publications that move away from an individualised understanding of mental health and mental illness and see mental health issues across the care-experienced community as a public health issue stretching across health and social care providers (Cocker et al, 2018; English et al, 2024). The following list from English et al (2024) incorporates a whole-systems approach to address the inequalities within mental health provision. This includes adopting a human rights-based approach (see Table 7.4).

This list articulates the knowledge and skills that social workers need to advocate effectively and provide services for minoritised children and young people. None of the listed recommendations are unachievable, but they do require social workers to be strong advocates, particularly when challenging systemic inequalities. In meeting the cultural needs of children and young people in care when it comes to mental health provision, social workers will need to actively support children and young people in care, recognising that each person has their own history and understanding of their identity, including experiences of discrimination. This should be acknowledged and validated.

Social workers will also need to work effectively with professional networks, including foster carers. We know how disruptive changes in placement can be for a child or young person. Effective placement matching is essential so that minoritised children and young people can have their cultural needs met by their carers and in their placements. Establishing positive working relationships with foster carers is also important in terms of supporting the placement and again ensuring that the cultural needs of children and young people are being met. There is a need for ongoing training to ensure that foster carers are aligned with equality, diversity and inclusion principles underpinning foster care services, including race equality.

In advocating for children and young people at all stages in their care journey, it is important that minoritised children and young people receive services where required but are not 'over-diagnosed' or over-problematised regarding their behavioural or emotional difficulties. No CAMHS clinician would want to diagnose a child or young person with a mental illness without evidence that such a diagnosis is accurate. It is also important to consider whether the reverse (under-diagnosing) is also occurring because social workers might not want minoritised children and young people (or any child or young person) to receive a diagnosis. This is an understandable concern; however, a lack of diagnosis may mean that a child or young person may be denied the opportunity to receive a treatment that could make a palpable difference to their mental health and wellbeing (Hiller et al, 2023; McGuire et al, 2025).

One of the other critical areas to raise is how CAMHS professionals understand the cultural needs of Black and minoritised children and young people who are care-experienced and work to address it. In my experience CAMHS professionals can be effective advocates for the children and young people they see and bring a different perspective to how trauma is understood and has affected a child or young person. This should not be underestimated. However, there are a couple of longstanding contentious issues between social services and CAMHS. It is good to see the work of Professor Hiller, and particularly recommendation 13: 'Mental health services should not reject a referral on the grounds of it being a "social care issue", unless a comprehensive mental health assessment has been completed showing no mental health concern'; and recommendation 14: 'Mental health services should not be able to automatically reject or close a case due to placement

Table 7.4: Actions needed now to address the mental health crisis for care-experienced children and young people

- 'Adopt a human rights-based approach that upholds children's rights to the highest attainable standard of health and social care provision without discrimination and abolish policies that undermine these rights for minoritised children
- Incorporate anti-racist health, social care and research practice into the health system's functioning and commissioning, including by increasing engagement during decision making, and co-creation of processes, policies, and procedures with minoritised communities to foster greater trust
- Integrate anti-racist training within health-and social care curricula to ensure that the next generation of health workers, social care works and educationalists have the information and skills to recognise and combat racism in the health system
- Embed professional accountability to uphold anti-racist principles and practice into the health and social care systems, including by embedding anti-racism within the annual appraisal process as a professional requirement
- Ensure that data and evidence collected and valued by the health and social care systems incorporate the voices and inputs of communities, delivering epistemic justice
- End structural discrimination in institutions and systems that shape children's interactions with the health and social care system, and separate policing and prison systems from health and social care
- Uphold equality, diversity, and inclusion commitments and funding and allocate funding to dismantle racism and white supremacy in the UK health system
- Co-create anti-racist and anti-oppressive services with minoritised communities, providing a viable alternative to oppressive systems and structures'

Source: English et al (2024, pp 1535–36)

instability' (Hiller et al, 2025), which builds on the work of the psychotherapist Margaret Hunter (Hunter, 2001), to encourage social care and NHS CAMHS to work more closely together.

Understanding equity, equality, diversity and inclusion from a whole-systems approach (Cocker et al, 2024) offers the opportunity to also consider other intersecting issues that minoritised young people in particular may experience, and what the impact on their lives might be. For example, for Black and minoritised LGBTQ+ young people in care – what are the specific issues affecting their lived experience of care? (Schaub et al, 2022). The same question can be asked of Black and minoritised children and young people in care who have disabilities, including neurodiverse conditions. Are the issues the same or different than for children and young people with disabilities who are not Black or minoritised? This is where systemic racism can affect outcomes for children and young people.

Why this is important: the impact of 'weathering' throughout the lifespan for Black and minoritised care-experienced young people

There are long-term negative effects for individuals related to a history of being in care (Sacker et al, 2024). This includes enduring inequalities in social and economic outcomes related to poorer educational outcomes and poorer mental health. Worryingly, Sacker and colleagues found in their longitudinal study in England that used data over a 30-year period (1971–2001), that adults who are care-experienced tended to die at a much earlier age than adults in the general population. Their study found that the type of placement that a child or young person experienced mattered considerably, with care by a relative being the best, foster care being next best and residential care predicting the worst outcomes for children and young people as adults (Sacker et al, 2022). The research team stated, 'Promoting kinship care is a public health measure, not just a social welfare concern' (Sacker et al, 2021, p 3).

However, with regard to the effect of ethnicity on care outcomes, Sacker et al (2024) query the way in which previous studies have contextualised their findings and question the impact of ethnicity on care outcomes for Black and minoritised children and young people. They point to four difficulties:

1. There are ethnic inequalities in outcomes in adulthood more generally. Most research on ethnic differences in outcomes after care has sampled care-experienced children only, with no comparison group.
2. Most research in this area is retrospective, and reliability is therefore affected.
3. Many studies have small samples, are unrepresentative or collect qualitative data which tends to involve small non-random samples.
4. Almost all published studies relate to the US where ethnicity and race have different meanings and implications from those in the UK.

In their study, Sacker et al (2021, p 4) found that:

> The widespread assumption that there are more negative adult outcomes among ethnic minority groups following care in childhood was not supported by our study. Previous reports of the negative impact of care on Black people's lives appear to have been misattributed to the experience of care when it is a feature of all Black people's lives. We found no interaction between Black ethnic identity and experiences of care affecting adult outcomes: the disparities seen for children in care were the same as those pervasive in society for the wider Black population.
>
> (Sacker et al, 2021, p 4)

The impact of racism on all Black and minoritised people's lives is considerable and this impact is the same for care-experienced children and young people as it is for Black people within the general population (Barnardo's, 2023; Sacker et al, 2021). We need further research in this area to explore the impact of changes in the care system since 2000 and understand the implications of racism within the care system.

Conclusion

This chapter has examined the relationship between racism and mental health within the care system. There is a lot we still do not know. From the existing evidence, there is an intersection between race and other forms of oppression and discrimination that is individual, social and structural. The effects that this has on Black and minoritised children and young people who are care-experienced is vital for social workers and other professionals to mitigate. Relational work is important in this regard, as is helping children and young people stay connected to family, friends community and culture.

As well as providing an overview of the literature and how it relates to racism within children's safeguarding work generally and within the public care system, four specific domains have been presented to help social workers explore the interface between intersectionality and care experience. The intersectional identities of any care-experienced child or young person will affect their experience of care. However, it would appear that the social and structural discrimination that all Black and minoritised people experience may have a larger effect on children and young people's experiences as adults. This needs to be considered at every stage of work with Black and minoritised children and young people in order to mitigate the irreparable harm that such discrimination can cause throughout the lifespan for people with care experience.

8

Adolescence and managing transitions into adulthood with care-experienced young people

Introduction

This chapter looks at transitions for care-experienced young people. Despite some improvements since the mid-2010s, the support available to young people leaving the care system still has weaknesses and is inconsistent across the sector. One of the areas where this is most apparent is when young people turn 18 and are no longer eligible for CAMHS/CYPMHS support if the 'cut-off' age is 18, although some services will work with young people up to ages 21 or 25. Most young people are not then eligible for support from adult social services or adult mental health services, as they do not have 'care and support needs' or 'serious and enduring mental illness' and so they do not meet the eligibility criteria under the Care Act 2014 or the Mental Health Act 1983/Mental Health Act 2007. This chapter outlines the policy framework underpinning leaving care services and also outlines policy guidance on transitions from health and youth justice services into adult health and criminal justice services.

In the latter part of the chapter, several other topical issues affecting care-experienced young people and mental health are discussed. These include involvement with youth justice, child criminal exploitation (CCE) and child sexual exploitation (CSE) and their interface with mental health, as these areas are concerning topics for practitioners and can contribute to the impact on those young people's mental and emotional wellbeing while in care and after care.

Transitions

It is important to begin by defining what we mean by transition before thinking about what it means for care-experienced young people, as although the transition from childhood to adulthood is a developmental pathway for most adolescents, it is experienced differently by each person. A transition refers to a process an individual goes through to move from one situation, state, condition or age to another (Johansson, 2021). Munro and Simkiss (2020, p 175) describe transitions as 'the process of moving from a child focussed system to an adult orientated system'. Transition to adulthood is not a single event and yet it is often portrayed as such, solely linked to the date of a young person's 18th birthday; young people are children up to 17 years and 364 days of age and then adults from the day they turn 18. However, the boundary between childhood and adulthood can be difficult to define (Valentine, 2003), and context is important to understanding the meaning of transitions for individual young people (Johansson, 2021).

'Transitions' is often understood as transitions planning for young people with special educational needs and disabilities (SEND), young people involved with youth justice services and care leavers, that is. young people already known to health and social care services. For those young people, this process may involve moving from children's to adults' services/systems. Each of these formal transitions processes has been created by policy, legislation, services and structures, which often create barriers and challenges for those navigating their transition. It is not a 'level playing-field'. Racism, homophobia and poverty, among other factors, can and do exacerbate inequalities (Cocker et al, 2024, 2026).

Transitions and care: what do we know?

For care-experienced young people the experience of moving into adulthood is different than for other young people who do not have experience of the care system. Their journey to adulthood often starts before they turn 18. The UK Government has statutory responsibilities to provide support to care-experienced young people aged over 16 years of age leaving local authority care. These services differ in each of the four countries of the UK and are delivered by a range of agencies including local authorities. Concerns have been expressed throughout the sector about the state's failure to support care-experienced young adults (Stein, 2004, 2006), despite significant legislation and guidance in place to address this. In England, there have been a number of government strategies published since 2016 (HM Government, 2013; National Audit Office, 2015; Department of Health & Department for Education, 2016; HM Government, 2016, 2018; OFSTED, 2022) that set out to address the poor life outcomes that care-experienced people often achieve. In Scotland, an Independent Care Review was established in 2016 to investigate the shortcomings of public care. On 5 February 2020, the Review published *The Promise*, a document that set out an ambitious programme of change (Independent Care Review, 2020). The Scottish Government accepted all the recommendations of the Review and made a pledge to deliver significant change by 2030. In 2025 the Oversight Board published their third progress report, indicating there was still significant work required to deliver the change agenda by 2030 (The Oversight Board, 2025).

Despite these reports raising many of the same issues, they have not had the desired effect on improving the experiences of care leavers or the life chances available to them (Sacker et al, 2021). This would suggest that trying to address and change the experiences of our care leavers is a 'wicked problem' (Camillus, 2008). This is because of the complexity of the situations many young people face, with systems and structures that do not support them adequately. This occurs when organisations face constant changes and challenges. The problems faced by care-experienced young people are decades long in the making, with local authorities, health and education services facing significant challenges over a sustained period. Such complex problems thrive within a context of organisational or multi-agency stress, and this confusion, discord and lack of progress are the telltale signs of a 'wicked issue' (Cocker et al, 2024).

Legal guidance for transitions planning for care-experienced young people

In England, the Children Act 1989 (section 24) states that all young people qualify for advice and assistance from the local authority to promote their welfare when they cease to be looked after. Each local authority determines the level of support it provides in discharging its duties. There are three principles for transition set out in the Children Act 1989 guidance for young people leaving care, which should govern practice when talking to the young person and when making any decision about them. These are:

- Is this good enough for my own child?
- Providing a second chance if things don't go as expected.
- Is this tailored to their individual needs, particularly if they are more vulnerable than other young people?

(Department for Education, 2025)

The Children Leaving Care Act (CLCA) 2000 strengthens this by creating a statutory duty to assess and meet the care and support needs of eligible,[1] relevant,[2] and former relevant[3] young people. This includes appointing a personal adviser for them and developing a pathway plan from the age of 16. The CLCA 2000 says that this support should be available to care leavers up to age 21 and has been extended to age 25 in some cases, covering education, training, career plans and support (Cocker et al, 2024). The Children and Social Work Act 2017 states that personal adviser support can continue to age 25 for all care-experienced young people, not just those in education and employment.

There are also duties on other agencies, such as health and education, to work together to support the wellbeing of young people who receive leaving care services, and to safeguard and promote their welfare (Children Act 2004, sections 10 and 11).

The Care Act 2014 is the primary legislation for social care with adults in England. The duty under section 58 requires the local authority to carry out a needs assessment for a young person before they are 18 to identify whether they have care and support needs. If they do, there should be careful planning to meet their care and support needs as they transition into the adult world at age 18. This is particularly important if a young person is care-experienced. The statutory guidance (Department of Health & Social Care, 2023) states that an assessment should be carried out if a young person is 'likely to have needs', not just those needs that will be deemed eligible under legislation (that is, those requiring care and support arising from or related to a physical or mental impairment or illness).

The guidance also defines a reciprocal duty for relevant partner agencies to cooperate for the purposes of supporting transitions work. This includes, for care-experienced young people:

> Local authorities should have a clear understanding of their responsibilities, including funding arrangements, for young people and carers who are moving from children's to adults' services. Disputes between different departments within a local authority about who is responsible can be time consuming and can sometimes result in disruption to the young person or carer. (Department of Health & Social Care, 2023, para 16.43)

There is a great deal of guidance available to support timely transitions planning, particularly where young people are already known to social services. I next highlight several salient pieces of guidance to outline current legal requirements in England to support care-experienced young people, where the state has legal duties and responsibilities regarding transitions planning (Department for Education, 2025).

National Institute for Health and Care Excellence (NICE) guidance

There are two National Institute for Health and Care Excellence (NICE) guidance documents that cover transition from children's to adults' health and social care services (NICE, 2016a, 2016b). Both guidance documents cover issues relating to transition to adulthood; however, their core focus is on those young people who are already deemed eligible for adult health or care services and so are going through 'transition' in the service-jargon sense. Many care leavers will not fit this category. The key principles underpinning transitions planning are that:

- young people and family members are involved in planning (section 1.1.1),
- the process is developmentally appropriate (section 1.1.2),
- support is strengths based (section 1.1.3),
- is person centred (section 1.1.4)

(NICE, 2016a)

Again, for care-experienced young people, there are challenges ensuring that family members are involved, as their involvement might not be appropriate.

NICE guidance indicates that planning for transitions should start early in year 9, where a young person is aged 13 or 14, or if they come to the notice of children's services after year 9, then transitions planning should begin immediately. This is two years before pathway plan meetings usually begin for care-experienced young people. For those young people covered by health and social care or education legislation, including young people with education, health and care plans (EHCPs), early transition planning is already a legal requirement (ICE, 2016a); however, for too many young people, this planning does not happen. Helpfully, the NICE guidance mentions the need to ensure that transitions planning is not based on a rigid age threshold and that it should take place at a time of relative stability for the young person (NICE, 2016b, p 8). Again, there are gaps in the practice realities of this for care-experienced young people.

NICE guidance about young people using health or care services includes references to safeguarding roles and responsibilities. It cites 'information sharing regarding safeguarding issues' as a key principle; specifying that 'every service involved in supporting a young person should take responsibility for sharing safeguarding information with other organisations, in line with local information-sharing and confidentiality policies' (NICE,

2016a, section 1.1.7, p 34). Following the young person turning 18 and being seen by adult health or social care services, the guidance suggests that any non-attendance or non-engagement by the young person should be addressed within safeguarding protocols by adult services. However, knowledge about the legal context and frameworks relating to consent and safeguarding is important here, as adult safeguarding protocols are very different to children's services and if a care-experienced young person does not have care and support needs then it is unlikely adult services will get involved. Leaving care services may well be asked to step in. Practitioners are advised in the NICE guidance to contact family members and others to support the process (NICE, 2016a, pp 14–15). Again, this can be difficult for care-experienced young people who are living independently post-18, as they may be estranged from their birth family and may have limited contact with previous carers. The personal adviser may or may not be able to take on this role.

Special Educational Needs and Disabilities (SEND) Code of Practice

The Special Educational Needs and Disabilities Code of Practice (Department for Education & Department of Health, 2015b) describes the duty placed on education, health and social care to work together to plan and jointly commission services for young people with special educational needs and/or disabilities whether or not they have an EHCP. These duties are set out under the Children and Families Act 2014, the Care Act 2014 and the National Health Services Act 2006. Partnership working is critical to successful transition planning, particularly for young people with special educational needs and disabilities. This includes care-experienced young people with special educational needs and/or disabilities.

The Code of Practice sets out commissioning responsibilities and joint working protocols for delivering services for young people during this point of transition from children to adult services:

> local governance arrangements must be in place to ensure clear accountability for commissioning

> services for children and young people with SEN and disabilities from birth to the age of 25. There must be clear decision-making structures so that partners can agree the changes that joint commissioning will bring in the design of services. This will help ensure that joint commissioning is focused on achieving agreed outcomes. Partners must also be clear about who is responsible for delivering what, who the decision-makers are in education, health and social care, and how partners will hold each other to account in the event of a disagreement. The partners must be able to make a decision on how they will meet the needs of children and young people with SEN or disabilities in every case. (Department for Education & Department of Health, 2015b, para 3.25)

It is positive that this guidance applies until a young person is 25. However, once again there is a mismatch in this transitions guidance between the eligibility or qualifying criteria for adult services, so this guidance excludes the great number of care-experienced young people who have some needs, but receive no statutory support post-18 or post-25 for these needs. This is because many care-experienced young people are not considered eligible for adult social care services, including mental health services, after they turn 18.

Responsibilities across geographical boundaries

For those young people, including care-experienced young people, who reside or are educated away from home with SEND, specific mention is made in the NICE guidance document of the need to begin transitions planning early for those in 'out-of-authority' placements (NICE, 2016a, p 7). The local authority guidance for care leavers also mentions the importance of planning for a young person's transition to adulthood as soon as possible, ideally before a young person reaches 16 (Department for Education, 2025). For care-experienced young people living out of area, there can be confusion about which local authority is responsible for taking action to support them. There are many occasions where services from different local authority areas are involved in supporting a care-experienced young person and it is important to emphasise that there are duties for organisations to cooperate in transition planning to support these young people across geographical boundaries (Department of Health & Social Care, 2023, para 16.43).

However, this is a complex area and who is responsible for what can be confusing. There are two key tests that apply to different duties for health and social care when young people move across local authority boundaries: 'ordinary residence' and 'physical presence'. Ordinary residence describes the place that a person 'has adopted voluntarily and for settled purposes as part of the regular order of his life for the time being, whether of short or long duration'.[4] 'Ordinary residence', however, does not apply when a child is in care or accommodated by the local authority. A person's 'physical presence' means that responsibility sits with the area where the person is physically located at the time of an incident or an admission into a health setting.

The local authority that is responsible for meeting a person's needs under the Care Act 2014 is the one where the person is 'ordinarily resident'. If they have no settled residence, the test is 'physical presence', and the local authority carrying out the assessment has responsibilities for: arranging an advocate, if they need one, to engage with the assessment, and for organising an Approved Mental Health Practitioner (AMHP) if required. The local authority where someone is physically present (even if only temporarily) is responsible for carrying out any safeguarding inquiry under section 47 of the Children Act 1989 or safeguarding enquiry under section 42 of the Care Act 2014, and for arranging an advocate if needed.

For services to meet someone's needs under section 117 of the Mental Health Act 1987, the local authority where the person was 'ordinarily resident' at the time they were detained under the Mental Health Act, is responsible, even if they have subsequently moved to a new area after discharge from hospital. Similarly, the local authority where the person is ordinarily resident is responsible for carrying out a Best Interest Assessment and authorising a Deprivation of Liberty Safeguards (DoLS) application under the Mental Capacity Act 2005, appointing an

Independent Mental Capacity Advocate, making accommodation decisions, and instigating care reviews (Cocker et al, 2024).

Mental capacity

Mental capacity relates to a young person's ability to make a specific decision, not just a generic statement about decision-making potential. The Mental Capacity Act (MCA) 2005 applies to young people from the age of 16. Young people over 16 years old, including care-experienced young people, are deemed to have mental capacity, unless assessed otherwise, and can make 'bad' or 'unwise' decisions. Some practitioners can over-rely on the 'bad' or 'unwise' decisions to then consider that young people have made 'lifestyle choices' when they may be facing harm or experiencing abuse, including exploitation. Applying an understanding of executive mental capacity and how adverse childhood experiences, trauma and 'enmeshed' situations can affect decision making, including making 'unwise' decisions, is essential when considering need for protection alongside upholding young people's rights. There is a danger of 'victim blaming' here, in terms of suggesting young people are making 'poor' or 'risky' choices. NICE (2018) guidance advises assessments should take into account observations of the person's ability to execute decisions in real life situations, highlighting the situational aspect of decision making. Where there is evidence that outside of an assessment environment the person is not able to understand or weigh up information to enact a decision, this should be thoroughly explored. The presumption of capacity under section 1 of the MCA 2025 does not override professional and statutory duties to ensure that young people or adults with care and support needs are safe from abuse, neglect or exploitation. 'There is a difference between someone who has an appreciation of risk and yet goes on to take the risk – albeit unwisely – and someone who … lacked awareness of the risk and sufficient problem-solving ability.'[5]

Mental capacity can also change over time, or depending on different circumstances (for example, when under the influence of substances). Where young people are approaching age 18, mental capacity assessments may need to be carried out before the young person turns 18, to assess whether they have the capacity to choose where to live and in what type of accommodation, carry out key life skills independently and recognise and take steps to mitigate risks (Cocker et al, 2024).

Madeleine's case is an example of poor practice in exercising responsibilities across boundaries, Care Act 2014 assessments and transitions planning between children and adult services (Bateman & Cocker, 2021, pp 3–4):

Madeleine was of mixed ethnicity (White British/Black Nigerian), she was 18 years old when she died and was well known to many services. She had a long history of mental health (CAMHS) support from a very young age, including being an inpatient when she was 9. At 16 her parents were told that CAMHS had 'tried everything' so they should ask for help from social care.

Madeleine had a diagnosis of Autistic Spectrum Disorder, 'emotional dysregulation' and Obsessive-Compulsive Disorder. She had an Education, Health and Care Plan but despite this had been excluded from schools because of her behaviour which was described as 'challenging'. She was first assessed by social care services when she was 12 and at 16, she was taken into care. She experienced 8 different placements in 5 months and was then placed in secure accommodation in Scotland. Shortly before her 18th birthday she moved from there to an Independent Living facility in Croydon. Despite having reached adulthood, coordination of her care needs remained the responsibility of LB Wandsworth's Children's Social Care. Many people were involved in supporting Madeleine and a good number of assessments were undertaken by social care and health colleagues in the year before she died, including a Care Act 2014 assessment, which found that Madeleine had care and support needs. However, this was never enacted.

On the evening of the 13 August 2020, whilst at her placement, Madeleine took ketamine. Staff called 111 for advice. A short time later, staff found her suspended from her door. She was taken to hospital and died on 16 August 2020.

Source: Case study taken from Cocker et al (2024, pp 157–158)

Madeleine was living in a different local authority area at the time of her death to the one responsible for her. This complicated planning arrangements for her. In complex cases, transitions planning requires careful multi-agency working and this was lacking with Madeleine, particularly around her mental health and placement provision. In situations like this, practitioners should remain curious and tenacious in seeking ways to engage young people, particularly where there are complexities, such as mental health and substance misuse, which compound their experience of services. The Safeguarding Adult Review about Madeleine identified many gaps in the service that Madeleine received, with no one person co-ordinating her support across the many agencies involved from health and social care (Bateman & Cocker, 2021).

Interface with CAMHS and adult mental health

A recurrent theme for care-experienced young people is a disconnect in their experience of service support and transfer between CAMHS/CYPMHS and adult mental health services. This is a longstanding issue. Young people talk about experiencing a cliff edge at age 18:

> There's no outside support. Like, adult mental health services is incredibly difficult to get. Because up until you're 18 you have services like CAMHS who will work with you weekly. But as soon as you turn 18 there is nothing. (Cocker et al, 2024, p 28)

Care-experienced young people may need additional mental health support in their early adulthood to help them make sense of their life experiences of separation, loss and trauma. Some care leavers are able to make good use of leaving care services, including the support of their personal adviser. However, others may need the support of adult mental health services, because of specific difficulties they face. Barnardo's found that 46 per cent of care leavers had been identified as having a mental health concern (Smith, 2017). Of those, 65 per cent were receiving no service and only 9 per cent were on a waiting list for NHS mental health services.

The variation of services and support available to care-experienced young people across the country is not helpful. A survey completed by London Innovation and Improvement Alliance (LIIA) found that there is:

- variation in support across London,
- variation in support for care leavers living outside of their home borough,
- high thresholds for Adult Mental Health Services,
- long waits for accessing Adult Mental Health Services.

(Transformation Partners in Health and Care, 2023)

There are no easy answers regarding solutions to the shortage of mental health services to meet the needs of care-experienced young people in their early adulthood. While this document points to the ambition of the NHS long-term plan (NHS England, 2019) to create a comprehensive mental health service for those aged between 0 and 25, the political changes made to NHS commissioning following the Labour government taking power in 2024, and the ongoing scrutiny of budgets within the public sector, mean that there are some questions about what change is possible/deliverable in the near future.

Interface with youth justice

There are a significant number of care-experienced young people in the youth justice population. Around half of care-experienced children will have a criminal conviction by early adulthood (HM Inspectorate of Probation, 2024). In 2017 the Farmer Review highlighted the over-representation of care-experienced young people in prison, and the significant adversities they face (Farmer, 2017). This led to the creation of the Ministry of Justice Care Leaver Covenant, and the creation of a toolkit to support prison establishments in working with care-experienced young people (Barnardo's, 2019).

HM Inspectorate of Probation reports that one in three care-experienced children (33 per cent) born between 1996 and 1999 received a youth justice caution or conviction between the ages of

10 and 17, compared to 4 per cent of those without care experience. In addition, 92 per cent of care-experienced children in England in 2022 who had received an immediate custodial sentence by age 24 were identified as having special educational needs. However, the SEND Code of Practice excludes young people in the justice system. Section 10 includes children and young people with SEND who are in youth custody, but section 10.61 says, 'This section does not apply to children and young people serving their sentence in the community, to persons detained in a Young Offenders Institution for 18- to 21- year-olds or to persons detained in the adult estate' (Department for Education & Department of Health, 2015b, p 223). This approach does not reflect the intersectionality of young people's lives and separates some young people in conflict with the law from their peers and adds further complexity to transitions planning for care-experienced young people.

There is a national protocol for managing transitions for young people moving from Youth Offending Teams (YOT) to the National Probation Service (NPS) (HM Government, 2021). This guidance sets out the responsibilities for each of the organisations that are involved in the transitions planning for young people. It refers to the Youth Justice Board Case Management Guidance,[6] which details the supporting principles of transition from YOT to the NPS and good practice for working with children in the youth justice system, and the Youth to Adult Transitions Framework Process Map 2021.[7] Despite these requirements, research notes that 'young people turning 18 while in contact with the justice system face a steep cliff edge, leaving them at risk of harm and continued contact with the criminal justice system' (Harris & Edwards, 2023), p 4), although most young people known to youth justice services do not transition to probation services at age 18. They see out their sentence in youth justice services and if they reoffend as adults, they move immediately into probation, most often with no handover and no information sharing between probation and youth justice workers (Cocker et al, 2025).

Interface with child criminal exploitation

There is no legal definition of child criminal exploitation (CCE). The Department for Education's definition in 'Working Together' guidance is:

> Child Criminal Exploitation occurs where an individual or group takes advantage of an imbalance of power to coerce, control, manipulate or deceive a child or young person under the age of 18 into any criminal activity (a) in exchange for something the victim needs or wants, and/or (b) for the financial or other advantage of the perpetrator or facilitator and/or (c) through violence or the threat of violence. The victim may have been criminally exploited even if the activity appears consensual. Child Criminal Exploitation does not always involve physical contact; it can also occur through the use of technology. (HM Government, 2023, p 154)

The Alliance for Youth Justice report about the criminalisation of victims of CCE and the transition to adulthood points out that this definition is not used consistently among policy documents (Harris, 2025), although it is used by the Home Office (HM Government, 2018). There is acknowledgement that young people who experience CCE may have been criminally exploited even if the activity appears consensual, and that adults may also be victims (Home Office, 2023). One of the most common and commonly associated CCE activities is 'county lines', where young people travel around the country to sell drugs. However, CCE can also involve many other activities, such as growing cannabis, transporting weapons, theft, shoplifting, burglary, fraud and street crime like begging and pickpocketing, as well as modern slavery, sexual exploitation and cuckooing (Jay, 2024).

In terms of CCE and links with care-experienced young people, research tells us that for a number of reasons connected to their 'looked after' status and deficiencies within the care system, care-experienced young people are particularly vulnerable to exploitation (Shaw & Greenhow, 2020). In 2023 the Tackling Child Exploitation Support Programme launched eight practice principles to underpin the work of the multi-agency professional network responding to child exploitation and extra-familial harm (Research in Practice et al, 2023). These include:

- Put children and young people first
- Recognise and challenge inequalities, exclusion and discrimination

- Respect the voices, experiences and expertise of children and young people
- Be strengths-based and relationship-based
- Recognise and respond to trauma
- Be curious, evidence-informed and knowledgeable
- Approach parents and carers as partners wherever possible
- Create safe spaces and places for children and young people

These principles are relational and should guide approaches to work with all young people, including those that are care-experienced. The complexities of many young people's lives, including the impact of poverty and homelessness for many care leavers, should not be underestimated.

Interface with child sexual exploitation

Working Together guidance defines child sexual exploitation as:

> a form of child sexual abuse. It occurs where an individual or group takes advantage of an imbalance of power to coerce, manipulate or deceive a child or young person under the age of 18 into sexual activity (a) in exchange for something the victim needs or wants, and/or (b) for the financial advantage or increased status of the perpetrator or facilitator. The victim may have been sexually exploited even if the sexual activity appears consensual. Child sexual exploitation does not always involve physical contact; it can also occur through the use of technology. (HM Government, 2023, pp 154–155)

The literature identifies the over-representation of disabled young people, young people in residential care and young people who go missing from care in the groups of young people targeted by perpetrators of CSE. And at age 18 there is a danger that they move from being seen as a 'victim' to 'perpetrator' (Brown et al, 2016). This leads to further concern about care-experienced young people being over-criminalised in early adulthood, which in turn impacts on their mental health.

> This risk of criminalisation is influenced by race, class and gender-based biases. In particular, it increases with age: the older a child is, the less likely they are to be viewed and treated as a victim, with a significant shift in this perception and treatment at age 18. … Upon legally becoming an adult at 18, thresholds for support are higher, criteria for being protected from prosecution are stricter, sentences are harsher, and young adults are at risk of being charged with the exploitation of children despite their own continued victimisation. (Harris, 2025, p 4)

When things go wrong: Transitional Safeguarding issues for care-experienced young people

Transitional Safeguarding is 'an approach to safeguarding adolescents and young adults fluidly across developmental stages which builds on the best available evidence, learns from both children's and adult safeguarding practice and which prepares young people for their adult lives' (Holmes & Smale, 2018). It is concerned with how to effectively safeguard and support young people across the period of late adolescence and early adulthood. It is the age of 18 years that determines the difference between the legal safeguarding frameworks for children and for adults. We have a binary approach to safeguarding in England; children and adult social care services have a different understanding of the management of risk with young people. As with other topics covered in this chapter that show the challenges care-experienced young people face moving into adulthood, there is a different eligibility for adult safeguarding enquiry and support, which then raises issues about what happens to those young people who do not meet the required threshold

> a person over 18 facing harm may not receive a safeguarding response if they do not meet the criteria set out in the Care Act 2014. So, it is 'not safeguarding' if the person does not receive a safeguarding response, and they do not receive a response if their situation is understood in procedural terms to be 'not

> safeguarding'. This self-reinforcing loop, with terms defining actions that in turn prescribe the terms, undermines the sector's ability to adapt and refine its response to emerging need and evidence. (Holmes, 2022, p 9)

This is particularly relevant, given the dominant focus of children's safeguarding on abuse that happens in children's own homes in children's services (Firmin, 2020) compared with adult safeguarding. Firmin's work has transformed the sector's understanding of safeguarding adolescence in the presence of extra-familial harms – that is, harms that happen outside the home.

Transitional Safeguarding is still an emergent approach. It involves multiple organisations that work with young people, not just social care services. It provides a language to describe a complex area of practice and policy concerned with supporting young people to be as safe as possible in a way that meets their developmental needs. It is not a prescribed model that can or should be replicated identically across geographical or service areas, rather it is an approach where local areas can innovate; health, social care and voluntary sector services are encouraged to work together to prevent and meet the safeguarding needs of young people in their locality and in a way that reflects the dynamic processes of transition (Cocker et al, 2024). For care-experienced young people, Cocker et al (2024) outline several salient themes from work they completed analysing a number of Safeguarding Adult Reviews and Child Safeguarding Practice Reviews where care-experienced young people have died. Themes emerging included:

- poor planning for transitions and poor multi-agency/inter-professional communication;
- poor assessments and poor relational practice;
- lack of recognition of the risks and vulnerabilities that young people faced and their contexts;
- weak legal literacy;
- lack of engagement with and participation by young people, as well as evidence of their 'voices', views and wishes; evidence of discriminatory practices, for example 'adultification'.

These reviews describe the multiple challenges for all practitioners and agencies in addressing practice and strategic issues to better prevent the tragedy of such deaths continuing (Cocker et al, 2024).

Equality and diversity issues

There are distinct limitations with normative models of transition that measure transition to adulthood by activities such as gaining employment, getting married or other 'conventional measures of autonomy' (Valentine, 2003, p 49). Racism, sexism, and homophobia towards young people are known to structure and exacerbate inequalities in health throughout the lifespan (Krieger, 2020). Structural inequalities will also affect young people and their experiences of transition, particularly those who face additional hurdles in childhood, such as experiences of abuse and neglect. However, 'many of those who might be defined as vulnerable or on the margins of society demonstrate great resilience in successfully attaining lifestyles of stability, productivity and well-being despite difficult childhood circumstances' (Valentine, 2003, p 49).

Chapter Seven reviewed what is known about the effects of racism for care-experienced children and young people. Chapter Seven also reported on the work of Sacker and colleagues (Sacker et al, 2021) about the long-term outcomes of care experience, including enduring inequalities in social and economic outcomes related to poorer educational outcomes and poorer mental health. Sacker et al (2021, p 5) recommend that, for all care-experienced adults, 'offering regular mental health MOTs to care leavers throughout their adult lives should become a core objective for local health authorities'.

Transitions panels

One of the criticisms from adult services staff about transitions planning is that referrals from children's services concerning care-experienced young people with care and support needs who are turning 18 come through very late, sometimes just a few weeks before a young person turns 18 (Cocker et al, 2024). A young person's 18th birthday should come as no surprise so timely referrals should always be made.

Many local authorities use transitions panels as a useful process to bring partners together to scrutinise and approve the transition plans for young people. This process enables senior managers from different services to review the support planning for young people as they move on and plan for how this will be delivered, including the commissioning and funding arrangements. All partner agencies can consider how they manage or commission services to bridge the transition from children's to adult support services, by designing bespoke services for young people aged 16+, extending children's services post-18 or allowing young people to join waiting lists for adult services pre-18.

An example of this process is outlined in Wallace and Cocker (2022), where a local authority's response to the death of Ms A, a care-experienced young person (Preston-Shoot, 2017), was to set up a transitions panel, a multi-agency planning forum comprising of representatives from children's social care, adult social care, the health foundation trust, police and the Department for Work and Pensions (explored later in the following case study). Its stated aims and objectives include creating opportunities 'through which information is shared to influence safe planning, options considered, and a learning environment promoted for all' (Dooley, 2019, p 2). The panel meets monthly to enable discussion of three or four young people. An indication of its effectiveness is that, in the first 18 months of thepanel's existence, there were no evictions of care-experienced young people. This is significant, given that one third of young people leaving care are reported as experiencing homelessness within two years of leaving care (Stein and Morris, 2010).

To facilitate transition planning in mental health, partners should agree a joined-up approach across the wider partnership too, which may involve a transitions panel or identifying a lead practitioner to coordinate the professional network, to enable the young person's needs and choices to be met during and post-transition. A number of NHS foundation trusts are now investing in transitions posts (for example, South London and Maudsley Adolescent and Young Adult Mental Health Specialist) and/or developed mental health transitions frameworks (Richmond and Wandsworth Safeguarding Adults Board, 2020).

An example of transitions planning

The following case study provides an example of how one local authority responded to the needs of their local community to develop services for young people. The information is taken from an article included in a Special Issue about Transitional Safeguarding (see : https ://www.tandfonline.com/toc/cpra20/34/1). It demonstrates how recommendations from a Safeguarding Adult Review led to the establishment of a multi-agency resource for care-experienced young people, co-produced with young people, and a transitions panel which provides ongoing oversight of transition planning.

Havering Cocoon service for care-experienced young people

In 2017 the London Borough of Havering (LBH) published a Safeguarding Adult Review concerning a care-experienced young adult, Ms A, who was receiving leaving care services at the time of her death at the age of 20 (Preston-Shoot, 2017). One of the recommendations was for the council to develop and strengthen services for young people in transition from children's services into adulthood, particularly care-experienced young people. This required children's and adult social care services to work closely together. Following a successful funding bid to the Department for Education, LBH made significant investment in its transition services, co-producing these with young adults themselves in conjunction with a mental health charity. This work resulted in the creation of The Cocoon, a new 'one-stop shop' onsite multi-agency service provision for care-experienced young people; and the transitions panel, a new multi-agency planning forum (Wallace & Cocker, 2022, pp 61–62).

The Cocoon is a hub for specialist multi-agency services to be provided to care-experienced young people, creating opportunities for them to meet with key workers and progress their personal development. Agencies involved in operational delivery include children's services, housing, police, mental health services and the Department for Work and Pensions (Wallace & Cocker, 2022, p 62). The development of The Cocoon involved co-production with care-experienced young people who named the space, created the branding, designed the layout of the premises and led on planning decisions. A youth management board meets monthly to discuss and plan young people's input into areas such as policy and group-based activity (Bostock et al, 2020, p 35). This has influenced a style of professional practice at The Cocoon that involves 'a commitment to co-produce pathway plans with young people based on mutually agreed goals and co-created solutions' (Bostock et al, 2020, p 22; Wallace & Cocker, 2022, p 63).

The monthly transitions panel is an ongoing collaboration with multi-agency engagement, discussion and planning, aiming 'to improve the shared responsibility, joint working and collaborative practice' required to deliver effective transitions services' (Dooley 2019, p 1, cited in Wallace & Cocker, 2022, p 64). Benefits from the transitions panel include improved cross-agency communication and joined-up thinking. Benefits for young people include reduced evictions (Dooley, 2019, p 8, cited in Wallace & Cocker, 2022, p 65).

Emerging impact

In terms of safeguarding issues for care-experienced young people, the Havering approach has been preventative, addressing a range of needs that they may have and aiming to improve a range of outcomes:

> the developments in Havering can be considered as contributing to preventing safeguarding risks through addressing a range of needs of care-experienced young people. These are a key group who may have a range of general safeguarding needs, due to their experiences of care and the reasons why they have been in care, compared to other people of the same age and can therefore fall through the 'safeguarding gap' when Leaving Care services are provided (Holmes & Smale 2018). However, many care-experienced young people may not have needs that are eligible for care and support under the Care Act, and as a consequence not be able to access ASC safeguarding services under section 42(2) of the Act (Department of Health & Social Care, 2025).

> Local Authorities do have broader powers regarding prevention of safeguarding risks, however a lack of resources and capacity can affect the ability of Local Authorities to respond to young people's safeguarding needs. Recommendations from the Ms A [Safeguarding Adults Review] highlight the issue of young people appearing not to meet thresholds, suggesting a broader and more flexible approach to interpreting the Care Act and safeguarding adult duties that does not focus solely on eligibility criteria. (Wallace & Cocker, 2022, pp 66–67)

Source: Case study taken from Cocker et al (2024, pp 165–166)

The Welsh government pilot: basic income for care leavers in Wales

In 2022 the Welsh Government introduced an ambitious pilot project to provide a basic income for care leavers in Wales (Welsh Government, 2022). As of 31 July 2024, over 600 young people leaving care have received an income of £1,600 (£1,280 after tax) per month for up to two years (Welsh Government, 2024).

This is an impressive national innovation designed to directly address the disadvantage in income and opportunity for care-experienced young people after leaving care. While an evaluation of the scheme is still forthcoming, and schemes such as this for care-experienced young people are rare, initial reports from the evaluation team highlight some of the complexities of basic income schemes generally, including the political tensions, along with the lack of consideration of the heterogeneity of care-experienced young people at project inception. The role of professionals in supporting care-experienced young people is vital and this is the subject of the first publication from the evaluation team (Roberts et al, 2026).

These debates do not detract from the ambition at a national level to do something radically different. However, material disadvantage is one part of the picture. Ongoing support and relationships are also key for care-experienced young people at this time, as are other intersecting factors (Roberts et al, 2026).

Conclusion

This chapter has provided an overview of how important good transition planning is for care-experienced young people. For years the support that care-experienced young people have received during and after their transition to adulthood has not been as good as it should be. This is despite a considerable number of government publications identifying the issues for these young people.

Each local area should know the needs of their young people, and within a multi-agency environment, consider how services can be designed or redesigned consulting with young people to improve their options and experiences. It is clear there are considerable pressures on capacity and resources across children and adult social care services and other services that support young people leaving care, including mental health, education and justice services. The two Safeguarding Adults Reviewss cited in this chapter illustrate how young people can fall through cracks. However, there are also positive initiatives in some areas to address the risks proactively. Regardless, there is compelling evidence that better use needs to be made of the guidance already in place to improve transitions work with young people.

9

Service models for best practice in providing mental health support for care-experienced children and young people

Introduction

This chapter presents a number of service models for providing mental health support for care-experienced children and young people. It uses data from my research findings where I describe three different typologies or models of CAMHS service integration from the specific services that were included in my study. These were:

1. highly integrated services, where CAMHS clinicians were based in the same team or building as the social workers;
2. moderately integrated services, where specialist CAMHS services were based in a local authority but not in the same building as local authority social workers;
3. non-integrated services, which refer to specialist services that were based in an NHS building separate from local authority social work services.

I also present one of the local authority highly integrated services as a 'case study' in this chapter. This local authority has high annual Department for Education SDQ returns, and an exceptional level of integration – it is a co-located service – with social workers and

CAMHS clinicians in the same office. There are several promising practice initiatives within this service, which are outlined.

Models of integration

My research used focus groups and semi-structured interviews to examine how social workers' (n = 58) understood the mental health needs of looked after children and their use of the SDQ in assessing these, as well as how CAMHS clinicians (n = 24) viewed the role of the social worker in assessing mental health problems. Social workers from nine local authorities and CAMHS practitioners from 11 health trusts in England took part in the research. I examined the level of integration of the specialist CAMHS services in the local authorities and health trusts that took part in my research. Table 9.1 includes a column that identifies which typology applies to each of the sample of local authorities/health trusts included in the study.

Table 9.1: Organisation of CAMHS in local authorities included in study

Local authority	Health trust	Specialist CAMHS service based in local authority?	Notes	Model of integration
A		No	Delivered at NHS community building	Non-integrated service
B	1	No	Delivered at NHS community building	Non-integrated service
C	2	Yes	Clinicians are based in social work 'units', which are small teams of social work qualified individuals. Clinician is 0.5 fte a week and is a psychotherapist.	Highly integrated service
D	3	Yes	Fully integrated into the LA and based on the same floor as the looked after children social workers	Highly integrated service

(continued)

Table 9.1: Organisation of CAMHS in local authorities included in study (continued)

Local authority	Health trust	Specialist CAMHS service based in local authority?	Notes	Model of integration
E	4	Yes	Based in the LA, in the same area as some children's services and has been since team inception in 1999	Moderately integrated service
F	5	Yes	Based in the LA in the same office as looked after children social workers	Highly integrated service
G	6	No	Delivered at NHS community building	Non-integrated service
H		Yes	Not in children's services building but in an adult social care building	Moderately integrated service
I		No	Delivered at NHS community building	Non-integrated service
	7	No	Delivered at NHS community building	Non-integrated service
	8	No	Delivered at NHS community building	Non-integrated service
	9	Yes	Based in the LA in the same office as looked after children social workers	Highly integrated service
	10	Yes	Based in the LA in the same office as looked after children social workers	Highly integrated service
	11	No	Delivered at NHS community building	Non-integrated service

Integration models: design of services and working relationships

Examining the effects of these three different models on social workers to then determine the 'best' model for CAMHS provision to looked after children from a social work perspective was difficult, and quite possibly overly simplistic, as the rationale for service design was more complicated in a service environment where everything was commissioned and costed.

Examples of different highly integrated services include:

- One specialist CAMHS service co-located in a local authority (Local Authority D) had developed a different approach to screen and review the mental health of care-experienced children and young people. Their role was described as one of 'gatekeeper': not to keep children out of the service, but to navigate a way into mental health services, should they be required to meet a child and carer's needs. Access to mental health services was not dependent on a social worker's perceived knowledge about a child, or how long a social worker had known a child, or how proficient the independent reviewing officer was in reviewing the care plans in place for a child. Rather, there was a separate but integrated layer of support available to the social worker that coordinated and monitored mental health issues for all looked after children, using the SDQ as the tool for this task. The team had begun using the teacher version of the SDQ in addition to the carer report version to begin to triangulate data received about children. This CAMHS service and local authority is used as a case study and explored further later in this chapter.
- Another integrated approach within a CAMHS service participating in my study (Local Authority C) involved CAMHS clinicians (psychotherapists) integrated into all social work units in the local authority on a 0.5FTE basis, taking a lead on ensuring that discussions on mental health were incorporated into all thinking, planning and work with children and their families. This local authority was reviewed in a service evaluation by Forrester et al, (2013), who report the following about the integration of CAMHS clinicians into social work teams:

> The role of the Clinician was another major difference between the units and the conventional teams. Clinicians did not lead on cases but had specific tasks on specific cases. They also took part in the staff meetings and provided therapeutic psychological or other alternative insight regarding both explanations of a client's behaviour and also methods of working with them. Clinicians typically worked on cases for which some extra work was required with a parent or a child. … In general, Clinicians were partly responsible for the fact that psychological theories (for example, attachment, psychodynamic, and social learning) and evidence-based research were a central part of the discussion of cases in some of the units. (Forrester et al, 2013, pp 97–98)

This local authority had adopted a particular theoretical approach (systemic approach) that underpinned all its social work practice, which was closely aligned to models used by its CAMHS clinicians. Again, children's access to mental health services was not dependent on an individual social worker's knowledge about mental health, as individual cases were allocated to the team with particular tasks assigned to team members. However, the CAMHS clinicians in this local authority commented on difficulties with regular clinical supervision because of staff vacancies and the fact that no one in the local authority was suitably qualified to offer supervision to these workers. This model had been independently positively evaluated (Cross et al, 2010, Forrester et al, 2013). The UK Government's innovation programme for children's social care (Department for Education, 2014) had seen many more councils across England adopt this approach. However, since Forrester et al,'s evaluation, the local authority in question had changed this model and psychotherapists were no longer integrated into every social work team.

However, there were some distinct advantages to each of the various integration service types. In highly integrated services, there was a lot more flexibility for CAMHS staff in the way they worked with children. This was the second-largest group of specialist CAMHS represented in my research. They did not solely offer an office-based service and were more likely to visit children in their placements and work outside of a 50 minute-long 'therapeutic hour' session.

> ... so we work in a quite flexible way, ... we will do things like go to, we will often go to children's homes, or sometimes meet them in the community if they are really difficult to engage, or they come here to a place that is a Barn. It is basically a building that doesn't have any mental health connotations. (Child psychologist; HT 5; highly integrated service)

> ...you are able to go and speak to social workers without having the barrier of trying to get to the building or trying to get through on the telephone ....for any professionals working with looked after children, to be co-located in the same building is a huge, huge benefit. (Care-experienced children nurse; HT 5; highly integrated service)

There were strong links between these specialist services and mainstream CAMHS. The disadvantage was that these specialist teams were more expensive than 'service as usual' for CAMHS and were therefore susceptible to cuts in times of austerity unless these were shown to be cost effective.

In the moderately integrated services, the advantage for the service was that it had some of the flexibility of the highly integrated services, in that the specialist service was not based within a health building and there was some flexibility about how services were offered by the specialist CAMHS practitioners. However, as it was not located in the same building as the social work services for looked after children, networking and liaison between these two services were not as integrated as in the highly integrated services. The distinct advantage of this model was that it was based in the local authority, as opposed to being in a community health centre, and therefore was not as stigmatising for children and young people to access. Only two of the specialist services included in this research were moderately integrated services. One specialist CAMHS service shared a building with the local authority's fostering and adoption service and was one of the original 24 CAMHS innovation projects established in 1999 (Local Authority E). The other specialist CAMHS service was based in a community building in the local authority (Local Authority H), whereas most of the council services in that local authority were in a central building in a business district some distance away. Both services were well respected by social workers in their local authorities.

In the non-integrated services, the lack of flexibility that traditional outpatient, appointment-based CAMHS had was problematic both for social workers and for care-experienced children, as children had to be seen at CAMHS offices at certain set times. Social workers reported a 'take it or leave it' attitude by some CAMHS staff; where young people missed appointments, CAMHS would often have a 'three strikes and you're out' approach where cases would be closed after non-attendance. Social workers were also critical of only one kind of CAMHS service being available for care-experienced children and young people, with minimal input from social workers about what that would involve. The advantage of this model was that the service was still separate from mainstream CAMHS but closely aligned with it. Professional supervision for staff occurred within the health trust, with suitably qualified managers. Social workers for care-experienced children were able to access specialist services more quickly than they would mainstream CAMHS. Half of the CAMHS included in this study were non-integrated services.

When considering how the three integration models affected the way in which social workers understood their role in using the SDQ, I did not have sufficient evidence in my data to show that the level of integration directly or indirectly linked to successful processes. The level of integration is not a determinant of change in embedding SDQ practice but it could be one factor in establishing the level of effective mental health processes. For example, the highly integrated CAMHS all had different approaches to the way in which they integrated within the local authority teams. Only one of the local authority teams in a highly integrated service (Local Authority D, or LA D) used the SDQ in their everyday work, but that was principally because the specialist CAMHS team did all the administration, all the scoring and wrote a report for the social worker to use in the child's annual review. The CAMHS team used a specialist model to normalise this work within the local authority, where the CAMHS team are the 'specialists' and do the work, and they then discussed the results of the SDQ screen with the social worker. In other models used by local authorities, for example LA H, where the specialist service was moderately integrated, social workers were responsible for completing the SDQ work themselves as part of their routine duties.

An examination of the relative strengths and weaknesses of these specialist vs generic models in explaining how the SDQ was normalised into practice was more useful than considering the level of integration of the specialist CAMHS service. However, these specialist services should not be viewed as static. If LA D were to have its funding cut or the service were to be recommissioned by the local authority and the clinical commissioning group with a smaller budget, this 'specialist' model, where CAMHS specialist services took responsibility for everything, might not be sustainable. It may be a stepping-stone to the 'reconfiguration' of services whereby activities supporting better integration of mental health issues in practice then become normalised into routine processes. The fear is that funding issues will be the driving factor for reconfiguring services rather than processes becoming embedded into everyday practice as a targeted and planned piece of work.

Case study: Local Authority D

A case study is an in-depth exploration and analysis of a specific case, organisation, team or event (Creswell, 1998). It enables an opportunity for detailed and intense analysis of complex phenomena in one case or multiple cases (Baxter & Jack, 2008). When examining the data gathered from the nine local authorities who took part in my research, one local authority in particular, LA D, appeared to have incorporated its specialist mental health services and the SDQ data collection process into its social work services in a more integrated manner than other local authorities. LA D is therefore used as a 'critical case' (Yin, 2003) to identify 'lessons learned' (Lincoln & Guba, 1985) about what worked well and identify any areas requiring further development.

The aims of this case study are:

- to describe the real-life context in which this local authority and CAMHS specialist team is located;
- to examine the way in which the SDQ data collection process is used by a social work team for looked after children and CAMHS specialist team in this local authority;
- to comment on whether the particular experiences of this local authority could offer ideas to other local authorities about how to achieve improvements in data collection and better use of the SDQ information by social workers.

The qualitative data used in this chapter comprised an interview conducted with the team manager of the specialist CAMHS team and the focus groups conducted with the social workers and the specialist CAMHS team working in LA D. These data are presented and discussed to investigate, firstly, whether LA D did include social workers who had higher-level understandings of mental health with care-experienced children and young people compared to those in the other local authorities included in this study; and, secondly, to elucidate any examples of promising practice.

I begin with a brief overview of LA D. Following this, the process used by LA D is evaluated against the statutory guidance to compare what is expected with what takes place in practice. A number of the models and typologies identified and discussed earlier in this chapter are then applied to LA D, with the ensuing discussion bringing together the promising practice in LA D with the findings from other local authorities.

An overview of Local Authority D

Local authority D is an Outer London Labour-controlled local authority based in the west of the city. The population of the local authority is around 288,000. Just over 44% of the population are White British, with 43.9% of people self-identifying as being of Black, Asian and Minority Ethnic origin. The population is more ethnically and linguistically diverse than the London aoverage, and is fluid, with a higher turnover of both international and domestic migrants compared to London and national averages (Office for National Statistics, 2021).

The children and young people living in LA D who are aged 15 and under comprise 19.4% of the total population (Office for National Statistics, 2021). Just under one third of the local authority's children are living in poverty (32 per cent), which is around the average for London.

Care-experienced children and young people in LA D

Over the previous five years (2020–2024), the local authority had an average of 285 children in care on 31 March of each given year (Department for Education, 2025), which is a rate of 42.6 in every 10,000 children. This is slightly below the average for the numbers of care-experienced children per 10,000 children in Outer London authorities (45.2 per 10,000) and below the average for authorities across England (69.4 per 10,000).

The looked after children's teams for the local authority were all located in the council's head office building. There were three different social work teams for looked after children: the 'through care' team, which worked with children aged between 0– and18; the 'late entry' team, which worked with children aged between 14 and 18; and the 'leaving care' team, which worked with young people aged between 18 and 25. All council services operated from this building.

The specialist health service for looked after children (from here on referred to as the specialist CAMHS team) was based on the same floor as the looked after children social work teams (so highly integrated). This specialist CAMHS team was established in 2009. It worked solely with looked after children and foster carers, offering outreach and consultation to social workers for looked after children and foster carers, and direct work with looked after children. Children had to live within the borough in order to be eligible for referral to this service.

The remit of the specialist CAMHS team included health and mental health issues. It comprised:

- two social workers, both of whom had additional mental health qualifications (for example, cognitive behavioural therapy, play

therapy, or family therapy), one of whom was a licensed clinical social worker (a qualification gained in another country);
- a clinical psychologist;
- a paediatrician (who undertook the annual health checks); and
- a paediatric nurse for looked after children.

The specialist CAMHS team's social workers were employed by the local authority and the health-based members of the specialist CAMHS team were employed by the mental health/community health trusts. The looked after children's teams and the specialist CAMHS team were managed by the same head of service based in the local authority.

SDQ processes in LA D

LA D used the SDQ in most of the ways outlined in the Statutory Guidance (Department for Education & Department of Health, 2015a). The SDQ carer report version was sent to the foster carer prior to the annual health assessment, and these were routinely completed by carers. In LA D, the SDQ was collected and scored by a member of the specialist CAMHS team, rather than a social worker, and this was the main way in which LA D differed from the suggested process in the Statutory Guidance. The SDQ information was made available electronically to both the looked after child's social worker and to the IRO for the looked after child's six-monthly review. Additionally, the specialist CAMHS team completed a brief report for social workers about every looked after child that gave a summary of background information, as well as the results of subscales where any issues that required monitoring or further referral were highlighted.

In the focus group, the specialist CAMHS team in LA D reported using the SDQ to monitor the mental health of the child or young person over time. The SDQ scores were available electronically for social workers (see Figure 9.1 for a flowchart of this process).

In LA D an assessment of the mental health of a looked after child involved members of the specialist CAMHS team receiving and scoring versions of the SDQ (carer/teacher and potentially self, depending on the age of the child), compiling a brief

Figure 9.1: The process for SDQ data collection and dissemination via local authority and CAMHS personnel in LA D

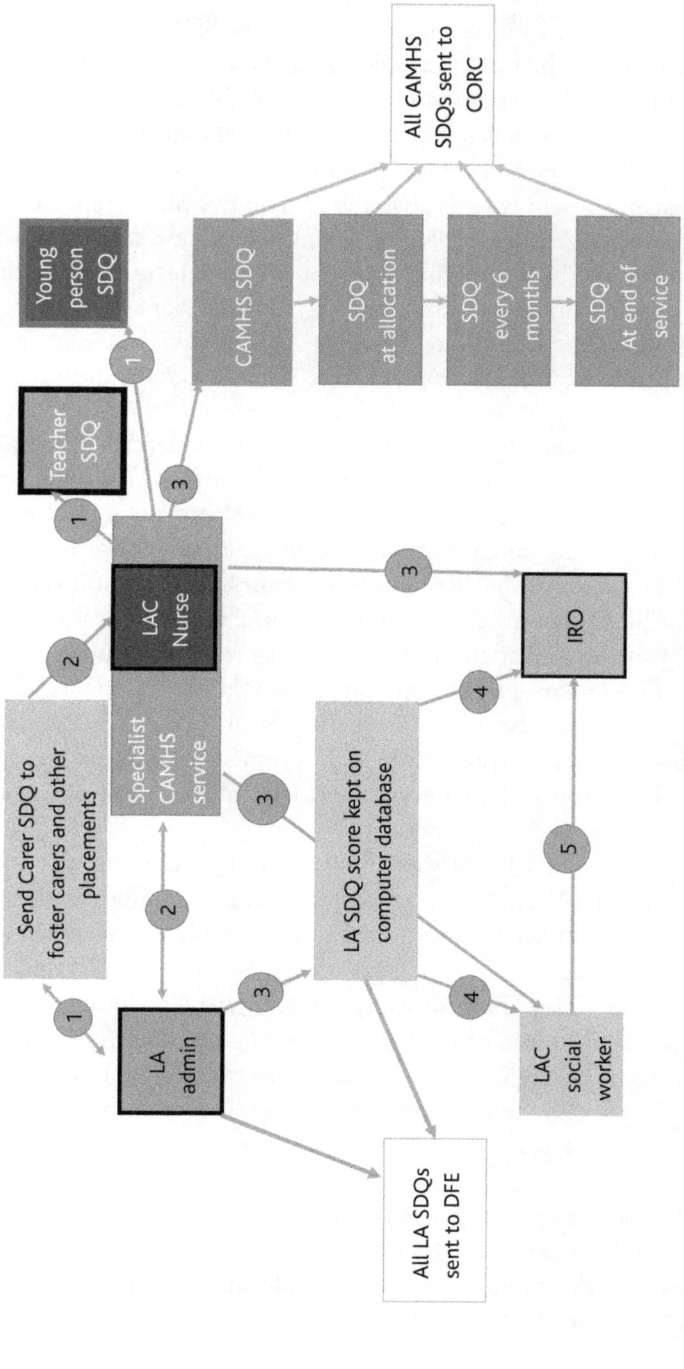

background statement about the individual child, and completing a statement summarising the results of the SDQ. This was carried out around the time of a child's annual looked after medical, with a view to this information being available for the child's next looked after review. Care-experienced children and young people who had been in care for a year or longer and had not changed placement had two reviews a year. The five SDQ subscales were used in the analysis, which was unusual as most local authorities used only the total difficulties score. This determined whether a child or young person's score was 'normal', or whether mental health difficulties were 'possible' or 'probable' in each of the subscales. From this information, social workers and members of the specialist health team decided together whether additional services might be required, and if so, what services might best meet the needs of the child or young person. According to the team manager for the specialist CAMHS team, social workers received this information, as did the specialist nurse for looked after children, the IRO and the business information officer. If the SDQ was showing something unusual then the team manager for the looked after children team also received copies.

The reason why the specialist CAMHS team undertook this task was because they found that social workers in the looked after children's teams were not routinely looking at the SDQ information and then using the data to inform decision-making:

> I think a lot of social workers don't even read these [SDQ] … but they know at the beginning of the month we'll come out there and we'll be talking about certain kids … we'll go talk to the social worker and say 'Hey, this is showing up, yeah, we'll go look at it', and so instead of them having to come to us, we will go to them, and they know that we are going to do that. We update this information every month. (Team manager; Specialist CAMHS team; LA D)

The advantage of the specialist CAMHS team having an overview of each looked after child in LA D was that they also knew what services the children or young people had already accessed. In an environment where social worker turnover was significant, this information was useful in ensuring that a 'scattergun' approach to referrals was avoided, and children and young people were not unnecessarily re-referred to services.

Because the specialist CAMHS team received the SDQs from foster carers, any training needs for foster carers in how to complete SDQs or about mental health were identified, and this training was organised and delivered by the specialist CAMHS team. The SDQ teacher versions were sent to schools by the specialist CAMHS team for looked after children of school age, and the results collected and reported alongside the carer version. The specialist CAMHS team also encouraged young people aged over 11 to complete self-report versions but tended to use the results of these as discussion starters between the specialist CAMHS team and young people about mental health, rather than analysing them alongside the carer and/or teacher SDQ versions.

The specialist CAMHS team was the gatekeeper for mental health services in the borough, and the team manager viewed this positively:

> I think we have assumed the role of the gatekeeper for mental health for children in care and I think it makes a difference because I'm not sure social workers can do that with all their cases, you know, I don't think they could do that. They're smart enough, but it's just the workload. (Team manager; Specialist CAMHS team; LA D)

The team had access to electronic information about all their care-experienced children and young people, including the SDQ data over a number of years. The team manager had created a management information system which provided the specialist CAMHS team with information about the mental health of every looked after child in the borough, including SDQ data, referrals, assessments, interventions and service refusals.

> I went through every one of the charts for every kid we had, it was 352, and pulled out every bit of information regarding referrals to mental health, any therapy that we know, everything I could do in that arena, with psychological behaviour and … we keep

> it caught up all the time so you can come to me about little Susie Q or Johnny, you know, and we can say, 'well three years ago they were offered a referral but they refused to come'. (Team manager; Specialist CAMHS team; LA D)

The team manager of the specialist CAMHS team emphasised two factors that they believed made a difference to the success of the team. The first was the 'business information officers', who were administrators located in every team responsible for data collection:

> So each business information officer sends out the Carer SDQs to the foster carers and they do a tremendous job. If they [foster carers] don't send it back right away they get on the phone, and all of our business information officers, except one really, are very pushy and very proactive. (Team manager; Specialist CAMHS team; LA D)

The second factor identified by the specialist CAMHS team manager as important for the team's success was the support received from the local authority service manager, who was the senior manager responsible for looked after children's services, and for this specialist CAMHS team for looked after children. Every local authority has its own arrangements for managing services run by the council and services run in partnership with health organisations. The model varies – the significance of the model for LA D was that the local authority service manager could create cultural expectations about cooperation and joint working between services they managed, which then supported effective completion of the SDQs and mental health support for care-experienced children and young people. The specialist CAMHS team manager described how the service manager was instrumental in influencing how well the specialist CAMHS team was embedded in the work of the looked after children service in this local authority. Having a clear organisational structure was a facilitator for better working relationships, but the additional leadership of the service manager was a critical factor in ensuring services worked well across teams.

The local authority service manager was also described by members of the specialist CAMHS team as their 'champion' at LA D's senior children's services management meetings, which ensured that the work of the CAMHS team was understood and valued at a senior level within the organisation. This relationship was viewed as vital in securing the long-term future of the specialist CAMHS team within LA D, and also in influencing practice outside the local authority:

> … where we could be in five years' time with the right sort of service manager, with the right funding in the future because actually it could be a beacon for outside of our borough because it [the specialist CAMHS team] is so helpful in a lot of ways … we've had some other people that worked for other boroughs, and they'd say we're doing so much more than everybody else does. (Team manager; Specialist CAMHS team; LA D)

These comments were echoed in the focus group that I did with the members of the specialist CAMHS team:

> We're very well managed ourselves with a manager who supports us in doing this work and sees the potential of it, and although she's a social worker, she has a background in mental health and I'm sure that that's had quite an impact on us. (Clinical psychologist; Specialist CAMHS team; LA D)

Following changes introduced in the late 1990s within mental health trusts, people appointed to management roles come from a range of professional groups, including social work. Within local authority children's services departments, senior managers are frequently social work professionals, but what is more unusual, such as in this case, is for these managers to have a mental health background as well.

The local authority service manager who was responsible for the SDQ returns to the Department for Education retired 18 months after I conducted initial interviews with staff working in the specialist CAMHS service. The team manager for the specialist CAMHS team had concerns about the impact that this might have on the service longer term, given the budget pressures and other factors affecting the local authority. LA D had already experienced the loss of some of their external services with other national providers, such as the NSPCC, because of funding restrictions.

In this local authority, one of the unique characteristics of the specialist CAMHS team was that the team acted as a universal referral point for access to additional mental health services. This ensured that children and young people were referred to services that would meet the specific needs they had, and social workers did not have to complete multiple referral forms for many different agencies.

> When we started centralising all mental health, they [social workers] would send out three or four referrals to every agency known that works with that kind of child, hopefully just to get someone on board. And so it wasn't well thought out. This process makes us think about the right pathway, … Every time a new social worker came in, especially the way they used to turn over, they'd say, 'Well, that kid needs therapy,' so they would do it, especially if it was an IRO or something. And so now we can see what is going on, so, 'No we don't need to do that. They were just there last year.' So it's very centralised with us and I think that's what makes it work. We've taken on the responsibility … and I know social workers appreciate it when I say, 'Don't worry about the referral to the [specialist service]. I'll write it out and do the letter.' It makes a big difference to them. (Team manager; Specialist CAMHS team; LA D)

In this local authority, the SDQ was part of the health assessment completed on looked after children. Given these processes strongly adhere to what is considered 'good practice', combined with the high rate of SDQ returns that LA D achieved, this local authority should be an environment where social workers had a 'high level' understanding of mental health, including using the SDQ in their work in order to deliver best outcomes for looked after children. So, what did social workers say about the SDQ?

LA D care-experienced children and young people social workers' perspectives on the SDQ

In terms of the value of the SDQ as a tool, the social workers in the focus group expressed a range of attitudes and ideas about its purpose and usefulness, very similar to the breadth of views expressed by social workers in other local authorities included in this study. Some of the data conflicted. A number of them commented that they did not use the SDQ in their practice, despite it being linked to and available on the child's/young person's electronic file.

> I never look at them. For me, it's information that's collected for the management information and it's not really collected for me. (SW1; care-experienced children team; LA D)

> We don't formally get sent them as far as I am aware, I haven't received any since I've been in practice but you do often find then on the file. I think they're quite out of date and you're like, 'This isn't relevant anymore'. (SW2; care-experienced children team; LA D)

As with social workers in other authorities, doubts were also expressed about the validity of the SDQ as an assessment tool, and value was instead placed on the relationship the social worker had with the child/young person and the foster carer, favouring this above relying on the results of the SDQ:

> It's just a tick box, little questionnaire and I found them useful as an activity to generate conversation and discussion when doing direct work or getting to know someone and doing your own assessments.

> But I wouldn't use it as a proper clinical assessment; it's not designed to be that. (SW1; care-experienced children team; LA D)

However, a number of participants challenged this view, recognising the contribution that the SDQs could bring to practice:

> I genuinely am really surprised that social workers aren't paying attention [to the SDQ] because you are right, you get very different information that comes in from each different one. The carers will probably be saying something very different to the child but that in itself is quite telling about the relationship, about what the child is thinking about that relationship. I think it's a bit sad it's literally being filed and no one's paying attention to it, because you can get quite a lot of really relevant stuff out of it. (SW3; care-experienced children team; LA D)

Overall, there did not appear to be any greater use of the SDQ by social workers in their day-to-day practice than in other local authorities. Even with the comprehensive processes in place for SDQ data collection in this local authority, including the high numbers of SDQs routinely returned, these views highlighted a potential gap between the process of SDQ data gathering, which happened outside of the social work teams in LA D, and the use of these data in practice across the social work teams. Given that its use by social workers in LA D was patchy at best, social workers described other ways in which they supported the mental health of looked after children, which included using the specialist CAMHS team:

> We are really lucky that we've got the specialist CAMHS team with clinical psychologists and social workers that we can go to, even if it's just for a consultation. So when we get that 'I'm out of my depth' feeling, we can go, 'This is what's going on. What do you think?' … I certainly would go to the

> LAC health team and seek their advice and if needs be a referral for them to work with the child.' (SW2; care-experienced children team; LA D)

> Our borough is quite unique in the sort of service we are able to provide for young people, because [the specialist CAMHS team] is round the corner from my office, I walk across and I go, 'I've got this young person, I don't know what to do …' (SW3; care-experienced children team; LA D)

However, a number of contradictions and disagreements were expressed between members of the focus groups in LA D about processes used for the SDQ and monitoring of care-experienced children and young people's mental health. Social workers knew that the business information officers sent out the forms to foster carers before the looked after child's bi-annual review, and that the looked after child's review was the appropriate place to discuss emotional and mental health issues. One of the contradictions in the data was that, despite all the social workers clearly reporting that they knew the SDQs were completed at the time of the looked after child's annual health assessment, one (SW2) said at another point in the conversation that the SDQ was not routinely sent to social workers. Others reported not seeing or using the summary reports that the CAMHS team prepared about the mental health of their looked after child. Some social workers were not aware that the teacher version of the SDQ was also routinely collected and that members of the specialist CAMHS team also worked with young people to complete the self-report version of the SDQ.

The focus group held with specialist CAMHS clinicians also raised issues about processes in looked after children's reviews in respect of how SDQs were used, how mental health issues were addressed and how CAMHS clinicians were involved in reviews:

> In the looked after children's review, it's variable in terms of not only whether mental health is covered, but how it's covered. I wouldn't go to a LAC review with a child that doesn't have emotional or mental

> health needs, so I don't know how that's covered when it's all kind of going well. But thinking about some of the young people that I see, I'm not even invited to LAC reviews or I'm invited the day before sometimes because people are just overwhelmed with work and they're not able to think far ahead. But then it is variable because others I do know invite me far in advance and it's really an important part of that social worker's relationship with the young person and the system around the young person to think about emotional wellbeing. So, you know, it's variable. (Clinical psychologist; specialist CAMHS team; LA D)

Problem areas for SDQ data gathering

One of the problem areas for SDQ data collection raised by social workers in every local authority included in the study, and not only LA D, was in respect of children in residential accommodation and/or those placed out of borough. Both the focus groups in LA D commented on how difficult it was for children placed outside of the borough to receive timely access to mental health provision.

> We're lucky in LA D that we have a health team and we also have an educational psychologist who does one or two days a week, but in the case I've just had, we can't get [a home county on the outskirts of London] to do the psychological assessment we need on the child. … I think out-of-borough placements are harder to keep your eye on but it's about the social worker keeping the child in mind the whole time and that's our role. (SW2; care-experienced children team; LA D)

> Young people in prison and, strangely enough, young people in very expensive residential placements … it's all around security and control and not around therapy. Somebody said about residential not doing SDQs and

> there might be an element of that, because they're out of sight. A lot of money has been spent. (SW1; care-experienced children team; LA D)

It was notable that this occurred despite both the Statutory Guidance suggesting clarifying which was the responsible Clinical Commissioning Group for funding services outside the borough and the existence of mechanisms to resolve any funding issues that arose (Department for Education & Department of Health, 2015a, pp 6, 23–4).

What makes a difference to social workers' understandings of the use of the SDQ?

The results discussed previously illustrated that, regardless of the promising context in which the SDQ data was gathered and made available to social workers and IROs who routinely worked with looked after children in LA D, understandings of the SDQ and use of the SDQ data by social workers in this LA appeared very similar to those of social workers in the other local authorities in my study. As with the other local authorities, some social workers demonstrated more skills and competence in mental health assessment, including knowing the point at which to ask for additional support, while others lacked the skills and knowledge to make what members of the CAMHS team described as appropriate referral decisions.

> Some experiences make me doubt a little bit their knowledge or interpretation, but it is variable and then there's social workers that'll be emailing you all the time and very much on the ball and wanting support or pathways to something different so it is variable, like in any profession. (Care-experienced children specialist nurse; LA D)

> You get some [social workers] who are great at communicating entirely appropriately, and checking in with very complex, worrying cases, then others not

> so... So that happens as well. (Clinical psychologist specialist health service; LA D)

Many of the points made by the specialist CAMHS team in LA D were also made by other specialist CAMHS teams in other local authorities. There were similar observations around the knowledge and skills deficits of many social workers in the area of mental health and the same problems were identified, with social workers thinking that therapy was the answer to a child's problems.

> I think there is a mindset within social work that says that therapy can solve it all and therapy is almost like this beacon that's held up and if we can just force these children through the doors and get them to sit down that everything will miraculously be okay. (Clinical psychologist specialist service; LA D)

The student social work experience of SDQ use in LA D

One of the participants in the specialist CAMHS focus group was a social worker who had previously been a student in the specialist CAMHS team and had completed and used the SDQ throughout her placement. Social work students in England undertake two placements for 170 days in total in two contrasting settings. A placement in the specialist CAMHS team had enabled this student to become familiar with the SDQ and with emotional and mental health issues for looked after children more generally. She then worked in another social work team elsewhere in the local authority. Her contribution to the focus group identified a number of challenges for specialist CAMHS practitioners in their work with social work colleagues to support the development of a particular mindset or way of thinking about mental health:

> I was just thinking that from doing the SDQs as a student, coming in and doing the self-report of the SDQs with the young people and then writing up about them and then looking back at their history and analysing it, you start to think in that

> way. Having done SDQs has made me think about mental health, has made me look into it, read up on it and really think more about it and to be more careful about it – as you were saying, not jumping in and saying 'Oh, I think it's this', and just looking at the basics of what begins, how it begins, where those signs are coming from and how it affects and seeing it through their history of how it's affecting them and how it develops. I feel that if the SDQ was piloted and other social workers were doing the SDQs themselves, generally it would make them think more about it, it would be a beginning point for them to understand it. (Social worker; ex-student in specialist health service; LA D)

This social worker was able to provide commentary on why looked after children's social workers' responses to mental health were varied, even in a borough where a separate team coordinated the SDQ, and identified ways in which all social workers could ensure that mental health issues were routinely addressed.

> Discussing mental health issues with social workers it was really varied, some of them don't see it as a health issue. They didn't connect it to the work that we did as within the looked after CAMHS team. Some people see it as a very negative thing and maybe mental health should be discussed not to be like 'is there any problems' but you know, 'How can we make sure that everything keeps going the way it is going? Are they participating in activities outside? Do they have one close person, a friend to speak to?' All this kind of thing and that's what should be discussed at every LAC review in my personal opinion. (Socialworker; ex-student in specialist health service; LA D)

The ex-student social worker's comments acknowledged that the process of social workers addressing mental health issues routinely in their work had to be more than just completing a form in order for the SDQ to have any meaningful impact on practice.

She highlighted how the overview reports that CAMHS completed were useful to social workers.

> with the SDQ returns themselves, I don't think they have had any impact on practice whatsoever … [so] I think it's good that there is that net outside of the social worker because I think there's a tendency to try and say, 'Oh well, the social worker can do that because it would be good for the social worker to know', and it's like, 'Well, actually, sometimes we can't do everything' and we have to be quite realistic about what we can do. So that kind of thing [report from the specialist team using SDQ data] is really helpful. (Social worker; ex-student in specialist health service; LA D)

The surprise, in the context of a 'good' local authority with high SDQ returns and good links between social workers and the specialist CAMHS team, was that some social workers disregarded the SDQ as meaningful. This particular social worker acknowledged that sometimes this may be about social workers' workload pressures or staff turnover, which was high, but the clinical psychologist thought that those social workers who understood the importance of mental health demonstrated good 'mind mindedness'. They were able to 'hold the child in mind' and alongside this, show good organisational skills. For example, where there were considerable mental health concerns for a child, this type of 'mind-minded' social worker would ensure that members of the specialist team were invited to the child's looked after review in a timely manner. Given that the dates for these reviews were set well in advance, this was a relatively minor communication issue which, when addressed, could encourage closer working between teams where this was necessary.

The specialist CAMHS team's observations about social workers and mental health knowledge

Many of the points about the mental health knowledge and skills of social workers made by specialist CAMHS teams in LA D were similar to those of staff working in other CAMHS teams. The clinical social worker in the specialist team thought that social workers still had a fear about mental health and about what the social work role with mental health entailed:

> I think there is a real level of panic around mental health, and wanting to try and fix it and make it better immediately, but not actually having as social workers the ability to do that because we are not trained mental health professionals and we're sort of the jack of all trades and micro-managers in what we do more than we are a specialist in anything. (Clinical social worker in specialist CAMHS team; LA D)

Other clinicians also showed some understanding about the pressures that social work colleagues were under in doing their jobs and had some suggestions for ways in which social workers could work more effectively in assessing and responding to mental health issues.

> They're not mental health specialists and we are not asking them to be, but I suppose to have some general knowledge about the kinds of signs and symptoms, the early signs and symptoms of mental health difficulties, so rather than going and to try to diagnose things, to know what the signs and symptoms are, to listen, to interview not just the young, obviously to interview and listen to the young person, but the people who know them best, because social workers are not going to have time to spend, you know, several hours a week talking to a young person. (Clinical psychologist specialist in CAMHS team; LA D)

Conclusion

There are benefits to examining a specific case and identifying and potentially extrapolating the factors that might be replicable in other authorities. Scrutinising a 'real life' case example also enabled the unforeseen and unintended consequences of specific actions and decisions to be better understood (Yin, 2003). One of the limitations of the case study approach is the lack of generalisability of the results of one case to wider environments or circumstances. However, some researchers who use this method say that this is not its purpose (Bryman, 2011). Lincoln and Guba (1985) discuss 'lessons learned' from case studies rather than focusing on generalisability. The 'lessons learned' from this case study were:

- Good administrative support for sending out and collecting SDQ data was essential to maximise compliance and high levels of data returns.
- Support from senior managers was essential in embedding the SDQ data into routine practice as this took time and resources. Senior management support could mean that the issue continued to be championed, alongside the constant pressure and distraction from other crises, initiatives, policy and practice developments within the service.
- A clear 'direction of travel' for the specialist CAMHS team contributed to effective SDQ data collection and interpretation for use with planning for both individual looked after children and strategic services. This specialist team had good ideas for further service development and a good understanding of the obstacles that might affect this progress.
- Good communication between the specialist CAMHS team and the looked after children's social workers was important to ensure that social workers approached members of the CAMHS team if they had concerns about any children they were allocated. Co-location was important here.

The work of the specialist team enhanced the social worker's role. The brief overview report that was prepared for the social worker raised the profile of mental health. However, there were downsides to this too. Taking responsibility for the SDQs and being the gatekeeper of mental health services could mean that social workers would then not respond to anything to do with mental health as they saw it as someone else's responsibility. This case study showed that co-located or integrated services do not necessarily mean that the SDQ is fully embedded into the practice of individual social workers and/or the strategic work of the local authority. Many of the views expressed by the LA D social workers and CAMHS clinicians were similar to those of social workers and CAMHS practitioners who I interviewed in other local authorities. The majority of social workers did not perceive that the SDQ had a role in their work.

LA D was the best in my sample at getting completed SDQ forms returned from foster carers, and was one of the best in the country at doing this, so clearly it was doing something right in terms of process. However, having a good data collection process was not enough to ensure that the SDQ was integrated within social work practice in the organisation, nor that this automatically led to benefits for children in terms of social workers making appropriate referrals on to services that they needed. The CAMHS specialists did have a good overview of the mental health history of all the looked after children in LA D, so there was a high likelihood that the CAMHS service would make appropriate referrals on to external mental health services, where this was needed. In terms of research question three, LA D could provide good SDQ information via the specialist CAMHS but the majority of social workers didn't use this themselves. The CAMHS staff collected and analysed the data and then made it available for social workers, most of whom did not make use of it.

LA D's specialist CAMHS team had a number of strengths, including its geographical location and the clear focus of its work championing the mental health of looked after children and maintaining the profile of mental health in the minds of social workers and IROs. In terms of research question four, interprofessional working relationships were excellent and had some impact insofar as the CAMHS staff were driving the use of the SDQ with social work colleagues. Change in a complex system takes time, effort, energy and resources, as this case study illustrates, and LA D had made good progress in its endeavours to advocate the use of the SDQ for looked after children with social workers via rigorous focus and process; however, further work was required to normalise the SDQ process among social workers.

Conclusion

This book captures the main debates about the mental health of care-experienced children and young people. I began with the voices of care-experienced young people, because their messages are essential to enabling us to know what works well and what needs to change in the current systems and structures within which we work. It is clear from their messages that there is still much to do to improve services for this group of children and young people both while they are in care and once they leave care.

These problems within the current services are not new and they are made all the more difficult with the squeeze on public spending within local government and the NHS. Even before COVID-19, referrals to CAMHS within the general population were increasing at an exponential rate, reflecting the stressors of modern life on many children and young people.

This is not to say that all is lost. There are many green shoots of opportunity. At a macro level, the English and Scottish Governments have announced plans to invest in services for children in care. In October 2025, the English Government announced £555 million to support the implementation of changes announced in the Children's Wellbeing and Schools Bill. This includes supporting care leavers via national 'Staying Close' support packages, investing in foster care recruitment and retention, and addressing the profiteering in the children's social care market (UK Parliament, 2025). This follows on from the publication of the Independent Review of Children's Social Care (MacAlister, 2022), which recommended an investment of over £2 billion to deliver the reform required to children's social care.

> The Government's current investment of over £2 billion over the three-year spending review period

> aligns with this ambition, particularly in prioritising preventative services through £1.57 billion investment in the Families First Partnership Programme. In addition, the Government has confirmed £555 million in Transformation funding to support the delivery of key social care commitments under the Children's Wellbeing and Schools Bill, and to continue our investment in family help, kinship and foster care reforms. On top of this, we are providing £560 million in capital funding to refurbish and expand residential care and provide more fostering placements. (UK Parliament, 2025, p 1)

In February 2026 the Scottish Government announced a £9.5 million investment in projects supporting the education and wellbeing of care-experienced children and young people (Scottish Government, 2026). This was announced on the sixth anniversary of The Promise of the Independent Care Review (Independent Care Review, 2020) and is part of a targeted resource provided to local authorities to support care-experienced children and young people from birth up to the age of 26.

> The Scottish Government is committed to Keeping The Promise by 2030, and we are seeing good progress across Scotland from education to justice – including a 18reduction since 2020 in the number of children identified as 'looked after'. …The funding we are announcing today, on the sixth anniversary of The Promise, takes the Scottish Government's total investment in the programme to just over £80 million since 2018 – showcasing how we are delivering for Scotland's care experienced young people and helping them get the best start in life. (First Minister John Swinney, in Scottish Government [2026, p 1])

As I mentioned in Chapter 8, the Welsh Government is piloting a project that sees all eligible care leavers in Wales receiving a basic income for two years after leaving care. As the 2025 interim statistical report states, 'No other basic income scheme has given regular payments as large as those received by young people involved in the pilot, nor have other basic income schemes been open to a national cohort of care leavers from the age of 18 for two years of payments' (Sanders et al, 2025, p 11).

These national investment plans are welcome. However, any changes introduced at macro and micro levels must be evidence informed. We need to see whether they work.

This book has provided an overview of research, examining issues arising in multi-disciplinary working, alongside hearing from young people themselves about what matters to them in relation to mental health support. There is some excellent research being funded by UK Research and Innovation bodies, which is helping to expand our knowledge about 'what works' with this group of children and young people, including the long-term impacts of not addressing this issue.

One of the most shocking discoveries for me in researching and writing this book was coming across the work of Professor Amanda Sacker and colleagues, evidencing the impact of public care on the reduced life expectancy of care-experienced adults (Sacker et al, 2021). My own work examining the situations of (n = 59) care-experienced young people who had died from abuse and neglect during late adolescence/early adulthood was also sobering (Cocker et al, 2024). At the most damaging end of the spectrum, young people face discrimination, homelessness, unemployment, poor mental health, and criminalisation, and can experience other factors related to multiple exclusion, such as drug addiction and exploitation. Having robust knowledge of how best to support young people who face these difficulties is essential.

Many of the messages for agencies working with care-experienced young people include:

- taking children and young people's views seriously;
- making sure that timely planning occurs for young people as they approach adulthood;
- acknowledging the complexity of lived experience and the heterogeneity for this group of young people;
- improving legal literacy;
- improving multi-agency communication;

- improving links between CAMHS and adult mental health services.

(Cocker et al, 2024)

While resources to invest in infrastructural change are welcome, they will not automatically create a better system for care-experienced children and young people. Once again, the issues affecting service structures are not new. We need to learn from our history. These problems are entrenched, and resourcing is only one part of a solution which is equally complex. It is essential that care-experienced children and young people remain at the very core of all we do. I still believe that supporting the mental health of care-experienced children and young people is essential to their overall wellbeing while in care and after they leave care, and is the lynchpin for everything else that follows. Of course, there are multiple challenges for all professionals working with care-experienced children and young people, but given the level of disadvantage that we know these young people experience, it is nothing short of a national disgrace that these disadvantages show very little sign of abating at a national level.

Social workers are important people in the lives of care-experienced children and young people and often underestimate the role they have in supporting, mentoring and advocating for them. It is often the little things that social workers do in relational practice that make the difference in how a child or young person feels about the events that happen in their lives. Kindness and tenacity are valued skills in working with young people, as are a great sense of humour and a vision for a different future. It is through relationships that magic happens – but these take time and investment. Building confidence about how to support children and young people who have experienced trauma, separation and loss is essential – including knowledge about mental illness and support for emotional wellbeing. It is an investment well worth making for you and for all the children and young people you will work with throughout your career. They need you to be the best you can be in advocating for them, in whatever role you have in your workplace.

Notes

Introduction

1 For clear information about mental health services and CAMHS for young people, parents/carers and professionals. See: https://hampshirecamhs.nhs.uk/issue/mental-health-and-mental-illness-professional/ and https://hampshirecamhs.nhs.uk/help/young-people/ and https://hampshirecamhs.nhs.uk/help/parents-carers/

Chapter 1

1 Tash is a personal adviser for an East of England Council's Leaving Care Service.

2 https://www.bbc.co.uk/news/articles/cj4dyy9kgrro

3 https://www.bbc.co.uk/news/uk-england-67123405

4 https://www.theguardian.com/education/2023/apr/16/buckling-nhs-fails-to-treat-250000-children-with-mental-health-problems; https://www.childrenscommissioner.gov.uk/blog/over-a-quarter-of-a-million-children-still-waiting-for-mental-health-support/

5 Emotionally Unstable Personality Disorder is linked to Borderline Personality Disorder. See: https://www.nhs.uk/mental-health/conditions/borderline-personality-disorder/symptoms/

6 Borderline Personality Disorder. See: https://www.nhs.uk/mental-health/conditions/borderline-personality-disorder/symptoms/

7 See: https://www.croydonsab.co.uk/about-us/safeguarding-adult-reviews/ and read 'Madeleine' published March 2022 and 'Sylvia' published May 2023.

8 https://www.childrenssociety.org.uk/information/young-people/well-being/services/time and https://www.childrenssociety.org.uk/information/young-people/well-being/services/pause

Chapter 3

1 See: www.sdqinfo.org for further information.

2 The International Classification of Diseases – Mental Health Disorders (11th edition) (ICD-11, 1993) came into use in World Health Organization Member States as from 2018.

3 The *Diagnostic and Statistical Manual of Mental Disorders* (5th edition) (DSM-V) is published by the American Psychiatric Association, Washington, DC (2013). This is the main diagnostic reference of mental health professionals

in the US. The original DSM published in 1952 listed 60 types and subtypes of mental disorder, while DSM-V, the current edition, contains well over 200. Difficulties experienced by children and young people represent one of the areas of classificatory expansion that has both reflected and inspired research interest in the field (Cocker & Scott, 2006).

4 See: www.dawba.info

5 Reliability is the ability of a measure to produce consistent results when the same entity is measured under different conditions (Field, 2013).

6 Validity is concerned with whether an instrument measures what it says it measures (Field, 2013). There are a number of different ways of establishing validity: face validity; construct validity and predictive validity (Bryman, 2011).

7 Measures the proportion of positives that are correctly identified by the measure or tool (Bryman, 2011).

8 Measures the proportion of negatives that are correctly identified by the measure or tool (Bryman, 2011).

9 See: https://www.gov.uk/government/collections/statistics-looked-after-children

10 See: https://www.england.nhs.uk/long-term-plan/

11 The Hawthorne Effect is a term that emerged from a study undertaken in a factory in Chicago in the early 20th century, where researchers observed the effect of changes to the quality of light in the factory on the productivity of workers. Worker productivity increased during the study but as soon as the study ended, productivity went back to the way it was prior to the research being conducted. Researchers thought that the changes occurred as a result to the workers receiving attention from the research team rather than from the change in light. In terms of how this might relate to care-experienced children and mental health, the change caused by the Hawthorne Effect would include undertaking activities, such as completing screening questionnaires, without this having an overall improvement on the mental health of care-experienced children and young people.

12 Virtual School Head (VSH): an officer employed by a local authority in England whose job is to ensure that the authority's duty to promote the educational achievement of the children it looks after is properly discharged. (Department for Education & Department of Health, 2015, p 35).

13 Child Outcomes Research Consortium. See: https://www.corc.uk.net/about-corc/

Chapter 4

1 See Department for Education & Department of Health (2015a, pp 13–14) for advice on the responsible commissioner, and guidance on out-of-borough placements and who pays. The guidance is clear that children in care should not be denied a service because they are placed out of borough.

2 A looked after child's review occurs every six months for all children who have been in care longer than four months and is the arena for gathering all involved agencies together with the child, parent (where appropriate) and

social worker to review the child's progress as well as permanence plans for the child.

Chapter 5

1 See: https://basw.co.uk/policy-and-practice/resources/reclaiming-social-work-evaluation-systemic-units-approach-delivering

2 The Child Outcomes Research Consortium (CORC) is the UK's leading membership organisation that collects and uses evidence to improve children and young people's mental health and wellbeing. See: https://www.corc.uk.net/

Chapter 6

1 See: https://www.adoption-focus.org.uk/sites/default/files/2021-03/Examples-of-theraplay-games.pdf

2 See: https://www.childhoodfirst.org.uk

3 See: https://www.thecaldecottfoundation.co.uk/residential-care/

Chapter 8

1 Eligible young people are aged 16 or 17, have been looked after for a period or periods totalling at least 13 weeks starting after their 14th birthday and ending at least one day after their 16th birthday, and are still in care. There is a duty to support these young people up to the age of 18, wherever they are living. (CLCA explanatory notes: www.legislation.gov.uk)

2 Relevant young people are those aged 16 and 17 who meet the criteria for eligible children, but who leave care. Regulations may exclude certain groups, such as children who return home permanently and children who receive respite care. Local authorities may, for example, take highly dependent children for short periods to give their carers a break. This group would remain the responsibility of their families and would not be eligible for the new arrangements even if their periods of respite care added up to the prescribed period for eligibility. (CLCA explanatory notes: www.legislation.gov.uk)

3 Former relevant young people are those who, before reaching the age of 18, were either eligible or relevant children. (CLCA explanatory notes: www.legislation.gov.uk)

4 *Shah v London Borough of Barnet* [1983] 1 All ER 226 (HL)

5 *Baker J, GW v A Local Authority* [2014] EWCOP20, para. 45

6 https://www.gov.uk/government/collections/case-management-guidance

7 Annex A, The Youth to Adult Transitions Framework Process Map 2021. See: https://assets.publishing.service.gov.uk/government/uploads/system/uploads/attachment_data/file/1001348/Annex_A_Youth_to_Adult_Transitions_Framework_Process_Map_2021.pdf

References

Abbo, C., Kinyanda, E., Kizza, R. B., Levin, J., Ndyanabangi, S., & Stein, D. J. (2013). Prevalence, comorbidity and predictors of anxiety disorders in children and adolescents in rural north-eastern Uganda. *Child and Adolescent Psychiatry and Mental Health*, 7(21). https://doi.org/10.1186/1753-2000-7-21

Achenbach, T. M. (1991). *Manual for the Child Behavior Checklist/4-18 and 1991 Profile*. University of Vermont, Department of Psychiatry.

Adjei, P. B., & Minka, E. (2018). Black parents ask for a second look: Parenting under 'White' child protection rules in Canada. *Children and Youth Services Review*, *94*, 511–524. https://doi.org/10.1016/j.childyouth.2018.08.030

American Psychiatric Association. (2013). *Diagnostic and Statistical Manual of Mental Disorders: DSM-5™* (5th edn). American Psychiatric Publishing, Inc. https://doi.org/10.1176/appi.books.9780890425596

Amstadter, A. B., Richardson, L., Meyer, A., Sawyer, G., Kilpatrick, D. G., Tran, T. L., et al (2011). Prevalence and correlates of probable adolescent mental health problems reported by parents in Vietnam. *Social Psychiatry and Psychiatric Epidemiology*, 46(2), 95–100. https://doi.org/10.1007/s00127-009-0172-8

Anselmi, L., Fleitlich-Bilyk, B., Menezes, A. M. B., Araújo, C. L., & Rohde, L. A. (2010). Prevalence of psychiatric disorders in a Brazilian birth cohort of 11-year-olds. *Social Psychiatry and Psychiatric Epidemiology*, 45(1), 135–142. https://doi.org/10.1007/s00127-009-0052-2

Archer, C. (2003). *Trauma, Attachment, and Family Permanence: Fear Can Stop You Loving*. Jessica Kingsley.

Audit Commission. (1999). *Children in Mind: Child and Adolescent Mental Health Services*. Audit Commission Publications.

Ayodeji, E., Dubicka, B., Abuah, O., Odebiyi, B., Sultana, R., & Ani, C. (2021). Editorial perspective: Mental health needs of children and young people of Black ethnicity. Is it time to reconceptualise racism as a traumatic experience? *Child and Adolescent Mental Health*, *26*, 265–266. https://research.ebsco.com/linkprocessor/plink?id=ec780e5e-5c92-319b-b227-251def6cedda

Bamford, F., & Wolkind, S. N. (1988). *The Physical and Mental Health of Children in Care: Research Needs*. Economic and Social Research Council.

Barnardo's. (2019). *Toolkit for Supporting Care Leavers in Custody*. https://www.nicco.org.uk/directory-of-resources/toolkit-forg-care-leavers-in-custody

Barnardo's. (2023). *Double Discrimination: Black Care-experienced Young Adults Navigating the Criminal Justice System*. https://www.barnardos.org.uk/sites/default/files/2023-09/Double%20Discrimination%20-%20Black%20care-experienced%20young%20adults%20navigating%20the%20criminal%20justice%20system%20report.pdf

Bateman, F., & Cocker, C. (2021). *Safeguarding Adults Review: Madeleine*. https://www.croydonsab.co.uk/wp-content/uploads/2022/03/PDF-Madeleine-SAR-Final-Report.pdf

Baxter, P., & Jack, S. (2008). Qualitative case study methodology: Study design and implementation for novice researchers. *Qualitative Report*, *13*(4), 544–559. http://search.ebscohost.com/login.aspx?direct=true&db=eric&AN=EJ824836&site=eds-live&scope=site

Beck, A. (2006). Addressing the mental health needs of looked after children who move placement frequently. *Adoption & Fostering*, 30(3), 60–65. http://search.ebscohost.com/login.aspx?direct=true&db=jlh&AN=2009320899&site=ehost-live

Becker, A., Woerner, W., Hasselhorn, M., Banaschewski, T., & Rothenberger, A. (2004). Validation of the parent and teacher SDQ in a clinical sample. *European Child & Adolescent Psychiatry*, 13(2), ii11–ii16. https://doi.org/10.1007/s00787-004-2003-5

Becker, A., Hagenberg, N., Roessner, V., Woerner, W., & Rothenberger, A. (2004). Evaluation of the self-reported SDQ in a clinical setting: Do self-reports tell us more than ratings by adult informants? *European Child & Adolescent Psychiatry*, 13, ii17–ii24. https://doi.org/10.1007/s00787-004-2004-4

Beecham, J. (2014). Annual Research Review: Child and adolescent mental health interventions: a review of progress in economic studies across different disorders. *Journal of Child Psychology and Psychiatry*, *55*(6), 714–732.

Beecham, J., & Knapp, M. (2001). Costing psychiatric interventions. In G. Thornicroft (Ed.), *Measuring Mental Health Needs* (2nd edn, pp 201–224). Gaskell.

Bele, S. D., Bodhare, T. N., Valsangkar, S., & Saraf, A. (2013). An epidemiological study of emotional and behavioral disorders among children in an urban slum. *Psychology, Health & Medicine*, 18(2), 223–232. https://doi.org/10.1080/13548506.2012.701751

Bernard, C., & Gupta, A. (2008). Black African children and the child protection system. *The British Journal of Social Work*, *38*(3), 476–492. http://www.jstor.org/stable/23724529

Bernard, D. L., Calhoun, C. D., Banks, D. E., Halliday, C. A., Hughes-Halbert, C., & Danielson, C. K. (2021). Making the 'C-ACE' for a culturally-informed adverse childhood experiences framework to understand the pervasive mental health impact of racism on Black youth. *Journal of Child and Adolescent Trauma*, *14*(2), 233–247. https://doi.org/10.1007/s40653-020-00319-9

Bignall, T., Jeraj, S., Helsby, E., & Butt, J. (2019). *Racial Disparities in Mental Health: Literature and Evidence Review*. https://lampardinquiry.org.uk/wp-content/uploads/2025/05/DC15-Race-Equality-Foundation-Racial-disparities-in-mental-health-Literature-and-evidence-review.pdf

Blower, A., Addo, A., Hodgson, J., Lamington, L., & Towlson, K. (2004). Mental health of looked after children: a needs assessment. *Clinical Child Psychology and Psychiatry*, *9*(1), 117–129.

Bogen-Johnston, L., Edelman, N., & Sellers, R. (2024). Interventions to support reproductive and mental health among care leavers: A systematic review. *Adoption & Fostering*, *48*(1), 82–104. https://doi.org/10.1177/03085759231212496

Bonfield, S., Collins, S., Guishard-Pine, J., & Langdon, P. E. (2010). Help-seeking by foster-carers for their looked after children: The role of mental health literacy and treatment attitudes. *The British Journal of Social Work*, 40(5), 1335–1335.

Bostock, L., Khan, M., Munro, E. R., Lynch, A., Baker, C., Newlands, F. and Antonpoulou, V. (2020). *Havering: Face to face pathways. Final evaluation report*. The Department for Education. https://assets.publishing.service.gov.uk/government/uploads/system/uploads/attachment_data/file/932347/Havering.pdf

Boyd, K., Balogun, M., & Minnis, H. (2016). Development of a radical foster care intervention in Glasgow, Scotland. *Health Promotion International*, *31*(3), 665–673.

Broad, B. (1999). Improving the health of children and young people leaving care. *Adoption and Fostering*, *23*(1), 40–48.

Broeders, M., Moss, S., Nyström, L., Njor, S., Jonsson, H., Paap, E., et al (2012). The impact of mammographic screening on breast cancer mortality in Europe: A review of observational studies. *Journal of Medical Screening*, *19*(suppl 1), 14–25. https://doi.org/10.1258/jms.2012.012078

Brown, S., Brady, G., Franklin, A., Bradley, L., Kerrigan, N., & Sealey, C. (2016). *Child Sexual Abuse and Exploitation: Understanding Risk and Vulnerability*. Early Intervention Foundation.

Bryman, A. (2011). *Social Research Methods* (4th edn). Oxford University Press.

Cabinet Office. (2018). *Race Disparity Audit Summary Findings from the Ethnicity Facts and Figures* London: HMSO. https://assets.publishing.service.gov.uk/government/uploads/system/uploads/attachment_data/file/686071/Revised_RDA_report_March_2018.pdf

Camillus, J. (2008). Strategy as a wicked problem. *Harvard Business Review*, *86*, 98–101.

Care Quality Commission (2019). *Brief Guide: Waiting Times for Community Child and Adolescent Mental Health Services*. https://www.cqc.org.uk/sites/default/files/Brief_guide_Waiting_times_for_community_child_and_adolescent_mental_health_services.pdf. Accessed on 13.6.26.

Chamberlain, P., Leve, L. D., Laurent, H., Reid, J. B., Price, J., & Landsverk, J. A. (2008). Prevention of behavior problems for children in foster care: Outcomes and mediation effects. *Prevention Science*, *9*(1), 17–27. https://doi.org/10.1007/s11121-007-0080-7

Chaudron, L. H., & Wisner, K. L. (2014). Perinatal depression screening: Let's not throw the baby out with the bath water! *Journal of Psychosomatic Research*, *76*(6), 489–491. https://doi.org/http://dx.doi.org/10.1016/j.jpsychores.2014.03.011

Clark, R. B. (1981). Community Action Programs: An appraisal. In J. Joffe & G. Albee (Eds.), *Prevention through Political Action and Social Change*. University Press of New England.

Cocker, C. (2003). *The Mental Health of Looked After Children in Public Care: Drop in the Ocean: An Examination of Current Specialist Mental Health Projects for 'Looked After' Children Within England*. Barnardo's. http://www.barnardos.org.uk/the_mental_health_of_looked_after_children_in_public_care.pdf

Cocker, C. (2019). *Social Workers' Views on the Use of the Strengths and Difficulties Questionnaire (SDQ) with Looked After Children*. PhD Thesis. University of Glasgow.

Cocker, C., & Allain, L. (2019). *Social Work with Looked After Children* (3rd edn). Sage.

Cocker, C., & Scott, S. (2006). Improving the mental and emotional well-being of looked after children: Connecting research, policy and practice. *Journal of the Royal Society for the Promotion of Health*, *126*(1), 18–23. https://doi.org/10.1177/1466424006061169

Cocker, C., Cooper, A., & Holmes, D. (2026). Transitional safeguarding and intersectionality. In C. Bernard, C. Firmin, & F. Keating (Eds.), *Handbook on Intersectionality and Social Work*. Edward Elgar.

Cocker, C., Holmes, D., & Cooper, A. (2024). *Transitional Safeguarding*. Policy Press.

Cocker, C., Larsson, B., Baruch, B., Rennolds, N., Holmes, D., Smith, L., et al (2025). *Transitional Safeguarding in Youth Justice and Probation Services: A Scoping Study*. HM Inspectorate of Probation Research & Analysis Bulletin 2025/02 Issue. https://cloud-platform-e218f50a4812967ba1215eaecede923f.s3.amazonaws.com/uploads/sites/32/2025/05/Transitional-Safeguarding-Research-Analysis-Bulletin-May-25.pdf

Cocker, C., Minnis, H., & Sweeting, H. (2018). Potential value of the current mental health monitoring of children in state care in England. *Bjpsych Open*, *4*(6), 486–491. https://doi.org/10.1192/bjo.2018.70

Collins, S. (2024). Love and social work in the UK: A critical evaluation. *Practice*, *36*(1), 69–86. https://doi.org/10.1080/09503153.2023.2267197

Comer, J. P., & Hill, H. (1985). Social policy and the mental health of Black children. *Journal of the American Academy of Child Psychiatry, 24*(2), 175–181. https://doi.org/10.1016/S0002-7138(09)60444-1

Cornish, C. (2024). A birthmother's counter-story of racism and oppression in children's social work: Carving an afro-centric space for sawubona in euro-centric social work education, practice, and the safeguarding system. *The British Journal of Social Work, 54*(3), 846–865. https://doi.org/10.1093/bjsw/bcae027

Cornish, C. (2025). Taking a stand against racism: The urgent need for SAWUBONA in child protection and foster care social work. *Children and Youth Services Review, 170*, 108140. https://doi.org/https://doi.org/10.1016/j.childyouth.2025.108140

Corsaro, W. A. (2018). *The Sociology of Childhood* (5th edn). Sage.

Cossar, J., Brandon, M., & Jordan, P. (2011). *'Don't Make Assumptions': Children's and Young People's Views of the Child Protection System and Messages for Change*. Office of the Children's Commissioner.

Cousins, W., Taggart, L., & Milner, S. (2010). Looked after or overlooked? An exploratory investigation of the mental health issues of adolescents living in state care in Northern Ireland. *Psychol Health Med*, 15(5), 497–506. https://doi.org/10.1080/13548506.2010.487110

Crenshaw, K. W. (1991). Mapping the margins: Intersectionality, identity politics, and violence against women of color. *Stanford Law Review*, 43(6), 1241–1299.

Creswell, J. (1998). *Qualitative Inquiry and Research Design: Choosing Among Five Traditions*. Sage.

Critical Appraisal Skills Programme. (2025). *What are Systematic Reviews? Why are they important?* Critical Appraisal Skills Programme. https://casp-uk.net/news/what-is-a-systematic-review. Accessed on 29.9.25.

Cross, S., Hubbard, A., & Munro, E. (2010). *Reclaiming Social Work London Borough of Hackney Children and Young People's Services. Part 1: Independent Evaluation. Part 2: Unpacking the Complexity of Frontline Practice – an Ethnographic Approach*. Human Reliability Associates and London School of Economics. https://secure.toolkitfiles.co.uk/clients/28663/sitedata/files/Eileen-Munro.pdf

Cummings, A., & Shelton, K. (2024). The prevalence of mental health disorders amongst care-experienced young people in the UK: A systematic review. *Children and Youth Services Review, 156*. https://doi.org/10.1016/j.childyouth.2023.107367

Dance, C., Rushton, A., & Quinton, D. (2002). Emotional abuse in early childhood: relationships with progress in subsequent family placement. *Journal of Child Psychology and Psychiatry and Allied Disciplines, 43*(3), 395–407. <Go to ISI>://WOS:000174469800011

Davies, J., & Wright, J. (2008). Children's voices: A review of the literature pertinent to looked-after children's views of mental health services. *Child and Adolescent Mental Health, 13*(1), 26–31. http://search.ebscohost.com/login.aspx?direct=true&db=eoah&AN=13517364&site=ehost-live

Davis, J., & Marsh, N. (2020). Boys to men: The cost of 'adultification' in safeguarding responses to Black boys. *Critical and Radical Social Work, 8*(2), 255–259. https://doi.org/10.1332/204986020x15945756023543

Davis, R. S., Devaney, J., Halligan, S. L., Meiser-Stedman, R., Oliveira, P., Smith, P., et al (2025). The feasibility and acceptability of delivering a group trauma-focused intervention to children in care. *British Journal of Clinical Psychology, 64*(1), 86–109. https://doi.org/https://doi.org/10.1111/bjc.12494

De Giacomo, A., Lamanna, A. L., Craig, F., Santoro, N., Goffredo, S., & Cecinati, V. (2012). The SDQ in Italian clinical practice: Evaluation between three outpatient groups compared. *Rivista di Psichiatria*, 47(5), 400–406.

Department for Education (2014). *Outcomes for Children Looked After by Local Authorities in England as at 31 March 2014*. https://www.gov.uk/government/uploads/system/uploads/attachment_data/file/384781/Outcomes_SFR49_2014_Text.pdf

Department for Education (2015). *Children Looked After in England (including Adoption and Care Leavers) year ending 31 March 2015*. https://www.gov.uk/government/statistics/children-looked-after-in-england-including-adoption-2014-to-2015

Department for Education (2018). *Applying Corporate Parenting Principles to Looked-After Children and Care Leavers: Statutory Guidance for Local Authorities*. Crown Copyright. https://assets.publishing.service.gov.uk/media/5a93eb3ae5274a5b87c2fde4/Applying_corporate_parenting_principles_to_looked-after_children_and_care_leavers.pdf

Department for Education (2022). *The Children Act 1989 Guidance and Regulations Volume 3: Planning Transition to Adulthood for Care Leavers*. https://assets.publishing.service.gov.uk/media/61f81624d3bf7f78df30b359/CA1989_Transitions_Guidance.pdf

Department for Education (2024). *Permanent Exclusions*. London: HMSO. https://www.ethnicity-facts-figures.service.gov.uk/education-skills-and-training/absence-and-exclusions/permanent-exclusions/latest/

Department for Education (2025). *The Children Act 1989 Guidance and Regulations Volume 3: Planning Transition to Adulthood for Care Leavers*. Crown Copyright. https://assets.publishing.service.gov.uk/media/67a0d251cae64da4967b3fdc/CA1989_Transitions_Guidance.pdf

Department for Education & Department of Health (2015a). *Promoting the Health and Wellbeing of Looked-After Children: Statutory Guidance for Local Authorities, Clinical Commissioning Groups and NHS England*. HMSO.

Department for Education & Department of Health (2015b). *Special Educational Needs and Disability Code of Practice: 0-25 Years. Statutory Guidance for Organsations Which Work with and Support Children and Young People Who Have Special Educational Needs or Disabilites*. Crown Copyright. https://assets.publishing.service.gov.uk/government/uploads/system/uploads/attachment-data/file/398815/SEND_Code_of_Practice_January_2015.pdf

Department for Education and Skills (2007). *Care Matters: Time for Change*. TSO.

Department for Education and Skills & Department of Health (2004). *CAMHS Standard, National Service Framework for Children, Young People and Maternity Services*. Crown Copyright. https://assets.publishing.service.gov.uk/media/5a7b4c2ce5274a319e77e590/National_Service_Framework_for_Children_Young_People_and_Maternity_Services_-_The_Mental_Health__and_Psychological_Well-being_of_Children_and_Young_People.pdf

Department of Health & Department for Education (2016). *Mental Health and Wellbeing of Looked-after Children: Government Response to the Committee's Fourth Report of Session 2015–16*. Crown Copyright.

Department of Health & Department for Education (2017). *Transforming Children and Young People's Mental Health Provision: a Green Paper*. Crown Copyright. https://assets.publishing.service.gov.uk/media/5a823518e5274a2e87dc1b56/Transforming_children_and_young_people_s_mental_health_provision.pdf

Department of Health & NHS England (2015). *Future in Mind: Promoting, Protecting and Improving Our Children and Young People's Mental Health and Wellbeing*. https://assets.publishing.service.gov.uk/media/5a80b26bed915d74e33fbe3c/Childrens_Mental_Health.pdf.

Department of Health & Social Care (2023). *Care and Support Statutory Guidance*. https://www.gov.uk/government/publications/care-act-statutory-guidance/care-and-support-statutory-guidance

Derluyn, I., & Broekaert, E. (2007). Different perspectives on emotional and behavioural problems in unaccompanied refugee children and adolescents. *Ethnicity & Health*, 12(2), 141–162. https://doi.org/10.1080/13557850601002296

Dimigen, G., Del Priore, C., Evans, S., Ferguson, L., & Swan, M. (1999). Psychiatric disorder among children at time of entering local care: questionnaire survey. *British Medical Journal, 319*(7211), 675. http://bmj.com/cgi/content/full/319/7211/675

Dooley, T. (2019). *Transitions Panel: Life in Motion – Does Age Matter?* (unpublished report), 20 May. Havering Safeguarding Adults Board.

Dozier, M., Peloso, E., Lindhiem, O., Gordon, M. K., Manni, M., Sepulveda, S., et al (2006). Developing evidence-based interventions for foster children: An example of a randomized clinical trial with infants and toddlers. *Journal of Social Issues*, 62(4), 767–785. https://doi.org/10.1111/j.1540-4560.2006.00486.x

Edbrooke-Childs, J., & Patalay, P. (2019). Ethnic differences in referral routes to youth mental health services. *Journal of the American Academy of Child & Adolescent Psychiatry, 58*(3), 368–375.e361. https://doi.org/10.1016/j.jaac.2018.07.906

Edney, C., Alrouh, B., & Abouelenin, M. (2023). *Ethnicity of Children in Care and Supervision Proceedings in England: Briefing Paper*. https://www.nuffieldfjo.org.uk/wp-content/uploads/2023/05/nfjo_briefing_paper_ethnicity_20230518_FINAL.pdf.

Egelund, T., & Lausten, M. (2009). Prevalence of mental health problems among children placed in out-of-home care in Denmark. *Child and Family Social Work*, 14(2), 156–165.

Ejegi-Memeh, S., Berkeley, R., Bussue, D., Mafoti, W., Mohamad, A., Myrie, U., & Samuels, S. (2025). The role of Black-led community organisations in supporting Black mental health: a Black emancipatory action research project. *Ethnicity & Health*, 30(3), 432–451. https://doi.org/10.1080/13557858.2024.2442323

Elhamid, A. A., Howe, A., & Reading, R. (2009). Prevalence of emotional and behavioural problems among 6-12 year old children in Egypt. *Social Psychiatry and Psychiatric Epidemiology*, 44(1), 8–14. https://doi.org/10.1007/s00127-008-0394-1

England, E., & Mughal, F. (2019). Underprovision of mental health services for children and young people. *Br J Gen Pract*, *69*(680), 112–113. https://doi.org/10.3399/bjgp19X701381

English, S., Deivanayagam, T. A., Bignall, T., Box, L., Butt, J., & Devakumar, D. (2024). Protecting children from racism: urgent health system actions. *The Lancet*, *403*(10436), 1535–1536. https://doi.org/10.1016/S0140-6736(24)00299-X

Evans, R., MacDonald, S., Trubey, R., Melendez-Torres, G. J., Robling, M., Willis, S., et al (2024). Interventions targeting the mental health and well-being of care-experienced children and young people: mixed-methods systematic review with stakeholder consultation to inform transportability and adaptability to UK context. *British Journal of Social Work*. https://doi.org/10.1093/bjsw/bcae061

Evans, R., MacDonald, S., Trubey, R., Noyes, J., Robling, M., Willis, S., et al (2025). How might we improve the mental health and well-being of care-experienced children and young people? Review and map of intervention theories. *Journal of Social Work*. https://doi.org/10.1177/14680173251336997

Everson-Hock, E. S., Jones, R., Guillaume, L., Clapton, J., Goyder, E., Chilcott, J., et al (2012). The effectiveness of training and support for carers and other professionals on the physical and emotional health and well-being of looked-after children and young people: aA systematic review. *Child: Care, Health and Development*, 38(2), 162–174. https://doi.org/10.1111/j.1365-2214.2011.01247.x

Fahlberg, V. I. (2012). *A Child's Journey Through Placement.* Jessica Kingsley Publishers. http://search.ebscohost.com/login.aspx?direct=true&db=cat01883a&AN=uea.003869641&site=eds-live&scope=site

Farmer, L. (2017). *The Importance of Strengthening Prisoners' Family Ties to Prevent Reoffending and Reduce Intergenerational Crime.* Crown Copyright. https://assets.publishing.service.gov.uk/government/uploads/system/uploads/attachment_data/file/642244/farmer-review-report.pdf

Field, A. (2013). *Discovering Statistics using IBM SPSS Statistics* (4th edn). Sage.

Firmin, C. (2020). *Contextual Safeguarding and Child Protection: Rewriting the Rules*. Routledge.

Flückiger, C, & Del Re, A. C. (2017). The sleeper effect between psychotherapy orientations: A strategic argument of sustainability of treatment effects at follow-up. *Epidemiology and Psychiatric Sciences, 26*(4), 442–444. https://doi.org/10.1017/S2045796016000780

Ford, T., Vostanis, P., Meltzer, H., & Goodman, R. (2007). Psychiatric disorder among British children looked after by local authorities: Comparison with children living in private households. *British Journal of Psychiatry, 190*(4), 319–325. https://doi.org/10.1192/bjp.bp.106.025023

Forrester, D., Goodman, K., Cocker, C., Binnie, C., & Jensch, G. (2009). What is the impact of public care on children's welfare? A review of research findings from England and Wales and their policy implications. *Journal of Social Policy*, 38, 439–456. https://doi.org/10.1017/s0047279409003110

Forrester, D., Westlake, D., McCann, M., Thurnham, A., Shefer, G., Glynn, G., & Killian, M. (2013). Final report of a comparative study of practice and the factors shaping it in three local authorities. London: TSO.

Forrester, D. (2024). *The Enlightened Social Worker.* Policy Press.

Foster, S. L., Schofield, G., Geoghegan, L., Hood, R., Sagi-Schwartz, A., Bakkum, L., et al (2025). Attachment theory and research: What should be on the core curriculum for child and family social workers? *Social Work Education*, 1–18. https://doi.org/10.1080/02615479.2025.2531859

Galvin, E., O'Donnell, R., Breman, R., Avery, J., Mousa, A., Halfpenny, N., & Skouteris, H. (2022). Interventions and practice models for improving health and psychosocial outcomes for children in residential out-of-home care: systematic review. *Australian Social Work*, *75*(1), 33–47. https://doi.org/10.1080/0312407X.2020.1856394

Geronimus, A. (2023). *Weathering: The Extraordinary Stress of an Ordinary Life in an Unjust Society*. Virago.

Geronimus, A. T., Hicken, M., Keene, D., & Bound, J. (2006). 'Weathering' and Age Patterns of Allostatic Load Scores Among Blacks and Whites in the United States. *American Journal of Public Health*, *96*(5), 826–833. https://doi.org/10.2105/ajph.2004.060749

Ghezae, F. T., Zungu, Z., John, A., Abdinasir, K., Bhui, K., Adebiyi, A., & Creswell, C. (2025). The association between experiences of racism and mental health on children and young people in the UK: Rapid scoping review. *British Journal of Psychiatry Open*, *11*(1), e26. https://doi.org/doi:10.1192/bjo.2024.836

Goldacre, A., Hood, R., Jones, E., King, A., & Wang, C. (2022). Reunification and re-entry to care: An analysis of the national datasets for children looked after in England. *The British Journal of Social Work*, *52*(8), 4756–4777. https://doi.org/10.1093/bjsw/bcac079

Göbbels-Koch, P. & Gupta, A. (2025). A socio-ecological exploration of suicidal ideation among people with care experience, *The British Journal of Social Work*, bcaf231. https://doi.org/10.1093/bjsw/bcaf231

Godden, N. J. (2017). The love ethic: A radical theory for social work practice. *Australian Social Work*, *70*(4), 405–416. https://doi.org/10.1080/0312407X.2017.1301506

Golding, K. S. (2008). *Nurturing Attachments: Supporting Children Who Are Fostered or Adopted*. Jessica Kingsley.

Gómez-Beneyto, M., Nolasco, A., Moncho, J., Pereyra-Zamora, P., Tamayo-Fonseca, N., Munarriz, M., et al (2013). Psychometric behaviour of the Strengths and Difficulties Questionnaire (SDQ) in the Spanish National Health Survey 2006. *BMC Psychiatry*, 13, 95. https://doi.org/10.1186/1471-244X-13-95

Goodman, A., & Goodman, R. (2012). Strengths and Difficulties Questionnaire scores and mental health in looked after children. *British Journal of Psychiatry*, *200*, 426–427. http://bjp.rcpsych.org/

Goodman, R. (1997). The Strengths and Difficulties Questionnaire: A research note. *Journal of Child Psychology and Psychiatry*, *38*(5), 581–586. https://doi.org/10.1111/j.1469-7610.1997.tb01545.x

Goodman, R. (1999). The extended version of the Strengths and Difficulties Questionnaire as a guide to child psychiatric caseness and consequent burden. *Journal of Child Psychology and Psychiatry*, 40(5), 791–799. https://doi.org/10.1111/1469-7610.00494

Goodman, R. (2001). Psychometric properties of the Strengths and Difficulties Questionnaire. *Journal of the American Academy of Child & Adolescent Psychiatry*, 40(11), 1337–1345. https://doi.org/10.1097/00004583-200111000-00015

Goodman, R., Ford, T., Corbin, T., & Meltzer, H. (2004). Using the Strengths and Difficulties Questionnaire (SDQ) multi-informant algorithm to screen looked-after children for psychiatric disorders. *European Child & Adolescent Psychiatry*, *13*(Suppl2), II25–II31. https://doi.org/10.1007/s00787-004-2005-3

Goodman, R., Ford, T., & Richards, H. (2000). The development and well-being assessment: Description and initial validation of an integrated assessment of child and adolescent psychopathology. *Journal of Child Psychology & Psychiatry & Allied Disciplines*, 41(5), 645.

Goodman, R., Meltzer, H., & Bailey, V. (2003). The Strengths and Difficulties Questionnaire: a pilot study on the validity of the self-report version. *International Review of Psychiatry*, 15(1–2), 173–177.

Goulet, J., Maltais, C., Archambault, I., Noel, V., & Gueriton, M. (2024). Supporting academic achievement of children in out-of-home care through effective interventions: results of a systematic review and meta-analyses. *Children and Youth Services Review*, *156*. https://doi.org/10.1016/j.childyouth.2023.107388

Gregory, A. (2024). NHS referrals for anxiety in children more than double pre-Covid levels. *The Guardian*, 27 August. https://www.theguardian.com/society/article/2024/aug/27/nhs-referrals-for-anxiety-in-children-more-than-double-pre-covid-levels-england

Harris, M. (2025). *From Exploited to Exploiter? Preventing the Unjust Criminalisation of Victims of Child Criminal Exploitation in the Transition to Adulthood.* https://static1.squarespace.com/static/5f75bfbbfb67fc5ab41154d6/t/68c1707d3795c66a6dda43ee/1757507709517/FINAL+AYJ-Exploited-to-Exploiter-CCE-Transition-to-Adulthood-Report+10.09.25.pdf

Harris, M., & Edwards, M. (2023). *Young People in Transitions in the Criminal Justice System: Evidence Review.* https://barrowcadbury.org.uk/wp-content/uploads/2023/06/FINAL-AYJ-Young-people-in-transition-in-the-criminal-justice-system-Evidence-review-April-2023.pdf

Herrman, H., Humphreys, C., Halperin, S., Monson, K., Harvey, C., Mihalopoulos, C., et al (2016). A controlled trial of implementing a complex mental health intervention for carers of vulnerable young people living in out-of-home care: The ripple project. *BMC Psychiatry, 16.* https://doi.org/10.1186/s12888-016-1145-6

Hill, C., & Mather, M. (2003). Achieving health for children in public care. *British Medical Journal, 326*, 560–561.

Hiller, R. M., Lehmann, S., Lewis, S. J., Minnis, H., Shelton, K. H., Tarren-Sweeney, M., & Taussig, H. N. (2023). Accommodating complexity: the need for evidence-informed mental health assessments for children in out-of-home care. *Journal of the American Academy of Child & Adolescent Psychiatry, 62*(1), 12–18. https://doi.org/10.1016/j.jaac.2022.06.021

Hiller, R., Duschinsky, R., Fearon, P., Holmes, L., Hood, R., McGuire, R., et al (2025). *Increasing Access to Evidence-informed Mental Health Service Provision for Children in Care in England.* University College London, UK Trauma Council. https://arc-nenc.nihr.ac.uk/wp-content/uploads/2025/05/National-Recommendations-MH-Provision-for-CiC84.pdf

HM Government (2013). *Care Leaver Strategy: A Cross-Departmental Strategy for Young People Leaving Care*. https://assets.publishing.service.gov.uk/media/5a7c531fe5274a2041cf33ea/Care_Leaver_Strategy.pdf

HM Government (2016). *Keep On Caring: Supporting Young People from Care to Independence*. Crown Copyright. https://assets.publishing.service.gov.uk/media/5a808389ed915d74e622ee47/Care-Leaver-Strategy.pdf

HM Government (2018). *Care Leaver Covenant*. Crown Copyright. https://www.gov.uk/government/collections/care-leaver-covenant--2

HM Government (2021). *Joint National Protocol for Transitions in England: Joint Protocol for Managing the Cases of Children Moving from Youth Offending Teams to the National Probation Service*. National Probation Service. https://www,gov.uk/government/publications.joint-national-protocol-for-transitions-in-england

HM Government (2023). *Working Together to Safeguard Children 2023 A Guide to Multi-agency Working to Help, Protect and Promote the Welfare of Children*. Crown Copyright. https://assets.publishing.service.gov.uk/media/6849a7b67cba25f610c7db3f/Working_together_to_safeguard_children_2023_-_statutory_guidance.pdf

HM Inspectorate of Probation (2024). *Youth Justice – Specific Sub Groups: Children with Care Experience*. https://hmiprobation.justiceinspectorates.gov.uk/our-research/evidence-base-youth-justice/specific-sub-groups/children-with-care-experience/

Holmes, D. (2022). Transitional safeguarding: The case for change. *Practice: Social Work in Action*, *34*(1), 7–23.

Holmes, D., & Smale, E. (2018). *Mind the Gap: Transitional Safeguarding – Adolescence to Adulthood: Strategic Briefing*. Research in Practice.

Holt, A., Melley, J., & Burns, J. (2025). Cost of children's homes doubles but care can be poor, says report, *BBC*. https://www.bbc.co.uk/news/articles/c4gj93d57pjo

Home Office (2023). *Criminal Exploitation of Children, Young People and Vulnerable Adults: County Lines*. https://assets.publishing.service.gov.uk/media/65322ad1e839fd001486720d/2023_FOR_PUBLICATION_-_Criminal_exploitation_of_children_young_people_and_vulnerable_adults_county_lines1.pdf

hooks, b. (2001). *All About Love: New Visions*. Harper and Collins.

House of Commons Education Committee (2025). *Children's Social Care: Fourth Report of Session 2024–25*. UK Parliament. https://committees.parliament.uk/publications/48718/documents/255354/default/

House of Commons Education & Skills Committee (2007). *Bullying: Third Report of Session 2006–07*. The Stationery Office.

Howe, D. (2005). *Child Abuse and Neglect: Attachment, Development and Intervention*. Palgrave.

Hunter, M. (2001). *Psychotherapy with Young People in Care: Lost and Found*. Routledge.

Independent Care Review (2020). *The Promise* (Scotland). https://thepromise.scot/resources/2020/the-promise.pdf. Accessed on 11.1.26.

Jacob, J., Merrick, H., Lane, R., Cracknell, L., Labno, A., D'Souza, S., et al (2024). 'Containing the network': Referrers' experiences of the community forensic CAMHS consultation and liaison model. *International Journal of Forensic Mental Health*, *23*(3), 264–276. https://doi.org/10.1080/14999013.2024.2350034

Jacobs, J. (2020). *Outcome Research Lowdown, July 2020: Dr Jenna Jacob Reflects on the Latest News on the SDQ*. https://www.corc.uk.net/news-blogs/2020/07/outcomes-research-lowdown-on-sdq/. Accessed on 16.5.26.

Javed, M., Sprecher, E. A., Carter, B., Elhassan, L., Hiller, R., Holmes, L., Park, J., et al (2025). A systematic review of ethnic representation in UK research involving children and young people living in care. *The British Journal of Social Work*, bcaf066. https://doi.org/10.1093/bjsw/bcaf066

Jay, A. (2024). *Shattered Lives, Stolen Futures: The Jay Review of Criminally Exploited Children*. https://media.actionforchildren.org.uk/documents/Shattered_Lives_Stolen_Futures_Report_-_Full_Report.pdf

Jee, S. H., Halterman, J. S., Szilagyi, M., Conn, A.-M., Alpert-Gillis, L., & Szilagyi, P. G. (2011). Use of a brief standardized screening instrument in a primary care setting to enhance detection of social-emotional problems among youth in foster care. *Academic Pediatrics*, *11*(5), 409–413. https://doi.org/http://dx.doi.org/10.1016/j.acap.2011.03.001

Jezzard, B. (1999). A better future for child and adolescent mental health services. *Mental Health Review Journal*, *4*(1), 18–21. https://doi.org/10.1108/13619322199900005

Johansson, T. (2021). Becoming and belonging: modern passages and transitions from childhood to adulthood. *British Journal of Sociology of Education*, *42*(3), 440–446. https://doi.org/10.1080/01425692.2021.1890408

Jones, R., Everson-Hock, E. S., Papaioannou, D., Guillaume, L., Goyder, E., Chilcott, J., et al (2011). Factors associated with outcomes for looked-after children and young people: a correlates review of the literature. *Child: Care, Health and Development*, 37(5), 613–622. https://doi.org/10.1111/j.1365-2214.2011.01226.x

Jones, R., Everson-Hock, E., Guillaume, L., Clapton, J., Goyder, E., Chilcott, J. et al (2012). The effectiveness of interventions aimed at improving access to health and mental health services for looked-after children and young people: A systematic review. *Families, Relationships and Societies*, 1(1), 71–85. https://doi.org/10.1332/204674312X633171

Khan, L., Saini, G., Augustine, A., Palmer, K., Johnson, M., & Donald, R. (2017). *Against the Odds: Evaluation of the Mind Birmingham Up My Street Programme*. https://www.centreformentalhealth.org.uk/publications/against-odds/

Knapp, M. (1997). Economic evaluations and interventions for children and adolescents with mental health problems. *Journal of Child Psychology and Psychiatry*, *38*, 3–25.

Knapp, M., Snell, T., Healey, A., Guglani, S., Evans-Lacko, S., Fernández, J. et al (2015). How do child and adolescent mental health problems influence public sector costs? Interindividual variations in a nationally representative British sample. *Journal of Child Psychology and Psychiatry*, *56*(6), 667–676.

Krieger, N. (2020). Measures of racism, sexism, heterosexism, and gender binarism for health equity research: From structural injustice to embodied harm—an ecosocial analysis. *Annual Review of Public Health*, *41*, 37–62. https://doi.org/https://doi.org/10.1146/annurev-publhealth-040119-094017

Kurtz, Z., & James, C. (2003). *What's new: Learning from the CAMHS Innovation Projects – Executive Summary*. Department of Health.

Lai, K. Y. C., Leung, P. W. L., Luk, E. S. L., & Wong, A. S. L. (2014). Use of the Extended Strengths and Difficulties Questionnaire (SDQ) to predict psychiatric caseness in Hong Kong. *Child Psychiatry and Human Development*, 45, 703–711. https://doi.org/10.1007/s10578-014-0439-5

Lehmann, S., Havik, O. E., Havik, T., & Heiervang, E. R. (2013). Mental disorders in foster children: a study of prevalence, comorbidity and risk factors. *Child and Adolescent Psychiatry and Mental Health*, 7, 39. https://doi.org/10.1186/1753-2000-7-39

Lewis, S. E. (2014). Assessment of mental health for looked after children (unpublished dissertation). University of Hull.

Lincoln, Y. S., & Guba, G. E. (1985). *Naturalistic Inquiry*. Sage.

Luke, N., Sinclair, I., Woolgar, I., & Sebba, J. (2014). *What Works in Preventing and Treating Poor Mental Health in Looked After Children?* NSPCC/Rees Centre/University of Oxford.

MacAlister, J. (2022). *The Independent Review of Children's Social Care: Final Report*. https://webarchive.nationalarchives.gov.uk/ukgwa/20230308122449/https://childrenssocialcare.independent-review.uk/final-report

Maguire, D., May, K., McCormack, D., & Fosker, T. (2024). A systematic review of the impact of placement instability on emotional and behavioural outcomes among children in foster care. *Journal of Child & Adolescent Trauma*, *17*(2), 641–655. https://doi.org/10.1007/s40653-023-00606-1

Mannes, J., Coughlan, B., Yoon, Y., Maorgan, T., Drayak, T., Crozier-Roche, F. et al (2024). *A Call for Change Tackling Inequalities in Access to Mental Health Support for Children with Social Work Involvement and Those Living in Poverty*. https://www.ncb.org.uk/sites/default/files/uploads/files/240813%20A%20call%20for%20change%20-%20COACHES%20report.pdf

Marmot, M. (2010). *Fair Society Healthy Lives: Strategic Review of Health Inequalities in England Post-2010 (the Marmot Review)*. Marmot Review/UCL.

Marmot, M., & Bell, R. (2012). Fair society, healthy lives. *Public Health*, *126 Suppl 1*, S4–S10. https://doi.org/10.1016/j.puhe.2012.05.014

Marquis, R. A., & Flynn, R. J. (2009). The SDQ as a mental health measurement tool in a Canadian sample of looked-after young people. *Vulnerable Children and Youth Studies*, 4(2), 114–121. https://doi.org/10.1080/17450120902887392

Marsh, P., & Fisher, M. (2005). *Developing the Evidence Base for Social Work and Social Care Practice*. Social Care Instititute for Excellence.

Martín, E., González-García, C., del Valle, J. F., & Bravo, A. (2020). Detection of behavioral and emotional disorders in residential child care: Using a multi-informant approach. *Children and Youth Services Review, 108*, 104588.

Mason, W., Chmelka, M., & Thompson, R. (2012). Responsiveness of the Strengths and Difficulties Questionnaire (SDQ) in a sample of high-risk youth in residential treatment. *Child and Youth Care Forum*, 41, 479–492.

McCambridge, J., & Day, M. (2008). Randomized controlled trial of the effects of completing the Alcohol Use Disorders Identification Test questionnaire on self-reported hazardous drinking. *Addiction, 103*(2), 241–248. https://doi.org/10.1111/j.1360-0443.2007.02080.x

McCann, J., James, A., Wilson, S., and Dunn, G. (1996). Prevalence of psychiatric disorders in young people in the care system. *British Medical Journal, 313*, 1529–1530. http://bmj.com/cgi/content/full/313/7071/1529

McCarthy, G., Janeway, J., & Geddes, A. (2003). The impact of emotional and behavioural problems on the lives of children growing up in the care system. *Adoption & Fostering*, 27(3), 14–19.

McGuire, R., Meiser-Stedman, R., Smith, P., Schmidt, D., Bjornstad, G., Bosworth, R., et al (2025). Access to best-evidenced mental health support for care-experienced young people: Learnings from the implementation of cognitive therapy for PTSD. *British Journal of Clinical Psychology, 64*(1), 63–85. https://doi.org/https://doi.org/10.1111/bjc.12471

McMurray, I., Connolly, H., Preston-Shoot, M., & Wigley, V. (2008). Constructing resilience: Social workers' understandings and practice. *Health & Social Care in the Community, 16*(3), 299–309. https://doi.org/10.1111/j.1365-2524.2008.00778.x

Meer, M., Dixon, A., & Rose, D. (2008). Parent and child agreement on reports of problem behaviour obtained from a screening questionnaire, the SDQ. *European Child & Adolescent Psychiatry*, 17(1), 491.

Meltzer, H., Gatward, R., Goodman, R., & Ford, T. (2000). *The Mental Health of Children and Adolescents in Great Britain.* The Stationery Office.

Meltzer, H., Gohuard, R., Corbin, T., Goodman, R., & Ford, T. (2003). *The Mental Health of Young People Looked After by Local Authorities in England: The Report of a Survey Carried Out in 2002 by Social Survey Division of the Office for National Statistics on Behalf of the Department of Health*. The Stationery Office.

Meltzer, H., Lader, D., Corbin, T., Goodman, R., & Ford, T. (2004a). *The Mental Health of Young People Looked After by Local Authorities in Scotland: The Report of a Survey Carried Out in 2002/2003 by the Office for National Statistics on Behalf of the Scottish Executive*. The Stationery Office. http://www.statistics.gov.uk/downloads/theme_health/Mentalhealth_Scotland.pdf

Meltzer, H., Lader, D., Corbin, T., Goodman, R., & Ford, T. (2004b). *The Mental Health Of Young People Looked After by Local Authorities in Wales: The Report of a Survey in 2002/2003 by the Office for National Statistics on behalf of the Welsh Assemby Government*. The Stationery Office. http://www.statistics.gov.uk/downloads/theme_health/mentalhealth_Wales.pdf

Mental Health Foundation. (1999). *Bright Futures: Promoting Children and Young People's Mental Health*. The Mental Health Foundation.

Mental Health Foundation. (2024). *Black, Asian and Minority Ethnic (BAME) Communities*. https://www.mentalhealth.org.uk/explore-mental-health/a-z-topics/black-asian-and-minority-ethnic-bame-communities

Midgley, N., Cirasola, A., Austerberry, C., Ranzato, E., West, G., Martin, P., et al (2019). Supporting foster carers to meet the needs of looked after children: A feasibility and pilot evaluation of the Reflective Fostering Programme. *Developmental Child Welfare*, *1*(1), 41–60. https://doi.org/10.1177/2516103218817550

Miles, A., Grey, J. E., Polychronis, A., Price, N., & Melchiorri, C. (2003). Current thinking in the evidence-based health care debate. *Journal of Evaluation in Clinical Practice*, *9*(2), 95–109. https://doi.org/10.1046/j.1365-2753.2003.00438.x

Ministry of Housing, Communities and Local Government (2024). *Statutory Homelessness in England: Financial Year 2023–24: Updated 30 October 2024*. UK Government. https://www.gov.uk/government/statistics/statutory-homelessness-in-england-financial-year-2023-24/statutory-homelessness-in-england-financial-year-2023-24

Minnis, H. (2013). Maltreatment–associated psychiatric problems: An example of environmentally triggered ESSENCE? *The Scientific World Journal, 2013*, 5, Article 148468.

Minnis, H., Everett, K., Pelosi, A. J., Dunn, J., & Knapp, M. (2006). Children in foster care: Mental health, service use and costs. *European Child & Adolescent Psychiatry, 15*(2), 63–70. https://doi.org/10.1007/s00787-006-0452-8

Minnis, H., & Del Priore, C. (2001). Mental health services for looked after children: Implications from two studies. *Adoption and Fostering, 25*(4), 27–38.

Minnis, H., Pelosi, A. J., Knapp, M., & Dunn, J. (2001). Mental health and foster carer training. *Archives of Disease in Childhood, 84*(4), 302–306.

Moody, G., Coulman, E., Brookes-Howell, L., Cannings-John, R., Channon, S., Lau, M., et al (2020). A pragmatic randomised controlled trial of the fostering changes programme. *Child Abuse & Neglect, 108*, 104646. https://doi.org/https://doi.org/10.1016/j.chiabu.2020.104646

Mount, J., Lister, A., & Bennun, I. (2004). Identifying the mental health needs of looked after young people. *Clinical Child Psychology and Psychiatry, 9*(3), 363–382.

Munford, R., & Sanders, J. (2015). Negotiating and constructing identity: Social work with young people who experience adversity. *British Journal of Social Work*, 45(5), 1564–1580. https://doi.org/10.1093/bjsw/bcu059

Munro, E. R., & Simkiss, D. (2020). Transitions from care to adulthood: Messages to inform practice. *Paediatrics and Child Health, 30*(5), 175–179. https://doi.org/https://doi.org/10.1016/j.paed.2020.02.007

Murray, E. T., Lacey, R., Maughan, B., & Sacker, A. (2020). Non-parental care in childhood and health up to 30 years later: ONS Longitudinal Study 1971–2011. *European Journal of Public Health, 30*(6), 1121–1127. https://doi.org/10.1093/eurpub/ckaa113

National Audit Office (2015). *Care Leavers' Transition to Adulthood*. Crown Copyright. https://www.nao.org.uk/wp-content/uploads/2015/07/Care-leavers-transition-to-adulthood.pdf

National CAMHS Support Service (2011). *Better Mental Health Outcomes for Children and Young People: A Resource Directory for Commissioners*. National CAMHS Support Service.

National Collaborating Centre for Mental Health (2015). *Children's Attachment: Attachment in Children and Young People Who Are Adopted from Care, in Care or at High Risk of Going into Care*. National Institute for Health and Clinical Excellence.

Neil, E., Gitsels, L., & Thoburn, J. (2020). Returning children home from care: What can be learned from local authority data? *Child & Family Social Work, 25*(3), 548–556.

Newlove-Delgado, T., Murphy, E., & Ford, T. (2012). Evaluation of a pilot project for mental health screening for children looked after in an inner London borough. *Journal of Children's Services*, 7, 213–225. http://www.emeraldinsight.com/products/journals/journals.htm?id=jcs

Newlove-Delgado, T., Marcheselli, F., Williams, T., Mandalia, D., Dennes, M., McManus, S. et al (2023). *Mental Health of Children and Young People in England, 2023*. NHS England. https://digital.nhs.uk/data-and-information/publications/statistical/mental-health-of-children-and-young-people-in-england/2023-wave-4-follow-up

NHS Advisory Services (1995). *Child and Adolescent Mental Health Services: Together We Stand*. HMSO.

NHS Digital (2016). *Mental Health and Wellbeing in EnglandAdult Psychiatric Morbidity Survey, 2014*. https://webarchive.nationalarchives.gov.uk/ukgwa/20180328140249/http:/digital.nhs.uk/catalogue/PUB21748

NHS Digital (2024). *Detentions under the Mental Health Act*. https://www.ethnicity-facts-figures.service.gov.uk/health/mental-health/detentions-under-the-mental-health-act/latest/#main-facts-and-figures

NHS England (2019). *The NHS Long Term Plan*. https://www.longtermplan.nhs.uk/

NICE (2016a). *Transition from Children's Services to Adults' Services for Young People Using Health or Social Care Services – NICE Guidance*. NICE. https://www.nice.org.uk/guidance/ng43/resources/transition-from-childrens-to-adults-services-for-young-people-using-health-or-social-care-services-pdf-1837451149765

NICE (2016b). *Transition from Children's to Adults' Services – Quality Standard*. NICE. https://www.nice.org.uk/guidance/qs140/resources/transition-from-childrens-to-adults-services-pdf-75545472790213

NICE (2018). *Decision Making and Mental Capacity*. NICE. https://www.nice.org.uk/guidance/ng108

NICE (2021). *Looked-After Children and Young People: Interventions to Promote Physical, Mental, and Emotional Health and Wellbeing of Lookedafter Children, Young People and Care Leavers*. NICE guideline NG205. https://www.nice.org.uk/guidance/ng205/resources/lookedafter-children-and-young-people-pdf-66143716414405

Niclasen, J., Teasdale, T. W., Andersen, A.-M. N., Skovgaard, A. M., Elberling, H., & Obel, C. (2012). Psychometric properties of the Danish Strength and Difficulties Questionnaire: The SDQ assessed for more than 70,000 raters in four different cohorts. *PLoS ONE*, 7(2), e32025. https://doi.org/10.1371/journal.pone.0032025

Norris, V., & Lender, D. (2019). *Theraplay: The Practitioner's Guide*. Jessica Kingsley.

Office for National Statistics (2021). *Census 2021: England and Wales*. HMSO. https://www.ons.gov.uk/census

Office for National Statistics (2022). *The Education Background of Looked-after Children Who Interact with the Criminal Justice System*. https://www.ons.gov.uk/peoplepopulationandcommunity/educationandchildcare/articles/theeducationbackgroundoflookedafterchildrenwhointeractwiththecriminaljusticesystem/december2022

OFSTED. (2022). *'Ready or Not': Care Leavers' Views of Preparing to Leave Care*. UK Government. https://www.gov.uk/government/publications/ready-or-not-care-leavers-views-of-preparing-to-leave-care/ready-or-not-care-leavers-views-of-preparing-to-leave-care

Okpokiri, C. (2020). Parenting in fear: Child welfare micro strategies of Nigerian parents in Britain. *The British Journal of Social Work*, *51*(2), 427–444. https://doi.org/10.1093/bjsw/bcaa205

Okpokiri, C. (2024). *An Evaluation of Requisite Parenting: An Optimal Black Parenting Style*. https://weareseen.org.uk/wp-content/uploads/2024/06/An-Evaluation-of-Requisite-Parenting-.pdf

Oswald, S. H., Heil, K., & Goldbeck, L. (2010). History of maltreatment and mental health problems in foster children: a review of the literature. *Journal of Pediatric Psychology*, *35*(5), 462–472. https://doi.org/10.1093/jpepsy/jsp114

Pearce, J. (1999). Collaboration between the NHS and Social Services in the provision of child and adolescent mental health services: A personal view. *Child Psychology and Psychiatry Review*, *4*(4), 150–152.

Petermann, U., Petermann, F., & Schreyer, I. (2010). The German Strengths and Difficulties Questionnaire (SDQ): Validity of the teacher version for preschoolers. *European Journal of Psychological Assessment*, 26(4), 256–262. https://doi.org/10.1027/1015-5759/a000034

Pez, O. (2012). Validation of the instruments: SDQ parent and teacher in eight European countries. *Neuropsychiatrie de l'Enfance et de l'Adolescence*, 60(5, Supplement), S100. https://doi.org/http://dx.doi.org/10.1016/j.neurenf.2012.05.420

Plowright, R. C. (2024). The significance of love in relation to looked-after children and child sexual exploitation. *Critical and Radical Social Work*, *12*(1), 40–57. https://doi.org/10.1332/204986021X16523430934288

Preston-Shoot, M (2017) *Safeguarding Adult Review: Ms A (Date of Birth: 20th March 1995)*. Havering Safeguarding Adults Board. https://www.havering.gov.uk/downloads/file/1408/ms_a_safeguarding_adult_review

Pritchett, R., Gillberg, C., & Minnis, H. (2013). What do child characteristics contribute to outcomes from care: A PRISMA review. *Children and Youth Services Review*, *35*(9), 1333.

Public Health England (2013). *NHS Population Screening Explained*. HMSO. https://www.gov.uk/nhs-population-screening-explained

Public Health England (2014). *Evidence and Recommendations: NHS Population Screening*. HMSO. https://www.gov.uk/evidence-and-recommendations-nhs-population-screening#evidence-review-process

Rainer, C., & Abdinasir, K. (2023). *Children and Young People's Mental Health: An Independent Review into Policy Successes and Challenges Over the Last Decade*. https://cypmhc.org.uk/wp-content/uploads/2023/06/Review-of-CYP-Mental-Health-Policy-Final-Report.-2023.pdf

Rao, P., Ali, A., & Vostanis, P. (2010). Looked after and adopted children: how should specialist CAMHS be involved? *Adoption and Fostering*, 34(2), 58–72.

Research in Practice, University of Bedfordshire, & The Children's Society (2023). *Multi-agency Practice Principles for Responding to Child Exploitation and Extra-familial Harm*. Research in Practice. https://tce.researchinpractice.org.uk/

Research in Practice (2025). *Why evidence-informed practice?* Research in Practice/National Children's Bureau. https://www.researchinpractice.org.uk/all/content-pages/about-us/why-evidence-informed-practice/. Accessed on 29.9.25.

Richardson, J., & Joughin, C. (2000). *The Mental Health Needs of Looked After Children*. Gaskell.

Richardson, R., & Lelliott, P. (2003). Mental health of looked after children. *Advances in Psychiatric Treatment*, *9*, 249–256.

Richmond and Wandsworth Safeguarding Adults Board (2020). *Minding the Gap: Mental Health Transitions Framework 2020–2023*. https://www.sabrichmondandwandsworth.org.uk/media/1449/mental_health_transitions_protocol.pdf

Roberts, L., Holland, S., Westlake, D., Mathur, V., Lloyd, H., Bezeczky, Z., et al (2026). Innovative and ambitious or unrealistic and risky? Initial professional perspectives on the basic income for care leavers in Wales pilot, *The British Journal of Social Work*, 56(1), pp 26–45, https://doi.org/10.1093/bjsw/bcaf124

Rock, S., Michelson, D., Thomson, S., & Day, C. (2015). Understanding foster placement instability for looked after children: A Systematic review and narrative synthesis of quantitative and qualitative evidence. *British Journal of Social Work*, *45*(1), 177–203. https://doi.org/10.1093/bjsw/bct084

Rosanbalm, K. D., Snyder, E. H., Lawrence, C. N., Coleman, K., Frey, J. J., van den Ende, J. B., & Dodge, K. A. (2016). Child wellbeing assessment in child welfare: A review of four measures. *Children and Youth Services Review*, 68, 1–16. https://doi.org/http://dx.doi.org/10.1016/j.childyouth.2016.06.023

Rushton, A., Quinton, D., & Treseder, J. (1993). New parents for older children: support during eight years of placement *Adoption and Fostering*, *17*(4), 39–45.

Rutter, M., Tizard, J., Yule, W., Graham, P., & Whitmore, K. (1976). Research report: Isle of Wight Studies 1964–1974. *Psychological Medicine*, *6*, 313–332.

Sacker, A., Murray, E., Lacey, R., & Maughan, B. (2021). *The Lifelong Health and Wellbeing Trajectories of People Who Have Been in Care: Findings from the Looked-after Children Grown Up Project*. Nuffield Foundation. https://discovery.ucl.ac.uk/id/eprint/10155700/1/Sacker%20A%202021_Report_The-lifelong-health-and-wellbeing-trajectories-of-people-who-have-been-in-care.pdf

Sacker, A., Lacey, R. E., Maughan, B., & Murray, E. T. (2022). Out-of-home care in childhood and socio-economic functioning in adulthood: ONS Longitudinal study 1971–2011. *Children and Youth Services Review*, *132*, 106300. https://doi.org/https://doi.org/10.1016/j.childyouth.2021.106300

Sacker, A., Murray, E. T., Maughan, B., & Lacey, R. E. (2024). Social care in childhood and adult outcomes: Double whammy for minority children? *Longitudinal and Life Course Studies*, *15*(2), 139–162. https://doi.org/10.1332/17579597Y2023D000000008

Samuel, M. (2025). Mental healthcare for looked-after children 'inadequate and unevidenced', warn experts. *Community Care*, 2 June. https://www.communitycare.co.uk/2025/06/02/mental-healthcare-for-looked-after-children-inadequate-and-unevidenced-warn-experts/

Sanders, J., & Munford, R. (2017). Hidden in plain view: Finding and enhancing the participation of marginalized young people in research. *International Journal of Qualitative Methods*, *16*(1). https://doi.org/10.1177/1609406917704765

Sanders, M., Schroeder, E., Fahr, P., Vallis, D., Mathur, V., Roberts, L., et al (2025). *Basic Income for Care Leavers in Wales Pilot Evaluation: Statistical Analysis Plan*. https://www.gov.wales/sites/default/files/statistics-and-research/2025-07/basic-income-for-care-leavers-in-wales-pilot-evaluation-statistical-analysis-plan-347.pdf. Accessed on 15.2.26.

Sayal, K., Owen, V., White, K., Merrell, C., Tymms, P., & Taylor, E. (2010). Impact of early school-based screening and intervention programs for ADHD on children's outcomes and access to services: Follow-up of a school-based trial at age 10 years. *Archives of Pediatrics & Adolescent Medicine* *164*(5), 462–469.

Schaub, J., Stander, W. J., & Montgomery, P. (2022). LGBTQ+ young people's health and well-being experiences in out-of-home social care: A scoping review. *Children and Youth Services Review, 143*, 106682. https://doi.org/https://doi.org/10.1016/j.childyouth.2022.106682

Schofield, G., & Beek, M. (2005). Risk and resilience in long-term foster care. *British Journal of Social Work, 35*(8), 1283–1301.

Schofield, G., & Beek, M. (2009). Growing up in foster care: Providing a secure base through adolescence. *Child & Family Social Work, 14*(3), 255–266. https://doi.org/https://doi.org/10.1111/j.1365-2206.2008.00592.x

Schofield, G., & Beek, M. (2014a). *Promoting Attachment and Resilience: A Guide for Foster Carers and Adopters on Using the Secure Base Model.* CoramBAAF.

Schofield, G., & Beek, M. (2014b). *The Secure Base Model: Promoting Attachment and Resilience in Foster Care and Adoption.* British Association for Adoption and Fostering (BAAF).

Schofield, G., & Beek, M. (2024a). *Introduction to the Secure Base Model.* https://www.uea.ac.uk/groups-and-centres/centre-for-research-on-children-and-families/secure-base-model/the-secure-base-model

Schofield, G., & Beek, M. (2024b). *Secure Base Caregiving Approaches.* https://assets.uea.ac.uk/f/185167/x/dd87126544/secure-base-caregiving-approaches-17feb21.pdf

Scott S. (2004). Reviewing the research on the mental health of looked after children: Some issues for the development of more evidence informed practice. *International Journal of Child and Family Welfare*, 2(3), 86–97.

Scottish Government (2026). *Creating Opportunities for Care Experienced Young People.* https://www.gov.scot/news/creating-opportunities-for-care-experienced-young-people/

Scottish Institute for Residential Child Care (2006). *The Contemporary Role and Future Direction of Residential Care for Children and Young People in Scotland.* SIRCC.

Selwyn, J., Wijedasa, D., & Meakings, S. (2015). *Beyond the Adoption Order: Challenges, Interventions and Adoption Disruptions.* BAAF. http://search.ebscohost.com/login.aspx?direct=true&db=cat01883a&AN=uea.003878659&site=eds-live&scope=site

Sempik, J., Ward, H., & Darker, I. (2008). Emotional and behavioural difficulties of children and young people at entry into care. *Clinical Child Psychology and Psychiatry*, 13(2), 221–233.

Sen, R. (2018). *Effective Practice with Looked after Children*. Palgrave Macmillan.

Shah, P., & Mountain, D. (2007). The medical model is dead – long live the medical model. *The British Journal of Psychiatry*, *191*(5), 375–377.

Shaw, J., & Greenhow, S. (2020). Children in care: Exploitation, offending and the denial of victimhood in a prosecution-led culture of practice. *British Journal of Social Work*, *50*(5), 1551–1569. https://doi.org/10.1093/bjsw/bcz137

Simkiss, D. E., Stallard, N., & Thorogood, M. (2013). A systematic literature review of the risk factors associated with children entering public care. *Child: Care, Health & Development*, *39*(5), 628–642. http://ovidsp.ovid.com/ovidweb.cgi?T=JS&CSC=Y&NEWS=N&PAGE=fulltext&D=ovfto&AN=00002703-201309000-00002

Sinclair, I., & Wilson, K. (2003). Matches and mismatches: The contribution of carers and children to the success of foster placements. *British Journal of Social Work*, *33*(7), 871–884.

Smales, M., Savaglio, M., Webster, S., Skouteris, H., Pizzirani, B., O'Donnell, R., & Green, R. (2020). Are the voices of young people living in out-of-home care represented in research examining their health?: A systematic review of the literature. *Children and Youth Services Review*, *113*. https://doi.org/10.1016/j.childyouth.2020.104966

Smith, M. (2009). *Rethinking Residential Child Care: Positive Perspectives*. Policy Press.

Smith, N. (2017). *Neglected Minds: A Report for Mental Health Support of Young People Leaving Care*. Barnardos.

Smith, A., Fairclough, S., Kaehne, A., Liverpool, S., & Maden, M. (2024). *Children and Young People's Mental Health and Physical Activity: An Independent Evidence Review Commissioned by Sport England*. https://sportengland-production-files.s3.eu-west-2.amazonaws.com/s3fs-public/2024-10/Smith%20et%20al%20Evidence%20Review%20Final%20Oct%2024-

South, R., Jones, F. W., Creith, E., & Simonds, L. M. (2016). Understanding the concept of resilience in relation to looked after children: A Delphi survey of perceptions from education, social care and foster care. *Clinical Child Psychology and Psychiatry*, *21*(2), 178–192. https://doi.org/10.1177/1359104515577485

Sprang, G. (2009). The efficacy of a relational treatment for maltreated children and their families. *Child & Adolescent Mental Health*, 14(2), 81–88. https://doi.org/10.1111/j.1475-3588.2008.00499.x

Stanley, N., Riordan, D., & Alaszewski, H. (2005). The mental health of looked after children: Matching response to need. *Health & Social Care in the Community*, *13*(3), 239–248.

Stein, M. (2004). *What Works for Young People Leaving Care?* Jessica Kingsley Publishers.

Stein, M. (2006). Wrong turn. The consensus that children in care are failing, and that the system is to blame is plain wrong. *The Guardian*, 6 December. http://www.theguardian.com/society/2006/dec/06/childrensservices.guardiansocietysupplement1

Stein, M and Morris, M (2010). Increasing the number of care leavers in 'Settled, Safe Accommodation'. Research Report. *Knowledge Review*, 3. C4EO.

Stokes, M., Mellor, D., Yeow, J., & Hapidzal, N. F. M. (2014). Do parents, teachers and children use the SDQ in a similar fashion? *Quality and Quantity*, 48(2), 983–1000.

Swann, R. C., & York, A. (2011). THINKSPACE—The creation of a multi-agency consultation group for looked after children. *Clinical Child Psychology and Psychiatry*, *16*(1), 65–71. https://doi.org/10.1177/1359104509355018

Talbot, R. (2002). *Young Minds: Looking After the Mental Health of Looked After Children*. Pavilion.

Tanabe, T., Kashiwagi, M., Shimakawa, S., Fukui, M., Kadobayashi, K., Azumakawa, K., et al (2013). Behavioral assessment of Japanese children with epilepsy using SDQ (Strengths and Difficulties Questionnaire). *Brain & Development*, 35(1), 81–86. https://doi.org/10.1016/j.braindev.2012.03.008

Tarren-Sweeney, M. (2007). The Assessment Checklist for Children — ACC: A behavioral rating scale for children in foster, kinship and residential care. *Children and Youth Services Review*, 29(5), 672–691.

Tarren-Sweeney, M. (2013). The Brief Assessment Checklists (BAC-C, BAC-A): Mental health screening measures for school-aged children and adolescents in foster, Kinship, residential and adoptive care. *Children and Youth Services Review*, 35(5), 771–779. https://doi.org/10.1016/j.childyouth.2013.01.025

The Child Safeguarding Review Panel (2025). *"It's Silent": Race, racism and safeguarding children: Panel Briefing 4*. Crown Copyright. https://assets.publishing.service.gov.uk/media/67cb0a9d5993d41513a45c5b/Race_Racism_Safeguarding_March_2025.pdf

The Oversight Board (2025). *For the Promise* Report THREE, February. https://oversightboard.scot/ob-resources/2025/oversight-board-report-three.pdf

Transformation Partners in Health and Care (2023). *Meeting the Mental Health Needs of Care Leavers Guidance for Leaving Care Teams and Integrated Care Boards*. https://www.transformationpartners.nhs.uk/wp-content/uploads/2023/11/Meeting-the-mental-health-needs-of-care-leavers_guidance.pdf

Treisman, K. (2017). *Working with Relational and Developmental Trauma in Children and Adolescents*. Routledge.

Trubey, R., Evans, R., McDonald, S., Noyes, J., Robling, M., Willis, S., et al (2024). Effectiveness of mental health and wellbeing interventions for children and young people in foster, kinship, and residential care: systematic review and meta-analysis. *Trauma, Violence, & Abuse, 25*(4), 2829–2844. https://doi.org/10.1177/15248380241227987

Turner, W., Macdonald, G. M., & Dennis, J. A. (2005). Cognitive-behavioural training interventions for assisting foster carers in the management of difficult behaviour. *Cochrane Database of Systematic Reviews, 2*. https://doi.org/10.1002/14651858.CD003760.pub2

UK Parliament (2025). Children's social care: Government Response – Fifth Special Report of session 2024–26. https://publications.parliament.uk/pa/cm5901/cmselect/cmeduc/1350/report.html

Utting, W. (1997). *People Like Us: The Report of the Review of the Safeguards for Children Living Away from Home*. Department of Health.

Valentine, G. (2003). Boundary crossings: transitions from childhood to adulthood. *Children's Geographies*, *1*(1), 37–52. https://doi.org/10.1080/14733280302186

Van Roy, B., Kristensen, H., Groholt, B., & Clench-Aas, J. (2009). Prevalence and characteristics of significant social anxiety in children aged 8–13 years: A Norwegian cross-sectional population study. *Social Psychiatry and Psychiatric Epidemiology*, 44(5), 407–415. https://doi.org/10.1007/s00127-008-0445-7

Wallace, M., & Cocker, C. (2022). Following the death of Ms A: A local authority response to transitional safeguarding. *Practice*, *34*(1), 61–69. https://doi.org/10.1080/09503153.2021.1976130

Ward, H., & Holmes, L. (2008). Calculating the costs of local authority care for children with contrasting needs. *Child & Family Social Work*, *13*(1), 80–90. http://search.ebscohost.com/login.aspx?direct=true&db=psyh&AN=2008-00534-010&site=ehost-live

Waterhouse, R. (2000). *Lost in Care: Report of the Tribunal of Inquiry into the Abuse of Children in Care in the Former County Council Areas of Gwynedd and Clwyd since 1974*. The Stationery Office.

Weekes, A. P., & Ward, S. (2025). Parenting is not easy in a racialized society: Decolonizing childcare practice. *The British Journal of Social Work*. https://doi.org/10.1093/bjsw/bcaf031

Welsh Government. (2022). *Basic Income Pilot for Care Leavers: Overview of the Scheme*, https://gov.wales/basic-income-pilot-care-leavers-overview-scheme

Welsh Government. (2024) *Basic Income for Care Leavers in Wales Pilot Statistics: August 2022 to July 2024. Basic Income for Care Leavers in Wales pilot statistics: August 2022 to July 2024*. https://www.gov.wales/basic-income-care-leavers-wales-pilot-statistics-august-2022-july-2024-html

Werner, E. (2000). Protective factors and individual resilience. In J.P. Shonkoff & S.J. Meisels (Eds.), *Handbook of Early Childhood Intervention* (pp 115–132). Cambridge University Press

White, S., Edwards, R., Gillies, V., & Wastell, D. (2019). All the ACEs: A chaotic concept for family policy and decision-making? *Social Policy and Society*, *18*(3), 457–466. https://doi.org/10.1017/S147474641900006X

Whyte, S., & Campbell, A. (2008). The Strengths and Difficulties Questionnaire: A useful screening tool to identify mental health strengths and needs in looked after children and inform care plans at looked after children reviews? *Child Care in Practice, 14*, 193–206. http://www.tandf.co.uk/journals/titles/13575279.asp

Williams, S., & Cocker, C. (2023). *Safeguarding Adults Review – Sylvia: Overview Report*. https://www.croydonsab.co.uk/wp-content/uploads/2023/05/Sylvia-Final-Report-pdf.pdf

Wilson, B., & Barnett, L. M. (2020). Physical activity interventions to improve the health of children and adolescents in out of home care: A systematic review of the literature. *Children and Youth Services Review, 110*. https://doi.org/10.1016/j.childyouth.2020.104765

Wilson, J., & Jungner, G. (1968). *Principles and Practice of Screening for Disease*. World Health Organization.

Wilson, P., Minnis, H., Puckering, C., & Gillberg, C. (2009). Should we aspire to screen preschool children for conduct disorder? *Archives of Disease in Childhood, 94*, 812–816.

Winter, K. (2006). The participation rights of looked after children in their health care: A critical review of the research. *International Journal of Children's Rights, 14*(1), 77–95.

Woerner, W., Fleitlich-Bilyk, B., Martinussen, R., Fletcher, J., Cucchiaro, G., Dalgalarrondo, P., et al (2004). The Strengths and Difficulties Questionnaire overseas: Evaluations and applications of the SDQ beyond Europe. *European Child & Adolescent Psychiatry*, 13, ii47–ii54. https://doi.org/10.1007/s00787-004-2008-0

Wolkind, S., & Rutter, M. (1973). Children who have been 'in care': An epidemiological study. *Journal of Child Psychology and Psychiatry, 14*(2), 97–105.

World Health Organization (1946). *Preamble to the Constitution of the World Health Organization as adopted by the International Health Conference, New York, 19–22 June, 1946; signed on 22 July 1946 by the representatives of 61 States and entered into force on 7 April 1948.* Official Records of the World Health Organization, no. 2, p 100.

World Health Organisation (2001). *Strengthening Mental Health Promotion Factsheet No. 220*. https://www.who.int/en/news-room/fact-sheets/detail/mental-health-strengthening-our-response.

World Health Organisation (2024). *Clinical Descriptions and Diagnostic Requirements for ICD-11 Mental, Behavioural and Neurodevelopmental Disorders (CDDR).* https://www.who.int/publications/i/item/9789240077263

Yin, R. K. (2003). *Case Study Research: Design and Methods* (3rd edn). Sage.

York, W., & Jones, J. (2017). Addressing the mental health needs of looked after children in foster care: The experiences of foster carers. *Journal of Psychiatric and Mental Health Nursing*, *24*(2–3), 143–153. https://doi.org/https://doi.org/10.1111/jpm.12362

Young Minds (2018). *Impact Report 2018–2019.* https://www.youngminds.org.uk/media/o25lazbr/youngminds-impact-report-2018-19.pdf. Accessed on 30.12.25.

Yuill, C., Crinson, I., & Duncan, E. (2010). *The Social Model of Health. Key Concepts in Health Studies.* Sage. https://doi.org/doi:http://dx.doi.org/10.4135/9781446251676

Zakaria, Z., & Yaacob, M. J. b. (2008). Psychiatric morbidity among children and adolescents Living in orphanages, Kota Bharu, Malaysia. *International Medical Journal*, 15(3), 183–188.

Index

References to figures appear in *italic* type;
those in **bold** type refer to tables.

B

C

D

G

H

I

N

O

P

R